D1395119

Nature
Watcher's
FIELD GUIDE

Nature Watcher's

FIELD GUIDE

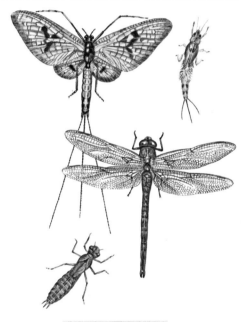

Derek Hall
Andrew Cleave
Paul Sterry

TREASURE PRESS

Foreword

It is unlikely that one book could ever tell you all there is to know about nature watching – and this one does not claim to do that – but we hope to have laid the foundations for anyone wishing to absorb themselves in this fascinating pursuit.

We make no apologies for the often-repeated advice concerning concealment and 'being in the right place at the right time', for they are of paramount importance. Equally we make no apologies for reminding the reader that laws regarding conservation are designed to protect and encourage wildlife so that ultimately there is more to be enjoyed by everyone; the welfare of the plants and animals in a particular habitat should always be put before the interests of the naturalist. In Britain, anyone wishing to ensure that their nature watching activities are not endangering rare or protected species should obtain a copy of the Wildlife and Countryside Act 1981, or should consult one of the many conservation organizations.

Finally, we acknowledge our debt to the various published works and personal anecdotes of other naturalists which have helped and inspired us, and in particular would like to thank Dr Jim Flegg who read the manuscript. His comments and suggestions were especially helpful.

D.H., A.C., P.S.

Acknowledgements

Photographs
Biofotos: 143. Format Publishing Services: Derek Hall 9,13,15,17,22,24,33 (top),37,43,46,47,51,53, 54,58,60,63,64,65,66,71,74,77,78,79,82,83,84,85,86,87,96 (left),98,100,101,103,104,110,113,116,117, 119,121,123,124,125,130,132,134,135,136,137,144,145,148; Brin Edwards 94. Leigh Jones: 49. Nature Photographs Ltd: Leo Batten 133; Frank Blackburn 32,52,62,75,111; R.B. Burbidge 147; N.A. Callow 29; Andrew Cleave 39,48; Michael Leach 40 (top); L. MacNally 67; Hugh Miles 33 (bottom); Owen Newman 96 (right); W.S. Paton 120; Derick Scott 115; David Sewell 95; Don Smith 80; Paul Sterry 40 (bottom).

Illustrations
Colour plates by Mick Loats and David Thompson/Linden Artists, Brin Edwards/Format Publishing Services, and Ian Willis
Line drawings by Phil Weare/Linden Artists and Brin Edwards/Format Publishing Services

First published in Great Britain in 1985 by
The Hamlyn Publishing Group under the title *Successful Nature Watching*

This edition published in 1989 by
Treasure Press
Michelin House
81 Fulham Road
London SW3 6RB

Copyright © Hamlyn Publishing 1985
a division of the Hamlyn Publishing Group Limited

ISBN 1 85051 469 0

Printed in The Canary Islands

Lito. A. Romero, S. A. - D. L. TF. 1.164-1989

Contents

Introduction

This book has two chief aims: firstly to enable you to put a name to many of the animals to be found in the countryside, and secondly – and perhaps more importantly – to help you to *see* these animals in the first place. Quite often a trip into the country (or local park) can be disappointing: very little is seen apart from a few obvious birds and insects. But this does not mean that nothing else was there; it is more likely that many other creatures were overlooked, or frightened away. There are many field guides on the market whose only real use is for identification. We believe, however, that many people have great problems in actually encountering much of our wildlife. Once seen, identification can often be a relatively simple matter. It is doubtful whether many people, if they came face to face with a badger, would be unable to recognize it. But how many people have ever seen one?

This book will help to rectify this problem by providing sound, thorough advice in the art of nature watching – as well as giving 'tricks of the trade' used by the experts. Following the advice in this book, which has been provided by naturalists with much experience of nature watching, will almost certainly increase – perhaps dramatically – the amount of wildlife you see. By providing the opportunity to get better views of more species – instead of just chance glimpses of a few – it allows you to devote more time to seeing animals in their environment: fox cubs gambolling in the spring sunshine, deer fighting over their harem or the courtship displays of birds, for instance. This is the point at which nature watching becomes really interesting and worthwhile.

It is important to stress at the outset that real success, as in almost any pursuit, can sometimes demand time and patience. For instance, you could chance upon a rare bird of prey at almost any time. Nevertheless to set out with the intention of seeing a particular species may take some time to achieve.

How to use this book

The book is divided into four main sections. The first section deals with essential aspects of nature watching such as the nature watcher's 5-point plan, general hints and advice, and the choice and use of equipment. The second section provides practical information about nature watching in specific habitats. The special features of each habitat are explained, together with the impact they have on the wildlife. If there is any reason for visiting a type of habitat at a particular time of year, this will also be mentioned. Then, within each habitat, we explain how to nature watch, using a unique combination of 'photokeys', practical photographs and explanatory text. This section will give you all the basic information to enable you to explore any habitat properly. The third section lists the main types of animals to be found within each habitat, and describes the techniques required to search for them. The fourth section is arranged as an identification guide to the more common animals to be found, so that once you have made a discovery, you can confirm identification.

The book can actually be used in several different ways. You can use it to look for a variety of wildlife in a particular habitat and then make an identification (you may eventually need additional standard identification guides to specific groups of animals as your powers of observation increase); or you can use the book for straightforward identification. Furthermore, you can set out with the intention of seeing, say, a buzzard, and then use the book to ascertain possible whereabouts and to discover *how* to look for buzzards in their likely haunts.

Notes on the identification section

Between pages 154 and 233 are described and illustrated, in systematic order, 430 of the British and European species most likely to be encountered. Whilst we have included many of the vertebrates that the naturalist will see we have, of necessity, restricted the treatment of invertebrates to usually no more than one representative of each group. However, since the purpose of this book is, essentially, to *see* wildlife, we strongly recommend the additional acquisition of a set of identification guides to all the major animal groups. They can provide details of many more species, and in greater detail, than can any single book devoted to the identification of all animals, and are the only satisfactory way of putting a name to any creature you may discover. A list of recommended books is included in the bibliography on page 234.

Although adult birds and mammals usually grow to a determined, constant size, many invertebrates and cold-blooded vertebrates grow to sizes determined by environmental conditions. Thus the sizes given here are maximums. Colours, particularly of cold-blooded vertebrates, usually refer to dorsal (back) views. *The close examination and handling of snakes, in particular, should in any case be avoided.*

The main habitats in which individual species may be found is denoted by a series of symbols:

◣	▭	⊡	⬆
mountain	moorland	heath and maquis	coniferous woodland

◉	▨	▨	⊟
deciduous woodland	lowland	fresh water	coast and estuary

The habitat in which the animal is most often encountered is shown first. The letter S or W placed before one of the symbols denotes that the animal is encountered in this habitat in only summer (S) or winter (W) in Britain and Europe. For birds, 'resident' means that it is present in a particular region all year; 'breeds' means that it is a summer visitor to a particular region for the

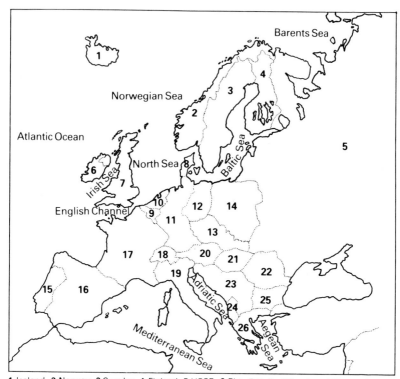

1 Iceland 2 Norway 3 Sweden 4 Finland 5 USSR 6 Eire 7 United Kingdom 8 Denmark
9 Belgium 10 Netherlands 11 West Germany 12 East Germany 13 Czechoslovakia 14 Poland
15 Portugal 16 Spain 17 France 18 Switzerland 19 Italy 20 Austria 21 Hungary 22 Romania
23 Yugoslavia 24 Albania 25 Bulgaria 26 Greece

This map shows the areas described in the identification section.

purpose of breeding. For all species ♂ denotes male and ♀ denotes female.
The area covered by this book is indicated on the map. For the purposes of
distribution we have distinguished between Britain, and the rest of Europe.
If the animal in question occurs in Britain this is stated; otherwise
distributions and areas refer to Europe only.

Some easy steps to successful nature watching

Although the most successful naturalists have spent years watching wildlife
and have a wealth of experience on which to call, you can improve your own
nature watching ability straight away if you remember:

The nature watcher's 5-point plan

1 THINK NATURAL: Where would *you* be if you were a shy creature like a
deer? Certainly not in the middle of a busy woodland path in broad daylight!

Concealment is the best way of increasing your chances of seeing shy species. Notice that the naturalist here, whilst fairly well hidden, still has a good view of the river and fields beyond.

Therefore, remember you are looking for creatures whose natural tendency may be to remain concealed, or to keep away from well-used paths. Remember also that animals such as many species of insects often stay close to their food plants, so this should be the place to begin searching for them.
2 TIME IT RIGHT: Many animals are nocturnal. Most mammals are likely to be encountered at night or early morning, and even some seashore creatures are only active at night. Apart from the differences of day and night, the seasons may be just as important. Certain species of birds are migratory. This means on the one hand that they are not actually present in some places for part of the year, but it also means that the times at which they gather for

migration or immigration, particularly in the case of wildfowl, are often especially fruitful. Many insects are also seasonal.

Birds are usually at their most active when feeding or during the nesting season, when their constant coming and going, as well as their territorial songs, advertize their presence to best effect. Some animals hibernate in certain parts of Europe during the winter and, again, this should be borne in mind if searching for a particular species.

Although winter tends to drive certain species to hibernate or to seek warmer parts of the world, those that remain are often much easier to see. Hunger may make traditionally shy species such as deer become quite bold and active even during the hours of daylight. Winter gives the naturalist a further advantage: the absence of leaf cover can make the task of actually seeing what is there much easier. Woodlands are one of the most fruitful places to visit in winter: they are usually a few degrees warmer than the open countryside, and may be found to support unusually high numbers of winter-feeding birds and insects.

3 BE QUIET: One of the main reasons why many people see few birds or mammals is because they tramp along woodland paths or over fields and moors, perhaps talking loudly to each other as they go. Any self-respecting mammal will simply melt into the depths of the wood, and most birds will just take to the wing at the first sight or sound of your presence.

The vibrations of your footsteps are equally alarming: tread quietly and carefully whenever you are nature watching. Stop frequently to listen and watch for possible signs of animal activity.

4 KEEP OUT OF SIGHT: Concealment is the naturalist's most important 'weapon'. Remember, that if you can see a bird whilst in the open, then the bird can certainly see you. (Some species can see thirty times better than humans!) If you are concealed, or can become part of the scenery, then the animal you are watching should have no need to run or fly off. Remember, too, that when watching mammals your scent is important.

5 USE YOUR EYES AND EARS: Many animals are not only well camouflaged, but some are also much smaller than most people realize. Therefore, look very carefully: search among fissures in tree bark with your hand-lens: look for unusual movements among trees; search on tree stumps, and beneath trees and bushes for feeding clues and droppings. Nature only advertizes its presence to those who know how to read the signs. Similarly, listen for sounds which will help you to locate animals.

What you can expect to achieve

As your experience grows and you become more attuned to spotting wildlife, almost every nature watching trip will yield *something* of interest – partly because, as your own knowledge increases, so hitherto insignificant features of the countryside become more interesting and relevant, but also because you genuinely should be able to see and identify more animals.

Naturally there will be days when, despite all expectations of a veritable wildlife bonanza, all will be relatively quiet and you may see very little. Just because a habitat is known to support a given number of readily identifiable animals, you shouldn't expect to see them all on one, or even a few, trips. At other times an unusual or interesting species – perhaps a rare vagrant bird – will cross your path by pure chance, and these occasions are also part of the reward for perseverance.

Inevitably, factors such as the inherent nature of the habitat itself, the time of year and local weather conditions, all exert a major influence on the movements of wildlife, and so it is always difficult to predict with any great certainty just what will be seen at any given time. Remember, too, that many mammals are rarely active by day. This means that special techniques must be employed to see them with any degree of certainty. These techniques will be explained in full in the relevant habitat sections.

The following list is a genuine record of some of the species seen on a short nature watching trip undertaken on a warm (10°C/50°F) sunny day with a light breeze at the very beginning of March. It doesn't reflect any great discoveries, but neither is it the most rewarding time to watch nature. Nevertheless, it is an indication of what can quite easily be seen by anyone even at a fairly modest time of year. If even the clues provided by this short trip were followed up (as described later), then it is likely that sightings of foxes and weasels could have been added to the list.

1 Woodland of coppiced hazel with oak and beech standards, bordering a larch plantation

snowdrops in flower

many other woodland flowers – such as dog's mercury, cuckoo pint, lesser celandine, primrose and bluebell – about to burst forth

Helotium fungus on dead tree branches

great tits (male proclaiming territory, female stripping bark for nest material)

flock of long-tailed tits

chaffinch

jay

great spotted woodpecker (drumming)

nuthatch

treecreeper

blackbird

wood pigeon

wren

robin

fox droppings

rabbit (crossing from conifer plantation to deciduous wood)

chewed split hazelnuts (identified as eaten by wood mouse, bank vole, grey squirrel, nuthatch)

2 Bog with alder carr and scrub woodland of ash, oak and Scots pine. Lake fringed with *Phragmites* reed and tussock sedge

brimstone butterfly (male) – just out of hibernation

flock of long-tailed tits

nuthatch

sparrowhawk

Canada geese, tufted duck (on lake)

centipedes, woodlice, spiders (under rotting wood)

roe deer footprint in mud by lake

2 roe deer, in grey winter pelage, disturbed from their cover

fox droppings

weasel droppings

amphibian skin (remains of meal)

chewed hazelnuts (result of wood mouse and bank vole)

grey squirrel

mole hills (on nearby farmland)

11

Habitats

A habitat can be described as an area with particular physical and climatic conditions, which gives rise to a characteristic assemblage of specially adapted plant and animal species. Some of these species may also be adapted to live in more than one habitat, however.

This book is divided into the major habitats of Britain and Europe. We have chosen to split the book into habitats because we believe that the reader will be able to apply more easily the techniques described in this way. It should also be pointed out that, just as some plants and animals are able to roam from one habitat to another, so some habitats can exist one within another and may seem sometimes to merge imperceptibly. Therefore, try to be flexible in your approach to investigating a habitat. For instance, you might try investigating the vegetation surrounding a woodland pond by applying the techniques of pond watching rather than those of woodland watching.

The species in a particular habitat are not necessarily unique to it; many birds, insects and mammals, for instance, are very wide-ranging, although their lifestyles (and in consequence the ways in which they might be encountered) may vary accordingly. To illustrate this point consider a fox: it might have its den in a woodland bank, but its hunting expeditions may take it across farmland, into gardens, on to heathland and downland and even on to beaches!

Recognizing a habitat

Most habitats are themselves quite easy to identify. There are few, if any, serious nature watchers who wouldn't recognize the difference between deciduous and coniferous woodland, for instance, but the distinction between, say, some of the freshwater 'wetland' habitats is often less precise. To assist in this respect, each habitat is preceded by an introduction which not only describes characteristic and diagnostic features to enable you to tell exactly what habitat you are in, but also explains the interrelationships between the species and their environment so that the art of nature watching becomes simplified.

Man-made habitats

Many books on wildlife devote whole chapters to – or are indeed wholly concerned with – the subject of the wildlife of towns, gardens and other man-made habitats. In this book we prefer to recognize many of the 'urban'

Several habitats are visible in this photograph: grazing pastures separated by hedgerows and trees, a deciduous woodland and, in the distance, arable land giving way to moorland. A mixture of habitats often results in a greater variety of species to be seen.

or at least man-made habitats as natural environments in their own right. For example reservoirs are important staging posts for thousands of migrant birds each year, as well as for smaller resident populations. Similarly gravel pits, canals and certain parks are so widely accepted by wildlife that they can be considered not only as true habitats, but also ones for which many of the nature watching techniques in this book apply. Of those man-made habitats which do not fall within the scope of the latter parts of this book, the following brief descriptions may encourage you to look for more of their inhabitants, and may help to suggest fruitful areas for investigation.

Roadsides

Many roadsides have become important havens for wildlife. In more rural areas the roads may be bordered by hedgerows – themselves favoured haunts of small mammals, birds, and invertebrates such as snails – as well as acting as bisectors of fields. This means that wildlife such as foxes and deer may cross the road to pass from one field to another, especially at night. Where trees are planted for amenity value, and where council cost-cutting schemes now mean less regular trimming of verges, an even more varied flora and fauna may develop. Drainage ditches are particularly worth inspection, for here aquatic insects such as dragonflies may be found. If you want to stand a good chance of seeing a kestrel – albeit a fairly fleeting glimpse as you hurtle past – get someone to drive you along a motorway. The verges provide plenty of food in the form of beetles and small mammals which these small birds of prey seek by hovering, head motionless, often only a few metres above the ground. Motorways have now become important wildlife reservoirs, with a varied collection of plants and animals.

Railway tracks

Because they are true highways and provide access from one place to another, and because they offer a degree of protection from predators and are allowed to become 'naturalized' to some extent, railway tracks provide many interesting opportunities for nature watching. Watching the track from a vantage point – such as a bridge – or even from the train itself may prove worthwhile. Lizards, foxes, badgers and voles are just a few of the animals which utilize railway tracks, and on nearby fields you may be able to spot rabbits, deer and many species of birds. If watching wildlife from a train, try to secure a seat in a forward carriage; some animals may be frightened off by the time the rest of the train rumbles past.

Towns

Most towns and cities are not the barren places devoid of wildlife which they might conjure up in our minds. Amenity planting of trees and shrubs, and the creation of parks, all help to provide a sanctuary for many forms of wildlife. Provincial towns surrounded by countryside, as well as the inner parts of larger cities, are frequently invaded by night-foraging foxes, and even badgers are regular visitors to some towns. Some of these bold creatures spend part of the day lying up beneath sheds, garages or other places of safety. For birds, the eaves of houses and the towers of churches and other buildings have long been important places to roost, or nest, and many species such as starlings, gulls, pied wagtails, black redstarts, house martins, sparrows and even kestrels frequently share man's environment.

On a more local scale, refuse tips, churchyards, walls – even the cracks between paving stones – can offer opportunities for some unusual forms of wildlife.

Gardens

With the increasing destruction of natural woodland, together with the expansion of housing schemes, more and more people are realizing the importance of gardens as wildlife sanctuaries. For birds, many gardens have become the new woodland edges – the traditionally favoured habitat for many species – and the provision of carefully sited nest boxes and feeding tables has encouraged them to an even greater degree. Even a fairly modest garden can attract a varied and interesting collection of wildlife – not to mention the invertebrate life already teeming beneath rockeries, soil and in compost heaps.

There are many books available which provide details on how to encourage wildlife into your garden by the judicious planting of native plant species, by providing small ponds, and by creating features which will emulate those found in the wild. It isn't necessary to turn your whole garden over to nature, and even if you do not feel inclined to plant specific natural species, a few buddleia bushes will provide plenty of butterflies, and a small patch of the garden 'left to nature' will soon become colonized with species such as clover and long-stemmed grasses which will attract insects for other creatures to feed upon.

We have already discussed the importance of bird tables for encouraging species and for studying their feeding habits, but of course hedgehogs can also be encouraged by the provision of food, and can be enticed to nest in the garden by building a suitable nesting chamber, details of which are available in many books concerned with garden wildlife.

Garden bird tables and food dispensers are also attractive to other wildlife.

General tips and techniques for nature watching

This section is intended to give the reader useful general tips, and to outline the techniques and codes of behaviour which apply to almost any form of nature watching. More specific advice is given, where relevant, in each of the sections relating to particular habitats, as well as in the sections on the choice and uses of equipment.

How to choose a habitat

Due to a variety of factors some habitats are richer in wildlife than others. On the other hand, there are some which *seem* to abound in wildlife just because the indigenous creatures have become accustomed to contact with humans. There are, for example, many places where species of deer – normally quite difficult to approach – can be seen at close quarters just because they are used to humans. Nevertheless, if the only site available to you at a particular time seems relatively impoverished, don't worry, there is probably more activity than you first realized. Whatever the habitat, the more often you visit it the greater your chance of adding to the list of species you encounter.

Today, most of us live quite close to at least a few good nature watching sites. The many conservation and local naturalists' organizations which exist mean that access is possible to a number of reserves and other places which have been set aside primarily for the encouragement of wildlife. Some of these sites may be quite small, and a few are fairly specialized, but by visiting a variety of them there is a chance of seeing not only a wide range of animals, but also perhaps more interestingly seeing animals (or indeed plants) which are on the organization's accompanying species list. This is of enormous help if you set out with the intention of seeing a particular creature, for your chances of encountering it in a known habitat – especially if the creature is uncommon – are greatly increased. There are several books available that include details of some of the many habitats to which the public or various naturalist club members have access, and local libraries also have details of many of the organizations from which further information may be sought. The value of joining nature organizations and visiting their reserves cannot be overstressed.

However, many other places also support rich populations of wildlife – beaches, local woods, hedgerows and country parks, for instance. All of these are worth a visit, although there is a good chance you will be sharing your habitat with other people less intent on maintaining the quiet, stealthy approach you are adopting! And this is where the advice given in the 5-point plan can be put into practice. For, if you do visit places where general

In any habitat, look for features such as this old watermill. Barn owls and several species of bat are highly dependent on such places for nesting or roosting, and can be seen leaving at dusk to hunt.

17

recreation is also a high priority, then at least plan to be there during times when others, bent on more noisy pursuits, may be absent.

When should you go?

A visit to many habitats can be more fruitful if you can gear this to a particular time of year. Sometimes this is not important: a rocky shore will have plenty of wildlife at any time – the seasons are not the governing factor here – but estuaries, ponds, downland and heathland are among those which provide greater opportunities for naturalists during particular seasons. For instance, some migrant waders congregate on estuaries during spring and autumn on their way to and from their breeding grounds, and others overwinter on them. Furthermore, if you know what species to expect at any given time, then the task of narrowing down the identification possibilities becomes simpler.

Similarly, the time of day or night is of great importance when looking for wildlife. Most mammals and many invertebrates are nocturnal (and so are some marine animals) and this must be borne in mind. Other species of invertebrates such as spiders are best seen early in the morning or evening when the air is still humid. And anyone who has ever been awakened by the 'dawn chorus' knows when birds are at their most vocal and active! More specific details concerning the best times to nature watch will be given in the relevant habitat sections.

Do not, however, make the mistake of dismissing winter as a barren time of year to be endured until spring arrives. After all, animals still need to eat and, since food is scarcer in winter, many may be bolder and easier to see. The lack of ground cover and general foliage also means that animals are less able to conceal themselves from view. Woodlands can be several degrees warmer than open countryside during winter, and may attract much of the local wildlife. Go out as soon as possible after snow has fallen, and follow any fresh animal tracks. They may lead you to a lair, and will certainly indicate the pathways used regularly by animals.

Field notes like these are an essential aid to identification.

Know your quarry

There is more to successful nature watching than just going to the right sort of habitat at the right time. It helps if you know what to look for as well as how to look. *How* to look is a major feature of this book, but you should also attempt to learn something of the lifestyles of as many of our native creatures as you can. Today there are plenty of books which will give you all manner of details about the lives and habits of the creatures you seek, not to mention television programmes and illustrated talks. Brief details about the lives of many of these animals are given in the checklist and identification sections of this book. A museum with an indigenous natural history collection is also helpful for there, at close quarters, you can note features of animals in a way that illustrations in books can never impart.

How to use an identification guide and a field notebook

This advice might seem obvious – particularly the first point – but like all 'working tools' there is a way of extracting the most from them. This book includes illustrations and identification details of 430 of the most commonly encountered British and European species or groups of species. For most purposes, you will find this sufficient; if you have seen and can identify everything in this book, consider yourself a naturalist!

However, it has not been possible to include different species of insects, for instance – only representatives of the major orders – and you will also invariably discover birds and other animals which are not illustrated. As you become more experienced, and perhaps wish to specialize, you will find it more helpful to use detailed identification guides devoted to particular groups in conjunction with this book. As with this book, learn how to use any guide before taking it into the field. Identification is much simplified if you have first discovered how the book in question is laid out, and how to use any identification keys it may be based upon.

For some wildlife – birds in particular – the best method of identification often lies in making field notes and a quick sketch, and then comparing these to an illustration in the guide. This has two advantages: firstly, you can make notes whilst the animal is still in view (or fresh in your memory), and secondly, having made a note of features such as wing patterns, bill length, etc., you will be less inclined to be distracted or influenced unduly by the illustrations in the guide. Ultimately, identification is not always merely a question of matching details against an illustration; sometimes, you must use your guide to eliminate certain species, and thus reach an identification. Often your view is poor, and some species – chiffchaffs and willow warblers are a classic case – require very good views, and details of their songs, to separate them. In such instances, and even in less critical ones than this, you must use a combination of physical and behavioural details. For instance:-

> Is the bird ever found in this habitat?
> Is it ever present at this time of year?
> Does it have a diagnostic call?

Assuming the animal to be identified is a bird, try to commit the following details to your notebook prior to making an identification:

Size (try to use nearby landmarks to gauge this)

General shape and proportions (make a quick sketch)

Bill length relative to body, and shape of bill

Plumage colour, pattern and extent of distinctive collars, breast and other markings

Tail or rump pattern in flight

Whether or not legs trail in flight

Add any details about its behaviour which will help identification:

Walking or hopping gait

Undulating or direct flight pattern

The same general rules also apply to mammals and many other animals. Certain species of deer display characteristic rump markings when moving away; the flight patterns of some butterflies and moths are their best identification feature. Don't forget to note down the type of habitat in which the animal appears. Generally speaking, you will see abundant species more often than rarer ones, so temper your final decision between two similar species with regard to this fact.

With experience, you will gain that perceptive ability to identify birds based on their 'jizz'. A bird's jizz is the characteristics which enable you to put a name to it without obtaining a good view. For instance, a white rump and flashes of black, blue and brown are all you need to know that, in woodland, you have alarmed a jay – even without hearing it calling.

One final word on birds' voices. Although many guides provide a descriptive sound of a particular bird's voice, many of these are still difficult to recognize in the field, for a written description to some extent is subjective, based on the listener's own interpretation of the sound. Furthermore many birds make a variety of sounds – alarm, contact, territorial, etc. – which further confuse the issue. The best advice is to borrow or buy one of the excellent recordings of bird songs which are available, and learn as many as you can. With practice, you can identify many species by call alone. (Remember, though, that birds are usually more vocal in spring and early summer.) An equally useful course of action is to accompany an experienced birdwatcher or join a birdwatchers' club outing, where an experienced group leader will initiate the novice from first-hand experience. Indeed, any nature watching trip that can be undertaken in the company of an expert will pay dividends.

Country code

1	Guard against all risk of fire;	5	Be careful not to damage hedges, fences or walls;
2	Keep all gates closed;	6	Take your litter home;
3	Keep dogs under proper control;	7	Safeguard water supplies;
4	Keep to the footpaths;	8	Protect all wildlife;

9	Go carefully on country roads;	11	Make no unnecessary noise;
10	Respect the life of the countryside;	12	Leave livestock, crops and machinery alone.

In addition to the above advice can be added the following:
1   Familiarize yourself with the laws relating to the collection or disturbance of species;
2   Photograph rather than take any specimens from their habitat;
3   Practice conservation by, if not actively joining conservation groups, at least ensuring that you do nothing to disturb or damage the habitats you are visiting;
4   Obtain permission before you venture on to private land;
5   Inform someone whenever you visit a habitat where there is a risk of becoming lost or cut off by tides, etc.

The art of concealment

Different wild animals adopt different strategies for remaining alive and safe. Some, many insects for instance, are masters in the art of camouflage; others just burrow or hide out of sight. Many mammals have become nocturnal, but even at night they are constantly on the alert for danger. The mammals and birds also rely on their acute senses to warn them of danger. Many birds can see much better than we can, and our own sense of smell is pitiful compared with that of, say, a fox which can detect us from about half a kilometre ($\frac{1}{4}$ mile) away.

The first consideration for the naturalist wishing to see timid species is to avoid giving his or her presence away to them. There are four main ways of doing this:-
1   Wear drab clothing. It is essential to wear sombre-coloured clothing which does not rustle when you move. If possible, cover your hands and face as well;
2   Keep downwind of mammals. Test the wind direction, and make a detour to get downwind of your quarry if necessary;
3   Try and use any possible cover – such as isolated trees and bushes – as 'staging posts' between you and your quarry. Avoid letting animals see the familiar human figure, by squatting down in front of anything which will break up your outline,
4   Move carefully and quietly. Walk on damp ground if possible, and avoid dry twigs. 'Freeze' if your quarry looks at you. Generally move slowly and avoid sudden movements. Wait until your quarry is feeding or has its attention focused away from you before moving closer.

Reading the habitat

A good naturalist can look at a habitat and, even without seeing any of its inhabitants, can assess whether it is rich or poor in species and even what its major species might include. Part of this 'insight' is common sense, and part is based on experience. First of all, what are your general impressions of the

You don't always need to set off into the depths of a woodland to nature watch. Standing still for a few moments to listen for birds alerted one of the authors to high-pitched squeaks coming from the undergrowth close to this path. Soon several water shrews made themselves visible.

habitat? Does it look attractive to wildlife? Are there trees of various species? Is there good ground cover? In a woodland, are the layers (see page 71) all developed? Are there plenty of nesting sites? Can animals move from one part to another in safety? Is there natural water? If so, is there good margin cover or is the water isolated from other natural cover? Are there plenty of tall grasses and wild flowers to attract insects? Asking yourself these and other questions will help to develop your own awareness of the habitat's potential as a place to watch nature. Clearly, some habitats will seem – and prove – to be richer than others.

Within the habitat, there are many other clues to the presence of wildlife. Feeding signs, droppings, tracks and trails all betray the species to be found. In many cases, these will be your only indication of the inhabitants. The importance of these animal 'calling cards' is discussed in more detail in the relevant habitat sections.

A word of warning

Nature watching is one of the safest of pursuits, but some habitats must nevertheless be treated with due respect. Always wear clothing (including footwear) appropriate to the habitat, and make sure that someone knows where you are going and when you expect to return. If this is not possible, leave a note on your car windscreen. Mountains and moorlands can be very cold, even in summer, and mists can easily envelop you causing a loss of orientation. A whistle and compass are essential here. *Any* aquatic habitat is potentially dangerous, and the best advice is to watch tides, keep away from fast currents and always test boggy ground with a stick before walking on it. If you can't swim, simply don't go so close to the water's edge that you might fall in. Keep to footpaths and other safe areas whenever possible. If in doubt, check local conditions with the relevant authority before venturing out into unknown territory.

Equipment

One of the advantages of natural history as a pursuit is that it can be indulged in without the need for very much specialist equipment. It may therefore come as a surprise to see the list of items which are now recommended! However, a glance will reveal that many of these are either optional, or are standard household utensils readily and inexpensively available.

Some of the more useful items of equipment for the naturalist.

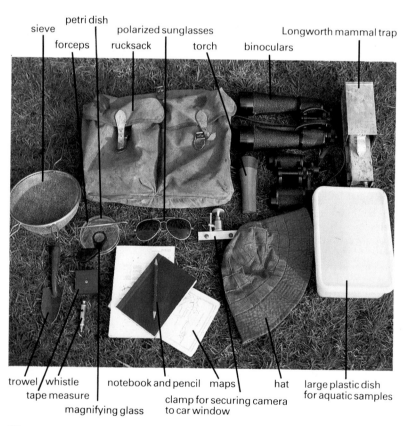

Binoculars

One of the few essential pieces of equipment. Although you can watch some wildlife without binoculars, few naturalists would seriously consider being without a pair. Apart from their obvious use for bird and mammal watching, they can also be used to identify butterflies and even distant flowers.

Choose the best pair you can afford. A more expensive pair really will enable you to see objects more clearly than a cheap pair of the same magnification and light-gathering intensity, and is likely to be more durable. Two numbers are stamped on binoculars, joined by a multiplication sign: for instance 8×40. The first number refers to the magnification, and the second to the diameter, in millimetres, of the objective lens. The greater the diameter, the greater the light-gathering properties of the binoculars. Dividing the objective lens diameter by the magnification gives you a figure called the exit pupil diameter; this should not be less than 5. For general nature watching 7×50 and 8×40 are ideal. Binoculars with magnifications greater than this require very steady hands, and of course become progressively more expensive. When buying binoculars, test them outside first. Ensure that there is no colour fringe around the image, and that vertical lines do not appear to bend.

One of the reasons why binoculars cause eye strain in some people, or just fail to perform properly, is because of incorrect adjustment. You will notice that one of the eye-pieces (usually the right one) has a separate focus. This is to compensate for the fact that each of our eyes differs slightly in strength. Close the right eye and focus on a distant object, using the central wheel. Now close the left eye and focus on the same object, but this time using only the eyepiece focus. The binoculars are now correct for both eyes, and you now only need to focus with the central wheel.

In the field, keep your binoculars handy, and with the main focusing wheel set near mid point, in case you want to look quickly at something. When not in use, keep them tucked inside your jacket to protect them.

Telescopes

For birdwatching on estuaries, reservoirs and coasts, a telescope may prove to be more useful than binoculars. Do not confuse nature-watching telescopes with those used for astronomy, however. Telescopes with magnifications of about 50 times are ideal, and modern types even have a zoom facility, enabling you to locate your subject from a wide field of view, and then to zoom in for detail. Telescopes need bright light to work at their best, and a tripod or some other steadying support is essential.

Camera

In terms of other optical equipment, a camera should be included, as it will prove invaluable for recording an attractive species or one that defies initial identification in the field. Nature photography is outside the scope of this book, although details of several useful guides to photography are given in the bibliography. Although you need quite sophisticated equipment to achieve shots of distant subjects, or to take photographs in extreme close up, whatever camera you own – range finder, compact or SLR, etc., – you can use it to advantage in the right circumstances.

Clothing

Clothing for nature watching must be versatile. It must keep you warm, dry and comfortable, but it must not rustle, and it must help you to blend in with your surroundings. The more pockets for maps, hand-lens, plastic bottles, etc., the better.

Footwear

Walking boots are the ideal footwear on moorland, mountains and drier habitats. Wellingtons are best for estuaries, bogs and seashores. Choose footwear which enables you to wear an extra pair of socks. These will keep your feet warm, and will prevent chafing.

General clothing

Strong trousers, shirts and a collection of pullovers which can be put on and taken off one by one to help regulate your body temperature are ideal. Waterproof leggings and an anorak are also essential, both to prevent chilling winds and the misery of trying to enjoy yourself when you are soaked through! Quilted waistcoats and similar items are also useful in some circumstances.

A woollen beret is useful (it helps to seal the gaps which anorak hoods often leave) and a peaked cap or similar is useful for avoiding the sun's glare. Gloves are essential both for keeping your hands warm and camouflaging your skin. (In this last respect, serious nature watchers should consider ways of making the human face a less obvious feature, by covering it with a makeshift veil or mask.)

General equipment

Most of the items listed here will be mentioned again in sections of the book where their application is useful.

Identification guides
Maps
Field notebook (spiral bound; keep in plastic envelope)
Pencil (sharpened both ends)
Small torch (with red filter if possible)
Polarized sunglasses
Hand-lens
Small polythene bags and plastic tubes with stoppers
Flat trays or shallow plastic boxes
Tweezers
Whistle
Compass
Trowel and sieve
Umbrella
Penknife
Pooter
Stick (for probing depth of water, firmness of ground, etc.)
Rucksack

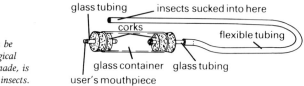

glass tubing   insects sucked into here
corks
flexible tubing
glass container   glass tubing
user's mouthpiece

A pooter, which can be obtained from biological suppliers or easily made, is useful for collecting insects.

Specialized equipment

There are a few items of equipment which you will need to purchase or make, but which will enhance your nature watching potential considerably in some circumstances.

DIP NET – essential for searching in the marginal water of ponds, rivers and streams.

BUTTERFLY NET – essential for catching insects in meadows and hedgerows. In use, the net is passed through the vegetation in one direction and then, in the same action, passed in the other direction. As the direction changes, the handle should be twisted and the net encloses any creature caught by the first sweeping action.

MAMMAL TRAP – Longworth or other mammal traps which do not harm the animals can be set next to likely small mammal pathways (for instance the edges of grass verges, holes in banks, etc.) The trap is baited with food (such as corn and other seeds for rodents, and a small amount of dog or cat food for small carnivores such as shrews) and is also provided with some straw for bedding. Inspect the trap at intervals of no more than twelve hours, for small mammals cannot survive in them for long periods. Non-lethal mousetraps are also available, which can also be used with success in certain instances for catching a variety of small mammals alive.

DREDGE – this is a group of large, hooked wires which is used to retrieve the bottom-growing weeds of lakes and rivers in order that their attendant animal life can be studied. The dredge, attached to a line, is thrown into the water and allowed to sink, and then withdrawn. It can also be used on the lower part of the seashore to bring in submerged seaweeds. Use this apparatus sparingly, since aquatic weeds often harbour eggs and juvenile animals.

MOTH TRAPS – mercury vapour moth traps are one of the best pieces of apparatus for trapping moths. Sometimes rare or unusual species are found, and catches may be extremely high in good conditions. A less expensive alternative to a mercury vapour trap can be created by using a bright camping light or Tilley lamp with a sheet of white paper underneath. Even leaving the light on in a room (with the door closed) overnight may attract quite a number of species. Other methods are shown on page 97.

TULLGREN FUNNEL – this piece of equipment is used for extracting the tiny animals in soil and leaf litter. It is simple to make at home, and the illustration on page 83 shows how this can be done.

Butterfly nets are used in a double action. The first sweep nets the insect, and the second sweep – made after rolling your wrist – prevents the insect escaping. In thick vegetation the stronger sweep net can be used.

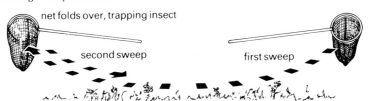

net folds over, trapping insect

second sweep

first sweep

Mountains

The dramatic scenery of mountain regions is the result of upheavals of the earth's crust and subsequent erosion by glaciation, climate, and clearance of the natural vegetation by man. Man's influence on the mountains is, however, far less marked than in many lowland regions. The inaccessibility, severe climate and poor soils of many mountainous areas have discouraged the spread of agriculture, although recreation may still have a detrimental effect in some areas.

Mountains composed of hard igneous rocks such as granite or quartzite have the most restricted flora and fauna; high rainfall usually washes the few existing minerals out of the soil, thus limiting the growth of plants to a few hardy species such as lichens, mosses, lady's mantle, heather, bilberry and mat-grass. This in turn limits the animal life to equally hardy grazing species like the red deer or mountain hare. Birds such as the ptarmigan are able to exist by eating the shoots of these hardy mountain plants, whilst migrants like the dotterel feed on the larvae of the few insects which can breed at high altitudes during the short spell of milder summer weather. Mountains composed of limestone, or other base-rich rocks, have a much richer flora, and subsequently support a wider and more varied collection of animals. (You can often identify limestone from a distance by its pale grey or white appearance.) The alpine meadows in summer are a delight, with an abundance of flowers and many butterflies, crickets and beetles to be found among them. These in turn provide food for a variety of birds and mammals, and as a result you are likely to see a much greater diversity of wildlife in a limestone area.

Altitude has a profound effect on the distribution of an animal, and before searching for a particular species its normal range should be considered. The alpine marmot, for example, rarely descends below the higher alpine meadows, and the snow bunting is restricted to the high tops in summer. It is not possible to state precisely where the alpine zone begins, or where one will find truly alpine species, as the altitude at which they are found varies from one region to another. As a general rule, however, moving north has the effect of lowering the altitude at which montane species occur, thus in the north of Scotland some species descend practically to sea-level, whilst in the Alps they are found only above the tree line.

A number of distinct zones can be identified on most mountains (the precise altitude at which these zones occur cannot be defined for reasons already given). The highest summits and steep, north-facing slopes and gulleys have permanent snow on them and thus have a very limited fauna; only migrant species or soaring birds are likely to be encountered there.

PHOTOKEY

steep crags provide safe nest sites   snow patches may show animal tracks

scan skyline for soaring birds of prey

use boulders to provide cover   tree line is upper limit for many species

Mountain scenery is often paralleled by similarly dramatic, or at least rare, animal species.

Below this occurs a zone of loose, broken rocks known as scree, which although snow-covered in winter is free of snow for the rest of the year. Plant life is sparse, consisting mainly of lichens, mosses and grasses, but here a few birds like the snow bunting and some small rodents may be found. Gradually the screes give way to the more luxuriant alpine meadows and pastures where the plants provide such a spectacle in early summer. Grazing mammals are more abundant here and many more insects are encountered, including a number of truly alpine butterflies. Ledges which are beyond the reach of most grazing mammals can be particularly rich in plant life and often provide safe nesting site or birds also. As insect and plant life become more abundant so, too, do the birds and this can be one of the most profitable areas for the naturalist to visit.

Finally the meadows give way to the wooded slopes where, unless they have been cleared by man, increasingly dense stands of birch, coniferous trees and low bushes – mainly willows – will begin to dominate the scenery. A feature of these lower slopes in many areas is the spread of non-native

29

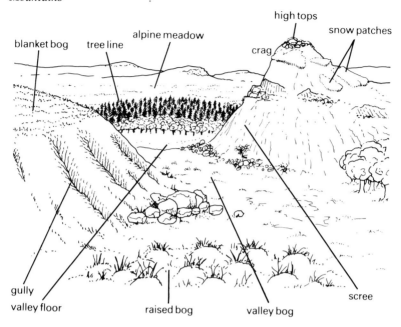

high tops

alpine meadow

snow patches

blanket bog   tree line

crag

gully

valley floor

raised bog

valley bog

scree

The main features of mountains. The height at which the zones occur differs according to location. For instance, the coniferous forest peters out at about 2600 m (8530 ft) on the southern Alps; in Scotland it does not grow above 600 m (1970 ft).

coniferous trees, planted by man either to replace the natural tree cover or to be harvested for economic return.

The cold conditions, coupled with rocks which often yield nutrients only slowly, mean that any upland lakes present are poor in plant and animal life, although they often provide nesting sites for unusual birds such as divers. The hardness of the rocks also reduces drainage so that hollows are often characterized by the formation of blanket bogs, in which sphagnum is the dominant plant.

Nature watching in mountains

Mountains are harsh environments for both the nature watcher and the animals and plants which live there. Food is often scarce and for this reason mountains do not support large animal populations. Birds of prey, for instance, are thinly dispersed and may range widely in search of food. However, what mountain animals lack in quantity, they make up for in quality for many are rare and spectacular, and will reward the nature watcher who devotes several hours of patient searching and observation.

Although, apart from the possibility of wooded slopes, mountains have

eagle   vulture   raven   harrier   buzzard

Flight silhouettes of soaring mountain birds.

little cover for the naturalist, they have an advantage over moorland in that the terrain is not only rocky but also that the landscape in general is usually steeply undulating. This means that you can move from one place to another, and still remain below the skyline and therefore out of view, and you can also use large rocks as temporary hides.

Before setting off to explore any mountain – even in summer – observe the following precautions:-

1   Check weather conditions and forecasts, and always inform someone of where you are going, even if it just means leaving a note on a car windscreen;

2   Carry a compass, a good map, whistle, torch and adequate food supplies (chocolate, fruit cake and glucose are good emergency rations);

3   Wear suitable warm, dry waterproof clothing (including an extra bright garment in case you need rescuing), and strong footwear with two pairs of socks;

4   Carry a watch, and allow time to make your descent in daylight.

When to go

Winter snow and short days make conditions dangerous, but with care it is possible to follow tracks and signs. Some species change colour to match the snow, but many leave the high tops until the weather improves. Most animals are spotted during spring and summer, although hibernation and migration causes a flurry of activity during the autumn.

Starting at the bottom

Many montane areas can be reached, in part, by road, and the car park can make a good starting point to nature watch. Birds and small mammals often congregate around these areas for picnic crumbs, etc., and from your car you may be able to watch several species. Whilst still in the car, scan the skyline above the mountains for a few minutes for large birds such as buzzards or ravens which may be soaring.

As you ascend the mountain, use any wooded areas as places of concealment from which to scan the rocks and skyline again for possible species. Scree slopes are an important habitat on mountain sides. They offer nesting and hiding holes for a variety of birds and small mammals, and the moist conditions attract many invertebrates such as centipedes, spiders and beetles. Lifting loose rocks may reveal some of these smaller creatures. The larger animals such as polecats, pine martens, and stoats are harder to see,

Your most likely sighting of an eagle is one soaring in the distance, but scanning inaccessible crags for likely nest sites may allow an exciting view like this.

and will usually require an early morning or late evening vigil from a well-concealed viewing place.

Higher ground

Streams are a feature of many mountains, and these can be examined for their animal life by following many of the techniques described on pages 117 to 124. In areas where drainage is poor bogs may also develop, and these also attract their own specific animal life.

Moving on upwards, it is useful to rest from time to time and to sit quietly and see if any birds are about. Birds of prey such as the golden eagle will use the updraughts created by the wind hitting the mountains to enable themselves to soar; often they will reach a great height and, despite their size, they will not always be visible to the naked eye. A useful clue to the presence of a bird of prey in the sky is the sound of a pair of mobbing ravens. These largest members of the crow family always take exception to the presence of other large birds in their territory and fly up to chase them off, calling loudly all the time.

The lack of trees in mountainous country makes any post, bush or prominent rock an attraction for small birds of prey such as the merlin, or perching birds like the wheatear. Droppings, or the remains of meals near such perching places are good clues, and it is usually worth retiring to a safe distance and waiting to see what uses the perch. When you approach a ridge or a high point try not to suddenly break the skyline. Large mammals such

(Above) The scarcity of natural cover means that you must keep below the skyline on open ground by moving forward in a prone position.

(Below) The mountain hare, seen here in its winter coat, is easily visible before snow covers the ground.

as red deer are always on the lookout, and being very alert they will soon spot you and move quickly away. Use what natural cover you are able to find to approach ridges, crouch low and scan the land ahead of you before moving out. Should you spot a herd of deer or a small group of chamois and wish to approach them more closely you must consider two things. Firstly, as you approach, are you going to appear above the skyline at any point or

33

move across open ground where your presence might attract attention? Secondly, is the wind going to carry your scent towards them? Of these two senses, the sense of smell is the keenest in most mammals, so work out the wind direction, bearing in mind that eddies and currents in narrow valleys can be quite complex.

If you are spotted as you move it is important to freeze instantly; most mammals spot movement fairly easily, but are unable to focus on stationary objects very clearly. If you are wearing clothing of subdued colours and have the wind blowing towards you there should be no problem. If you are stalking a group of mammals there might well be one which is on the lookout so great caution is needed, but following an individual mammal is easier if you move when it is moving and stop quickly when it stops. Ideally you should approach closely to watch the mammal without disturbing it and try to leave without it having been aware of your presence. This will make approaching the same mammal on a further occasion much easier.

Typical animals: fieldbrief

Phylum Arthropoda

Insects Because of the hostile nature of the environment few butterflies and moths are found. The small mountain ringlet is a characteristic upland species of butterfly found above 500 m (1640 ft). Only flies when the sun shines; when a cloud obscures the sun, it drops to the ground immediately. Pinpoint landing spot and search the grass carefully, as butterfly will crawl into cover. Other species sun themselves in the early morning or when sun breaks through after a cloudy spell. Many other species of 'brown' butterfly (Satyridae) occur in different areas of Europe; number of eyespots on wings useful in identification.

Montane species of moth may be disturbed when walking through vegetation. The black mountain moth is a small, dark species with butterfly-like flight. A daytime flier, on the wing in July. The broad-bordered white underwing is on the wing in May. It has a rapid flight, showing white on wings. Other species of moth have cryptic colouring and can be searched for on lichen-covered boulders.

Alpine meadows often support large populations of grasshoppers and bush crickets. Watch the ground in front of your feet for hopping insects. Males can be tracked down by their chirping songs. Sometimes mating pairs are encountered and are easier to follow when they hop.

Spiders These can be searched for in low vegetation by hand or by using a sweep net. Certain species such as crab spiders will be found under stones and boulders.

Phylum Chordata

Amphibians Some amphibians can be seen in mountainous areas. Look under stones and rotting logs in damp places, especially after heavy rain.

Birds BIRDS OF PREY Scan the horizon for soaring birds of prey. Best on a sunny day when there is more updraught and the birds rise on thermals. Golden eagle recognized by immense wingspan and wings held stiff in soaring flight. Griffon vulture is often seen in small parties soaring above carrion. A patient wait by a large carcase may be rewarded by a visit from several vultures or other birds of prey.

GAMEBIRDS Ptarmigan is a bird of boulder-strewn mountain-tops. Plumage provides excellent camouflage. Mottled grey, brown and white to match the lichens in summer, and white to match the snow in winter. In summer, scan likely areas and look for 'moving' boulders. In winter, look for shadow cast by bird on snow. Often completely indifferent to man, especially around ski resorts. Look for groups of droppings, which resemble cigarette ash.

WADERS Few wader species are seen on the mountain-tops, and they are initially difficult to spot. Their calls are often the first sign of their presence. Scan the horizon through binoculars at low level, whilst kneeling. Birds are more likely to be seen silhouetted against the skyline.

PERCHING BIRDS Several species of small perching birds occur in mountain areas, often in flocks. They can often be seen feeding around the base of boulders on scree slopes. In flight, the wing and tail patterns are useful identification features. Many mountain passerines are quite tame and will look for food in and around car parks; the car itself makes a good hide from which to view them. Most of these birds move down the slopes to lower altitudes in the winter. Ravens are very acrobatic in flight, often tumbling upside down. Frequently mob large birds of prey. Alpine choughs are found above the tree line in the Alps and Pyrenees. Often seen in groups, especially around ski stations, where they become very tame.

Mammals RED DEER and REINDEER are large obvious mammals but, as they are shy, need to be stalked carefully in order to obtain good views. Keeping below the skyline is of great importance here and a careful watch needs to be kept on the wind direction. CHAMOIS have size and approximate shape of small goat. Horns have characteristic hooked tips. Small parties often graze grassy slopes between the rocks. Very agile and nimble, even on precipitous rock faces.

Two other large mammals may be encountered on mountains in the Alps and Pyrenees. MOUFLON are the wild equivalent of sheep, and IBEX are the wild equivalent of goats. Scan rock faces for small groups. Males often stand guard on prominent rocks.

Some small mammals have a white winter coat which provides them with excellent camouflage. The black ear-tips of the MOUNTAIN HARE and black tip to the tail of the STOAT give them away when the animals move.

Scree slopes and mountain sides are worth scanning with binoculars for signs of other small mammals. Look for droppings and bait a likely spot; the animals may show themselves if you wait quietly behind a boulder.

Moorland

A moor is a bleak expanse of uncultivated land, devoid of trees, even though it is below the natural tree line. The lack of trees is usually the result of man's clearance of the native pines. Moorland soils are nearly always shallow, deficient in essential plant nutrients and acidic. Moorlands are usually associated with regions of high rainfall, and this climatic factor, coupled with poor drainage, has led to the development of a thick blanket of peat which can cover vast areas.

Unless extensive drainage and liming of the soil take place, moors are particularly difficult to cultivate. Left to nature, this has led to the development of a community of dwarf, shrubby species which can tolerate poor, acidic soils but not shading by trees or disturbance of the soil. Ling or heather is the dominant plant, growing to the exclusion of all else on some moors. It is a valuable food plant for insects, birds and mammals, and many moorland species depend on it. Old heather plants (some twenty-five to thirty years of age) are too woody to be eaten by many species, so some moorland farmers burn patches of heather to encourage it to regenerate; this burning is usually carried out on a ten to twenty year cycle.

Very wet moorlands support cross-leaved heath, whilst on well-drained slopes bell heather can grow. Other berry-bearing shrubs such as bilberry, cowberry and crowberry also occur, and these provide a valuable supply of food for migrant birds in the autumn. The bilberry is usually a relict of the former coniferous woodlands and usually grows on the drier soils. Where grazing is not too severe it can form quite a dense scrub. Mosses and lichens are common on rocks, stone walls and buildings, and in damp areas.

If a moorland has been heavily grazed by sheep, cattle or red deer, or if the burning has been particularly severe, the heathers will be replaced by a community of grasses and sedges, most moorland species having tough leaves which can resist both grazing and severe weather conditions. Mat-grass can form huge patches, whilst cotton-grass and deer-grass – which are not true grasses at all – are common in wetter areas.

Very wet hollows soon fill up with sphagnum moss, and in early summer cotton-grass produces a splash of white with its characteristic cotton-like seed heads. Many insectivorous plants live in these nutrient-deficient habitats, deriving nitrogen by trapping and digesting flies and other insects. Sometimes the tiny sundew can be so common that whole areas appear red and glistening as the sticky hairs on its leaves catch the light. Bog myrtle, a low shrub with pleasantly aromatic leaves, often grows in these boggy hollows or along the courses of tiny streams. It is a valuable plant as it supports symbiotic bacteria in its root system which are able to trap

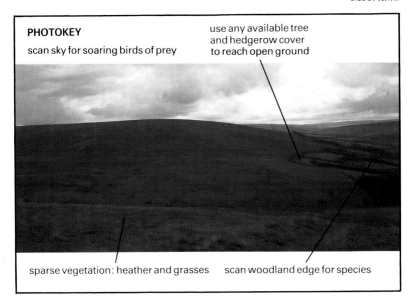

PHOTOKEY

scan sky for soaring birds of prey

use any available tree and hedgerow cover to reach open ground

sparse vegetation: heather and grasses   scan woodland edge for species

Despite its often bleak appearance, moorland supports a varied fauna.

atmospheric nitrogen and produce nutrients which are then made available to other plants.

In areas of high rainfall the sphagnum mosses continue to grow to such an extent that peat is still being formed, and often the level of the bog becomes higher than the surrounding land, forming what is known as a raised bog. It can even cover small pools and streams, leading to the formation of quaking bogs – so called because they literally shake when you walk on them – deep enough to engulf horses or people. A blanket bog forms in places where high rainfall and lack of disturbance or drainage by man allows the sphagnum mosses to grow unchecked, so that huge areas eventually become covered with a blanket of peat. Few animals live here, but midges and craneflies may be abundant, and beetles and dragonflies can also be found.

The low nutritional value of most moorland plants, and the lack of any dense cover, has a restricting effect on the animal life. The few species of grazing mammals which do occur usually search for the more succulent species growing among the heather: voles can sometimes be quite numerous, and red deer and mountain hares are also found. The open landscape means that larger animals will be difficult to approach. Some, such as red deer, will often stay in remote places, especially in summer when grazing is possible on the high ground. Mammals such as hares, and birds like grouse, spend much of the day lying up in the heather, and other non-migratory birds often fly low over the ground to avoid the attentions of the merlins, harriers and other birds of prey, all of which also rest on the ground.

Nature watching on moorland

Safety must be considered when visiting moorland. The high altitude means that dangerous weather conditions can be expected at any time in this bleak habitat. The safety rules for a walk in the mountains (see page 31) apply on moorlands as well. Some moorlands are used as military training areas, and these are always very clearly marked, both on the ground by marker posts and flags, and on most good maps. Always check very carefully about rights of access, firing times and restricted zones before entering such areas. When walking across moorland remember that bright green patches of sphagnum moss indicate where the plant is growing out over deep water. Valley bogs or mires can be very deep and should be approached with great caution.

When to go

Very few species remain on moorland during winter, but in spring displaying birds and emerging reptiles and insects are to be seen, and their numbers increase during summer. By the autumn most bird populations are at their highest.

Open ground

It is important to make use of whatever cover is available so that you do not get spotted too soon by birds or mammals. Dry-stone walls provide useful cover, and often conceal a few interesting species themselves. To help break up your outline, look round any cover if possible, rather than over it. (If you need to climb over a wall, do so very carefully and, should you dislodge any stones, be sure to replace them exactly as you found them. The walls are important stock-proof barriers and considerable damage and inconvenience can result from a gap being created in a wall.) Wheatears nest in crevices in these walls, and stoats use walls as cover when stalking their prey of rabbits or other small mammals. The regular runs of a stoat may be evident from droppings; you could also try to attract one by baiting near the wall. It is also worth searching among the stones for invertebrates for they, too, will find the cover and shelter useful. Snails are infrequent on moorland because of the lack of calcium and the high acidity, but slugs such as the large black *Arion ater* are usually very common. They feed on the mosses and lichens which grow on the stones. Spiders are widespread and they often emerge into the open in sunny weather (see page 102 for spider watching techniques). A few species of ants live under the stones and they are a further attraction to insectivorous birds like the wheatear.

Other mammals such as foxes and hares often lie up during the day in piles of stone or patches of gorse scrub and, in very remote areas, where human disturbance is rare, they can even be found sleeping in the sun on top of rocks. Bearing this in mind, it is always worth scanning any outcrop of rocks through your binoculars before approaching it too closely.

Prominent posts or rocks, or overhead wires, should be scanned for birds of prey which use them as perches. The merlin uses posts as resting places and for plucking its prey, which consists of small songbirds such as the

Look for dry-stone walls on moorland. They provide cover for the naturalist, and are also a rewarding place to find animals such as stoats, as well as attracting many invertebrates.

meadow pipit. Not all predatory birds use perches regularly, and those such as the hen harrier and short-eared owl are more likely to be seen as they fly low over the heather, rarely breaking the skyline. They both roost out of sight, low down in the heather, and hen harriers especially use communal roosts, flying in just before dusk to the same spot every night during the winter.

Moorland birds are mostly ground-nesting and ground-feeding species. The red grouse is the typical moorland bird in Britain, whilst on the

Rabbits and brown hares can be told apart at a distance by the relative lengths of their ears and heads.

(Left) This view of a curlew demonstrates the importance of scanning the habitat carefully with binoculars. At first sight you could easily miss it, or put it to flight inadvertently.

(Below) Emperor moths are typically found on ling.

Continent other species such as the willow grouse replace it. The grouse relies on the heather for its food and shelter. Often it can be seen feeding on the young heather shoots, but it is always worth searching for in open gravelly places such as along roadsides where it can be seen picking up the grit needed to aid digestion, or near small pools where it comes to drink. This usually takes place early in the morning, which is a good time for watching most moorland birds. As the red grouse is a popular sporting bird, much is done to encourage it, and many moorlands are preserved and managed solely for the grouse. These managed moorlands can be recognized by the patchy nature of the heather, a result of the burning of different areas to encourage new growth. Grouse feed on the new shoots, and so this is a good place to search for them.

Sweeping through the heather with a butterfly net (see page 27) will dislodge some of the insects which are feeding or resting on it. The caterpillar of the emperor moth is a very large and brightly coloured creature, yet it blends in with the heather surprisingly well, being very difficult to find simply by searching for it with the eye. Using a sweep net is much more likely to bring success, and many other insects will turn up as well. The cocoons of several moth species are best searched for in the heather in winter when they show up well in the old heather plants. When the heather is in full bloom in late summer many insects are attracted to feed on the pollen and nectar. The sweep net will be needed again, but be careful with angry bees! The leaf litter below the heather also supports insects and many species of spiders, and it is here that on the drier moorlands lizards and adders will be found. Sometimes the tiny heather beetle can be very numerous, and a variety of other beetles, larvae, spiders and harvestmen will be found if the leaf litter is searched thoroughly. Try sprinkling some of it on to a sieve to find the smaller organisms. Other flowering plants such as bilberry should also be examined, because they will also attract pollen-seeking insects.

After a severe winter some moorlands have a number of corpses of the mammals which could not withstand the weather. Quite large mammals can be found dead and decaying, as even the hardiest breeds of sheep or deer succumb to bad conditions at times. This carrion is a vital source of food to a number of species, and if it is possible to remain concealed near a carcase, behind a wall, for example, the scavengers can be observed. The carrion crow and raven soon find dead animals, and the buzzard uses its keen eyesight to locate food from a great distance. Foxes will take carrion, and at some carcases a variety of species will be found either feeding together, or

When stalking deer use all available cover and be aware of wind direction.

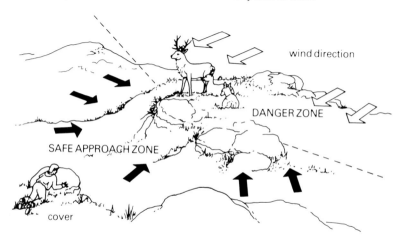

41

queuing up to take their turn. If no natural carrion is present then offal or a dead road casualty animal placed in a prominent position will attract the scavenging species. Erecting a photographic hide nearby will ensure closer views, as merely hiding behind a wall will not offer concealment from airborne scavengers. If it is not too unpleasant, the carcass should be turned over to look for beetles and their larvae. Sexton beetles are attracted by the smell of decay, and bury small pieces of flesh, and even whole small birds or mammals, so that they can lay their eggs on them. Many flies lay their eggs directly on the carcass and these develop into maggots which are a further source of food for birds.

Moorland streams

A moorland stream always attracts a variety of interesting species. Birds like the dipper and grey wagtail are rarely found far from running water, and they nest in river banks, under bridges or very close to the water. By working your way along the stream it should be possible to find these and other moorland-nesting species like the common sandpiper, together with the birds and mammals which come to drink or bathe.

The clear water of most moorland streams enables the careful observer to watch fishes as they face into the current waiting for their food to be swept down to them (see fish watching on pages 122 to 124). They dart away very quickly when frightened, so try not to let your shadow fall on the water, and remember also that the vibrations of heavy footsteps will be transmitted through the bank into the water. In the winter months salmon arrive at the upper reaches of moorland streams, having completed a long and hazardous journey from the sea in order to spawn in the clear, gravelly beds of the streams. They choose shallow pools where there is plenty of clean gravel and well-oxygenated water. The females construct small depressions in the gravel called 'redds' by making powerful sweeps with their tails whilst lying on their sides. It is quite easy to watch them doing this, as during spawning salmon seem oblivious to all disturbance. Watch out also for predators and scavengers, for the salmon often die after spawning, and when they are so weak after their long journeys upstream from the sea they are easy prey.

Examine the banksides for footprints and droppings of patrolling mammals, especially otters. Otters themselves are notoriously difficult to see. Being largely nocturnal, and having acute senses, they are rarely seen, even by the most experienced field naturalists. The first step in finding otters is to look for their oily droppings or spraints which are usually deposited on a prominent boulder or grass tussock. The characteristic webbed footprint is another useful clue and the remains of a partly eaten fish – usually the tail and head – left on the riverbank are also strong indicators that otters are in the vicinity. They are fairly wide-ranging, and might not use a particular stretch of river every night, so great patience is called for. They are particularly fond of eels, so muddy stretches where eels are likely to be more common are worth watching. Observing otters requires the same skills as watching badgers. Concealment on the part of the observer is most important, and note must be taken of the wind direction, as otters have an excellent sense of smell. Finally, if you do have the good fortune to

(Right) Upland pools may attract many animal species.

(Below) Sundews — easily recognizable as splashes of red colour in boggy places — often ensnare interesting insects.

have a successful otter watch, be sure to leave quietly without alerting the otters to your presence; this will make them less wary on future occasions.

Peat bogs

Most moorland streams have their sources in peat bogs; the precise sources are in fact rather difficult to locate, as the water seeps from the peat in tiny trickles which gradually join together to form the stream. These areas should be approached with care as the peat can be very deep, and there are often surprisingly deep pools between the raised hummocks of sphagnum moss and cotton-grass. Insects such as pond skaters occur on the surface of these pools and tiny, gyrating specks will turn out to be the very active whirligig beetles. Dragonfly larvae live in the water and the bottom ooze, but a net will be needed to find them; the pole makes a useful walking stick and can be used for sounding out the depth of any particularly dangerous looking patches of sphagnum. The raft spider, a large and attractive species, lives on the sphagnum and catches insects and other creatures by fishing for them in the water. If you approach the edge of the pool carefully, and try not to shake the moss too much, you should be able to see one in the 'fishing position' with its legs just touching the water.

Typical animals: fieldbrief

Phylum Mollusca
Slugs can be abundant on damp moorland, particularly after rain. *Arion ater* is a large black species which leaves a conspicuous slime trail over vegetation. The smaller, brown upland slug *Deroceras agreste* often grazes lichens off boulders. In dry weather search for slugs under stones, or at night with a torch.

Phylum Arthropoda
Insects Many lowland species of butterfly and moth wander on to moorland or breed in sheltered spots. The large heath is restricted to moorland, and is very active when sun shines but drops into cover the instant the sun is obscured by cloud. Search the vegetation where you think it landed. If unsuccessful wait by spot until sun reappears; subsequently the butterfly will also emerge. Moths may be disturbed as you walk through vegetation. Try sweeping vegetation with a net as you walk, and examine the catch. Several day-flying species can be observed on moorland, and these include emperor moth and fox moth.

Dragonflies may be found by streams. Those which are, tend to be very active, patrolling a particular stretch of water. They often fight aerial battles with rivals of same species. Easiest to observe resting early in the morning before sun has warmed them up. Larvae live in buried sand and gravel in stream bed. Species of *Sympetrum* dragonfly frequent moorland pools. Search the rushes and other poolside vegetation for mating pairs. Adults sometimes observed emerging from larval skin early in morning.

Moorland pools sometimes contain water bugs. Pond skaters skim the surface of the water, whereas water boatmen and other bugs are found below the surface. If disturbed, they quickly disappear from view but will return if you sit quietly for a few minutes.

Spiders Search heather and other vegetation for webs.

Phylum Chordata
Amphibians Frogs may be found in many moorland areas, mating and laying spawn in every conceivable stretch of still water, even in tyre ruts. Remains of unpalatable oviducts often litter ground around pools where predators have fed on frogs.

Reptiles Adders bask on sunny, bare, south-facing slopes. Particularly noticeable in early spring when just out of hibernation and less active. If disturbed while basking will frequently return to same spot later on. Mark spot and return cautiously. Lizards may be seen basking on sunny banks in summer.

Birds BIRDS OF PREY Hen harriers and merlins both fly low to the ground, and so are best seen by scanning the horizon whilst sitting low down yourself, so that they are more likely to break the skyline. Merlins habitually use posts and prominent boulders and walls from which to look for their prey and also to eat. These perches are often 'white-washed' with droppings. In winter, the larger peregrine can also be seen in this habitat. Look up and scan the sky for buzzards soaring; listen also for their 'mewing' call.

OWLS In contrast to most other owls, the short-eared owl hunts by day over moorlands. Sometimes it is flushed from dense vegetation whilst roosting. Snowy owl is a tundra species found mainly in Scandinavia; easily seen in summer as white plumage contrasts against dark vegetation. Generally seen in daytime sitting on rocks, etc.

GAMEBIRDS Many areas of moorland are specifically managed for gamebirds such as grouse. The heather is burned systematically to provide new shoots upon which the grouse feed, and it is worth concentrating your searches in such places. Red grouse have a characteristic laughing call and are often heard before being seen, crouching low in the heather before being flushed. Male black grouse use areas of bare ground as communal breeding display sites. Signs of such activity are feathers and droppings. Once located, return to the site on an early spring morning and wait quietly.

WADERS Many waders breed on moorlands in summer. They are most often located by a knowledge of their different calls. Golden plover and dunlin prefer to breed and feed in areas where the heather is short. Waders will use noisy alarm calls if you venture too near to their nests, and care should be taken not to disturb them on their breeding grounds. Look for common sandpipers along moorland streams, where they breed.

PERCHING BIRDS Due to the lack of trees, few perching birds are to be seen on moorlands, but several species such as twite and linnet exploit the abundant summer insect populations and breed on the moors. Meadow pipits habitually sit on the tops of heather clumps and boulders. Ring ouzels are wary birds of rocky crags, often detected by their loud clacking alarm; use an outcrop as cover when watching them. Some perching birds live along streams. Grey wagtails and dippers perch on mid-stream boulders; crouch down with your back to the bank and watch a likely spot. A boulder covered in droppings is probably a favourite place from which the birds start their hunting forays.

Mammals VOLES are common on moorland and can be seen by quickly turning over logs or corrugated iron under which they make their nests. A rustle in the grass may betray their whereabouts.

MOUNTAIN HARE Despite its name, is also found in moorland areas where it lies for most of the day in a scrape in the ground (form). Mountain hares feed on heather and make conspicuous trails through the vegetation. In winter they turn to other sources of food such as rowan and juniper. The twigs are bitten through to leave a characteristic, sloping cut. Tracks in the snow give away the presence of these animals in winter, as do their black ear-tips; the rest of the coat turning white and providing superb camouflage against the snow. Brown hare also found; usually close to farmland.

FOX Not common on moorland, but obvious when it does appear and easy to spot due to the lack of cover.

STOATS AND WEASELS Will occasionally forage over moorlands.

POLECAT Only found in wooded areas; keeps to cover, but may be seen as road accident victim.

RED DEER Sometimes occur on moors. They are particularly noticeable when disturbed or running, or when their outline breaks the horizon. As with all species of deer, a great deal of stealth and patience is required to stalk them properly.

Heathland and maquis

Heathland

Heathlands are lowland areas of heather, low shrubs and grassland which were once wooded. They were cleared of their trees many centuries ago, usually to provide grazing land, and then maintained as cleared areas by constant grazing and collecting of timber. Some heathlands were set aside as common land where the grazing was available to local people. Many of these have now been deep ploughed and swallowed up by modern farming.

The lack of plant cover over a prolonged period, coupled with the well-drained gravelly nature of the soil, has resulted in most of the minerals being leached out, giving the heathland soil a very characteristic appearance. The upper layer is usually shallow and dark and contains many plant and animal remains in it, and has the consistency of dry peat. Below this is a pale grey layer which has lost most of its soluble materials; these are deposited in the hard-pan layer immediately below it which has a striking orange coloration due to the presence of iron compounds. The hard-pan layer is really very hard, and it makes an effective barrier to the growth of tree roots which are

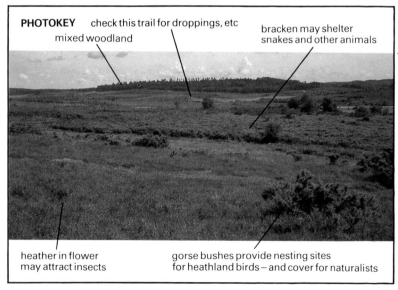

PHOTOKEY check this trail for droppings, etc
mixed woodland
bracken may shelter snakes and other animals
heather in flower may attract insects
gorse bushes provide nesting sites for heathland birds – and cover for naturalists

Heathland in summer; this habitat supports many unique and interesting species.

Birch scrub develops when heathland begins to revert to woodland.

quite unable to penetrate it. Finally, the lowest layer is the parent material, which is usually a gravel and sand mixture.

The most characteristic plants of heathland are the heathers, which in late summer cover the heaths with a purple carpet. Bell heather colonizes the drier areas, while ling grows on most soils. The wetter areas are colonized by cross-leaved heath and there are a number of local species of heather which are much more restricted in range. The dominant heathland shrub is common gorse, which turns many heaths bright yellow when it is in full bloom in the spring and fills the air with its heavy scent. The dense, prickly bushes are valuable nesting and feeding areas for many heathland birds, which can find protection in them throughout the year. The flowers are pollinated by bumble bees, but many other insects visit the gorse flowers, and even the seed-pods can be filled with tiny weevils. Heathland is also characterized by two other species of gorse which have similar flowers but do not reach such a great size: western gorse is most common in western Britain and Ireland, whilst dwarf gorse is more widespread in eastern Britain and on the Continent. Acid-tolerant grasses such as purple moor-grass and wavy hair-grass can flourish only where the growth of heathers has been checked in some way, perhaps by a fire or clearance. Patches of heathland may have only the sparsest covering of mosses or lichens on them, but even here some insect life may be found – usually tiny relatives of the grasshoppers called groundhoppers which blend perfectly with their background.

The light, sandy soils of heathlands provide ideal conditions for ants, which form large colonies, and for many other insects which can be found feeding on the heathland plants. Spiders are also numerous, feeding on the abundant insects, and they in turn are prey for the lizards and insectivorous birds which are so characteristic of this habitat. On the wetter parts of heathland, bogs similar in nature to the bogs of upland moors develop. These usually support some species less tolerant of the upland climate, such as marsh gentian or bog orchid.

Unless grazing, burning and collection of timber occur regularly, most heathlands, despite the low fertility of their soils, will revert to woodland. Birch colonizes very rapidly and Scots pine also invades heathlands when there are man-made plantations nearby. Alder and alder buckthorn usually grow in the wetter hollows, and eventually a closed woodland with a mixture of acid-tolerant species, including some oaks, will develop. A few remnants of the heathland vegetation will survive only as long as some light can reach the woodland floor, with ling usually being the last of the heathland species to be found.

Maquis

In southern Europe a slightly different type of heathland community develops, in which the gorse bushes are replaced by other low, spiny shrubs, and the dominant trees are usually the Aleppo pine or the maritime

PHOTOKEY
stony hillside attracts insectivorous birds and reptiles

sun-warmed boulders attract reptiles and small mammals

many insects live in thorny scrub
use any natural cover for concealment

A wooded region of the maquis in southern Europe.

pine. The origins of this maquis are similar to those of heathland. Clearance of the original plant cover, and then heavy grazing and the prevention of natural regeneration, has led to the development of plant species resistant to grazing and drought such as spiny broom and tree heather. Apart from their spiny nature, many of the shrubs of the maquis, including rosemary, have extremely aromatic leaves which deter grazing by mammals or invertebrates. Flowering usually takes place early in the year, and during the hot dry summer much of the vegetation will look very brown. There are many evergreen trees and shrubs in this habitat which are able to conserve moisture by having reduced leaves, or leaves with waxy outer surfaces; deciduous trees are unusual here. Insects are numerous in this habitat and there are many more insectivorous birds to be found here than on heathland, including many species of warbler. Where grazing is very severe the maquis will become even more restricted, forming a semi-desert of very low, spiny shrubs with many open patches of bare ground called garigue.

Nature watching on heathland and maquis

This habitat is an excellent one for insects, therefore much of the natural history interest focuses on either the insects themselves, or the species which prey on them. However, mammals such as rabbits – as well as larger species – will also be found.

This well-camouflaged wall lizard, like many other basking animals, prefers dark-coloured rocks since these absorb and then radiate more heat.

When to go

The most rewarding time to visit heathland or maquis is in warm sunny weather when the insect and bird activity is at its peak, and when reptiles are active. Some insects can easily be seen by direct observation, but it is advisable to take a butterfly or sweep net with you in order to catch any fast-flying species or any which are hiding in the vegetation.

Open ground and banks

Sunny banks where the sand is exposed and warmed by the sun are ideal basking sites for heathland reptiles. Approach these spots as stealthily as you approach a site in any other habitat, for snakes will feel the vibrations caused by heavy footsteps and disappear quickly. A further reason for approaching these sites carefully is that some snakes are poisonous, and it would be unwise to step on, or touch one of these, by mistake. Do not let your shadow fall on reptiles either, as this will cause as much alarm as heavy vibrations. In late spring male adders can be seen fighting near the basking sites, seeking the attentions of the females watching nearby. They are then least likely to take any notice of onlookers.

These same sunny banks are also the homes of insects such as predatory beetles or burrowing wasps so, having examined the site for reptiles, take a closer look for the holes made by smaller creatures. Trickling a few grains of sand down a hole, or poking a blade of grass down it will usually entice any resident out into the open. Have a specimen tube or a pooter handy to catch whatever comes out.

Other hiding places

In dull weather heathland reptiles make for cover, so any logs, sheets of corrugated metal or large rocks should be turned over carefully to search for them. Always replace these hiding places exactly as you found them as they provide vital cover for many other creatures apart from reptiles. Small

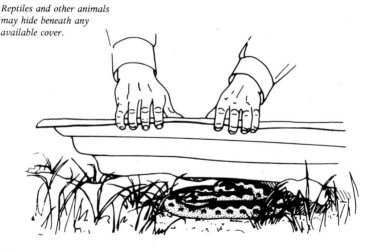

Reptiles and other animals may hide beneath any available cover.

Sandy patches often attract insects (especially beetles) and reptiles.

mammals such as voles also nest under logs or sheets of metal, although mammals are not common on heathland. Some reptiles also hide in the heather, and adders have been accidentally caught up in butterfly nets whilst sweeping through the vegetation!

Bushes and shrubs

Sometimes it is possible to find a thorny bush, such as hawthorn, adorned with the partly eaten and dried remains of lizards, small mammals, birds or beetles. These are likely to have been placed there by a shrike to act as a 'larder' or food store to be used in times of scarcity. Shrikes feed on a variety of small creatures, some of which they can swallow whole, whilst others need to be torn up. The spines of the hawthorn help them to do this, and any left-overs remain on the bush to be eaten later. In the Mediterranean the woodchat shrike is most likely to be encountered, whilst over much of the

The red-backed shrike builds its nest among spiny bushes and thickets.

rest of Europe the red-backed shrike is most common. The great grey shrike breeds further north than the other species, and moves south to spend the winter on heathlands. Shrikes are active, alert birds, frequently seen perching near the top of a bush where they watch for prey, so in order to watch them a very cautious approach is needed, using any cover available.

Birds are not abundant here, but are well worth searching for as some are rare and interesting species. Most nest on the ground and are therefore easily disturbed, so when searching for other species such as snakes, keep a watchful eye open for nests. Should you find one move away from it as quickly as possible to avoid disturbing the parent birds or young. Some species advertize their presence by using the tops of gorse bushes as song posts. Early mornings in late spring are ideal times to search for the singing males of species like the stonechat or Dartford warbler. Later in the season they can be watched as they search for the insect food needed to rear their growing families. Again, your best chance of success lies in using other bushes as natural cover. Don't forget to look upwards, too; birds of prey may be soaring high above, their keen eyes searching the ground for prey. A visit to a heathland at dusk in summer may give you the opportunity to hear the strange churring call of the nightjar. The males sit on a branch calling, turning their heads as they do so, and this most un-birdlike sound carries far across the heath. Try cupping your hands behind your ears to magnify the sound; this will make it easier to locate. When they fly they produce a whip-lash call, and they can sometimes be seen silhouetted against the sky as they chase night-flying insects.

From cover such as bushes and shrubs you can watch for mammals. Most mammals will emerge from refuges like adjacent woodland, so try and station yourself as close to this as possible, particularly at dusk when foxes, rabbits and deer come on to the habitat to feed. Remember to look for any signs such as footprints or droppings.

Low vegetation

Depending on the species, heather, bracken and other low-growing plants offer animals either a refuge or a source of food. Butterflies and bees feed on the flowers and can be caught with a sweep net, or can be seen by squatting down and carefully looking among the foliage. Crab spiders hide, perfectly camouflaged, in some flowers, awaiting visiting insects which they then capture. Use a stick to carefully part the bracken. This will avoid you stepping on any nests or resting snakes. If you encounter a nesting bird depart leaving your discovery undisturbed.

Look carefully among the heather and other low-growing plants for insects and spiders, especially those well camouflaged. A puff of cigarette smoke will often cause moths and other insects to break from cover.

Heathland and maquis

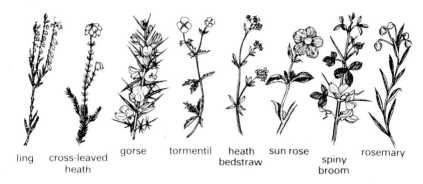

ling   cross-leaved   gorse   tormentil   heath   sun rose   spiny   rosemary
         heath   bedstraw   broom

Many insects are restricted to particular foodplants. Some of the most common plants on which to look for insects are illustrated here.

Animal trails are clearly visible on heathland, and should be examined for droppings and other signs, as well as the animals themselves.

Ponds and streams

A variety of aquatic insects are found wherever there are permanent pools or small streams, particularly dragonflies and damselflies. Adults are on the wing throughout most of the summer and are frequently seen hawking over the water or heather in pursuit of their insect prey. They can sometimes be caught in a butterfly net, but they have extremely good eyesight so you will have to be very quick. Many species follow the same route time and time again so if you miss one on the first attempt, you can often try again later. Early mornings are probably the best times for finding dragonflies and damselflies for they are then at their lowest level of activity; until they have raised their body temperatures slightly they are unable to fly very quickly, sitting on waterside vegetation with their wings outstretched to absorb the sun's heat.

Shallow pools which may even dry up in the summer are sometimes chosen as breeding sites by the natterjack toad. Its tadpoles seem to prefer rather warmer conditions than the common toad's, and so it has a more restricted range. As a prelude to spawning, natterjacks gather near the pool and set up a far-carrying chorus of croaking. This can be heard a great distance from the pool, but will suddenly stop if there is any disturbance. It is usually possible to creep up to the pool at dusk and listen quietly, but in order to make certain of success the best plan is to visit the pool during the day and look for an easy route to the edge of the pool which does not involve too much clambering over obstacles or through vegetation, the noise of which would alert the amphibians to your approach and cause them to take shelter in the water or nearby vegetation.

Try to find a place where it is possible to sit comfortably – there is less chance of you moving and causing disturbance then – and plan to make your arrival before the dusk chorus begins. Apart from the natterjacks, a number of other species should be seen at this time, such as roding woodcock or tawny owls. A torch with a red filter – red cellophane will do – can be used to observe the toads and other pond life without causing them too much alarm.

It is always worth searching the vegetation at the edges of heathland pools for the exuviae, or larval skins, of newly emerged dragonflies. The larvae develop under water, but when their development is complete they climb out of the water, usually at night, and cling to an upright stem. Some species synchronize their emergence, and so there are occasions when large numbers of newly emerged adults can be found drying their wings early in the morning. The larval stages can be found by sweeping a net through the water weeds or by sieving the mud at the bottom of the pool.

Typical animals: fieldbrief

Phylum Arthropoda

Insects There are several heathland butterflies and most, such as the silver studded blue, grayling and green hairstreak are strong, rapid fliers. These species need to be watched in the early morning or late evening when they are less active if close views or photography are required, otherwise they should be netted, identified and then released unharmed.

Many nocturnal species of moths may be disturbed from vegetation during the day or caught with a sweep net. Several heathland moths are daytime fliers and this makes them easier to spot. A number of heathland moths, the emperor and the fox moth for example, have large, strikingly coloured caterpillars and these can be searched for among the vegetation. Nocturnal species of moth may be attracted to your car headlights or a torch in heathland areas.

Several predatory beetles live on heathlands. Tiger beetles are very active and conspicuous during the day on heathland paths; they are easier to approach when a mating pair is discovered. Various species of bugs can be found by careful searching or beating of the vegetation. The larvae of many flies live in heathland pools and can be caught and examined with a net.

Dragonflies and damselflies are common and prominent members of the heathland community. Some of the larger species often have a favourite perch from where they watch for rivals or potential prey. They will return to the same spot repeatedly if you wait for them patiently. Mating pairs remain in tandem for some time and so are easier to approach. Adults generally metamorphose from the aquatic nymph stage at night, and a nocturnal search of pool-side vegetation with a torch can locate them. A search of rushes and sedges during the day should reveal cast nymphal skins which can be taken home and identified.

Many species of bees and solitary wasps frequent heathland. A patient watch near one of their burrows may be rewarded with the sight of an adult returning to it. Ants are often numerous on heaths; turn over stones to reveal their nest colonies and eggs, but always replace them afterwards.

Heathlands are excellent habitats for grasshoppers and crickets. The best time to watch them is on dull days or early in the morning when they are less active. Praying mantids, by contrast, are difficult to locate because they are so inactive, remaining motionless on vegetation, waiting for prey. Ant lions have larvae which bury themselves in sandy soil and form a soil funnel into which ants and other insects fall but cannot escape. Try dropping a few sand grains down the funnel and the insect may show itself.

Spiders and harvestmen Common on heaths, their webs sometimes cover the grass and heather.

Phylum Chordata

Amphibians Toads are particularly noticeable in the spring when they congregate in large numbers. Toad spawn appears as chains of eggs wrapped around water weeds. Outside the breeding season, toads are more terrestrial and can be found under stones and in damper places on the heaths. The natterjack toad remains hidden during the day and is only active at night. Listen for the mating calls of the males during the spring breeding season.

Several species of newts can be seen in heathland pools; catch them with a pond net and return them to their habitat when they have been identified.

Reptiles Heaths are undoubtedly the best habitat for watching reptiles. Slow worms and common lizards are widespread and are often seen basking in the sun or scurrying away when disturbed. Sand lizards particularly like to bask on patches of sand warmed up by the sun. Many other species of lizards occur in areas of maquis. As with most reptiles, spring is a good time to see them, since they will have recently emerged from hibernation and will not be too active. Adders sun themselves on bare slopes and even on top of the heather. They are always wary but will return to a favourite sunning patch eventually if disturbed. Smooth snakes have similar habits to adders but are more secretive. Look for them under sheets of corrugated iron and other debris in the early morning and late evening.

Birds BIRDS OF PREY The hobby is a characteristic heathland predator, especially where there are scattered pines for it to nest in. It is most likely to be seen in the early morning or evening when the birds upon which it feeds are leaving or arriving at their roosts. Watch for hobbies over water, too, for they will take dragonflies from the surface of heathland pools. Many other species of bird of prey visit heath and maquis to feed on insects, small mammals and carrion, but nest elsewhere. Scan the horizon in search of these raptors.

NIGHTJARS These are nocturnal birds, related to swifts. Listen for their churring calls at dusk, cupping your hands behind your ears to magnify the sound. Once pinpointed, watch for the birds on the wing, chasing after moths and other insects, capturing them with an audible snap of their gaping beaks.

HOOPOE An unmistakeable bird which is sometimes disturbed in scrubby patches of maquis.

ROLLER Vivid colours in flight; perches on bushes.

SHRIKES These impale their prey on thorn bushes in a so-called 'larder'. Insects, lizards and even small mammals are stored in this way.

WOODLARKS Look for these birds in heathland areas with some trees, which are used for delivery of the song. Notice rather bat-like flight silhouette.

WARBLERS Many different species nest on the scrubby areas of heath. The different songs are a useful identification clue, but the best way to see these sometimes elusive birds is to sit quietly overlooking a clearing and watch for them as they fly between the bushes.

STONECHAT A common bird of heathland and maquis. Scan the tops of heather clumps for singing males; the call sounds like a couple of pebbles being clacked together.

Mammals Most mammals seen on heaths and maquis are passing through or just visiting the area to feed.

BATS Various species may feed over heathland pools at dusk, catching midges and moths. They are difficult to identify in flight without aid of a 'bat detector', which enables high-pitched calls to be identified.

RABBITS May excavate their burrows in the sandy heathland soil. They are very wary animals and will disappear into their warrens at the first sign of danger, therefore watching from cover at dusk usually produces the best results.

VOLES AND MICE Some species are found on heathlands; small mammal traps can be baited near runs through the heather and scrub.

FOX Occasionally has an earth in sandy soil, particularly around roots or mature gorse bushes. Watch suitable holes from a distance with binoculars (see page 86 for identification of holes).

STOAT AND WEASEL These two wide-ranging carnivores prey upon rabbits and small mammals, and are occasional visitors to heathlands.

Coniferous woodland

Coniferous woodland is the natural climax vegetation in many upland regions of Britain, central Europe and Scandinavia. For instance, a forest of spruce would be the dominant vegetation in Scandinavia if all agriculture and other clearance ceased, whereas Scot's pine would be dominant in upland Britain. Pines thrive on shallow, gravelly soils which are fairly dry and low in nutrients, and they can even grow in places where there is no soil cover at all, surviving merely by rooting themselves in narrow rock crevices. Spruces, on the other hand, need damper conditions and a slightly

PHOTOKEY

open, sunny sites

canopy

extensive ground cover of bracken and shrubs

search for insects and pupae in the soil

Open, semi-natural coniferous woodland such as this is likely to contain more species than the more highly managed conifer plantations.

richer soil. Both species need some assistance in order to grow in these habitats, however, and this comes in the form of a mycorrhizal fungus which forms an association with the root system of the tree. This partnership, an example of symbiosis, facilitates the uptake of nitrates from the soil by the tree, and the fungus benefits by having a ready supply of plant food.

The dense carpet of needles on the woodland floor prevents the growth of many ground layer plants, but bilberry, which also has a fungal partner associated with its roots, is able to form a complete carpet where there is sufficient light. Wavy hair-grass and broad buckler fern can also grow in clearings or rides where some light penetrates, although they never form very dense stands. The dense canopy of many pinewoods effectively cuts out the sunlight, however, and often the only ground layer plants are the fungi, some existing as partners on the roots of the conifers and usually appearing as rings of toadstools, whilst others act as saprophytes, feeding on the slowly decaying needles, cones and branches.

Native coniferous woodlands, such as the Caledonian Pine Forests of Scotland, are far richer in associated species than man-made plantations, because the naturally spaced trees encourage a far greater diversity of microhabitats, including a thriving shrub layer and its attendant insect, bird and mammal populations. The man-made forests usually consist of a single species of tree only, often of a non-native variety, planted closely together. The trees will also be of the same age, having been planted together, so there is less likelihood of an old tree falling to the ground and thus allowing light to penetrate or providing some rotting timber. The only form of clearing is the woodland ride, but this is created to provide access for heavy machinery and is therefore kept fairly clear of undergrowth. The introduced conifers support only a few native invertebrates, so opportunities for feeding by birds are limited. When the trees have reached a suitable size they are felled and removed, rather than being left to die, so there is always a shortage of rotting timber. The forestry operations which involve the use of very heavy machinery greatly disturb the soil which means that the ground flora cannot establish itself very easily; foxgloves and rosebay willowherb do adapt to these conditions, however, and they often provide a splash of vivid colour in recently cleared areas.

When an area of bleak moorland is fenced off and planted up with young conifers there is always a dramatic increase in the ground cover of grasses and mosses due to the lack of grazing. This in turn supports a greatly increased vole population leading to an invasion of predatory birds such as the hen harrier and short-eared owl. When the young conifers grow taller and form a closed canopy the ground flora gradually disappears, and with it the small mammal and bird populations, to be replaced by other species. Once the conifers are mature and begin producing cones a new population moves in to feed on the new food supply, and the red squirrel and crossbill are good examples of species dependent on the mature forest. Although the food supply in plantations is rather limited, many of them provide shelter for species which feed elsewhere, but use the woods for nesting or hiding in during the day.

Nature watching in coniferous woodland

Although coniferous woodland does not support the diversity of animal life to be found in deciduous woodland, it is nevertheless an important habitat for wildlife, providing a niche for some unusual species seldom found in other habitats. One of the most noticeable features of a dense coniferous woodland is the silence. It is very important therefore that you should keep as quiet as possible yourself. Although the dense carpet of needles will deaden the sound of your footsteps, accidentally stepping on a twig and snapping it will produce a sound like a pistol shot and alert most birds and mammals to your presence. Move cautiously, watching where you place your feet, and stop frequently to listen for the sounds of birds.

When to go

Coniferous woodlands act as effective windbreaks, and in addition the ability of most species of conifers to retain their leaves all year means that they provide welcome shelter and food for animals even in the colder months, although insect populations will be higher during warmer months.

Canopy

As most conifer plantations have no shrub or ground layer the bird life is restricted to the tree canopy, and the species will be those which feed on the cones or on the specialized insects of conifers. Some birds can be located by

Where possible, break up your outline by crouching in front of trees. Do not forget to keep your elbows tucked in.

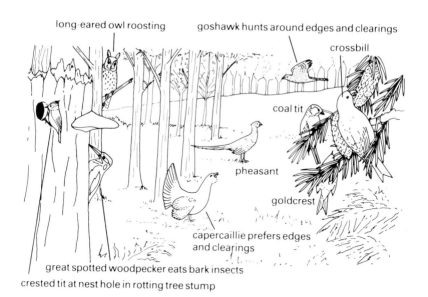

long-eared owl roosting

goshawk hunts around edges and clearings

crossbill

coal tit

pheasant

goldcrest

capercaillie prefers edges and clearings

great spotted woodpecker eats bark insects

crested tit at nest hole in rotting tree stump

The birds of coniferous woodland exploit various parts of the habitat. Try and learn the habits of different species – which ones move about in flocks, when they are most active, etc.

their calls, but should you hear a variety of birds scolding and calling in alarm it is worth trying to locate them as they will probably be mobbing an owl – which in conifer woods is likely to be a long-eared owl. The owl will sit motionless whilst the smaller birds fly round and round and perch near to it, calling furiously. Some pinewood birds are far less vocal, and sitting quietly and waiting at likely looking spots is the best approach, but others can be located in different ways. Crossbills, for example, need to drink daily, because their diet of dry seeds does not provide them with sufficient water, so an isolated pool will be quite an attraction to seed-eaters. Conceal yourself a short distance away from the pool to see which species use it. If no natural drinking pools exist, it is well worth making one of your own with a small sheet of plastic or a sunken dustbin lid. Keep it filled with water and it will soon begin to attract birds and mammals glad of the new water supply in an otherwise dry environment. Squirrels are common in pinewoods and, as in deciduous woodland, can often be detected by noting branches bouncing up and down as they leap from tree to tree, rather than swaying in the breeze.

Binoculars are important for the close observation of animals in the tree canopy and, because of the low levels of light in pinewoods, a pair with good light-gathering power is essential. Choose a pair with lenses which have a rating of 7×50.

Examine the bark closely with a hand-lens for insects and spiders

Coniferous woodland

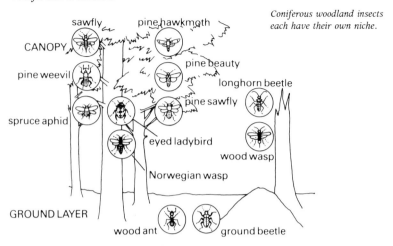

Coniferous woodland insects each have their own niche.

CANOPY

sawfly
pine hawkmoth
pine weevil
pine beauty
longhorn beetle
spruce aphid
pine sawfly
eyed ladybird
wood wasp
Norwegian wasp

GROUND LAYER

wood ant
ground beetle

The crested tit searches for food on tree trunks, and nests in stumps.

Examine the trunk closely with a hand-lens for insects, spiders and other small creatures.

crawling over the surface. The cones of coniferous trees are worthy of particular attention, since many insects live among the scales, feeding on the pollen in spring. The needles, or conifer leaves, should be examined for the larvae of insects which often resemble them closely.

Woodland floor

Pine cones will be found littering the woodland floor, and these should be examined carefully for signs of animals feeding. Cones which have been

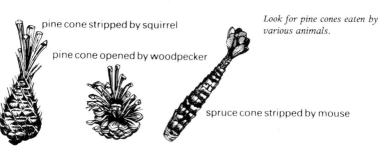

pine cone stripped by squirrel

pine cone opened by woodpecker

Look for pine cones eaten by various animals.

spruce cone stripped by mouse

63

(Above) Conifer plantations have closely planted trees, encouraging little or no undergrowth except fungi. However, the needle carpet itself is worth investigating.

(Below) Using a sieve to separate the larger particles of debris.

stripped down to a narrow stump will have been eaten by squirrels, but cones which have twisted and shredded scales will probably have been eaten by crossbills.

Old tree stumps should be examined for signs of feeding by woodpeckers, and for holes made by boring beetles. Low stumps often have on them the territorial markings of rabbits in the form of their droppings or urine. Nuthatches often wedge seeds or nuts in crevices in stumps to enable them to be opened more easily, so if you come across a stump with any of these signs on it, it is well worth visiting it on several occasions and waiting quietly to see what appears.

The damp conditions of autumn bring a crop of fungi to the woodland floor and these are a good source of food for many insects, particularly beetles. Their larvae can be found by breaking open the caps of the fungi; the adults often hide by day beneath the leaf litter or under logs, so these should also be searched. Remember that some fungi are poisonous, so always wash your hands after handling them.

Woodland rides
Although constructed primarily for management purposes, woodland rides become effective woodland edges, enabling a richer flora to develop, and encouraging a greater variety of insects and other animals. Conceal yourself among the trees, but with a view along the length of the ride, and wait for animals to show themselves. Woodland rides are often the site of ant hills — the homes of the wood ant. Alternatively, if you spot ants on the woodland floor you can often trace the nest by following them back to it. On no

By using natural cover, the observer has an excellent view along this grassy ride, but remains inconspicuous himself.

account should you disturb the nest by poking into the surface with a stick, for this will open it up to predators or the weather and seriously harm some of the pinewood's most valuable and interesting inhabitants. You may find that someone or something has already disturbed the surface of the nest, in which case it would be worthwhile observing it from a distance. Green woodpeckers are particularly fond of ants and use their long tongues to extricate them from holes in the nest. Some birds, such as jays and starlings, practice the peculiar habit of 'anting' in which they sit on the nest and lower their wings to enable the ants to crawl up them and on to the bird's body. The birds usually fluff out their feathers so that the ants can get close to the skin. There is no convincing explanation as to why the birds do this and subject themselves to the bites of the ants; it possibly has some connection with ridding the skin and feathers of parasites like lice, however, by the release of formic acid by the ants.

Since woodland rides are fruitful areas for wildlife, it is worth seeing if

A wood ants' nest; this one was about 30 cm (12 in) high.

The rare pine marten can sometimes be attracted to baited stumps in secluded parts of coniferous woodlands.

you can encourage other coniferous woodland mammals by baiting a likely spot for a few days. A carcase or road casualty bird may attract a weasel, fox or even a pine marten. Rabbit pellets can be used to encourage rabbits. One way of attracting small birds, or larger predatory species, is by making a 'squeaker'. This produces high-pitched notes similar to the calls of small birds or rodents. A ground-glass stopper in a bottle will produce the desired sounds, but even a pencil rotated inside a wooden cotton reel will do the trick. The secret is to make the sounds as realistic as possible whilst remaining fairly well concealed yourself. Goldcrests, coal tits and other small birds will soon come to investigate the source of the sound and eventually predators such as stoats will be drawn to it. One theory about the reason for the attractiveness of the sound is that the predators think that the sounds are being produced by an animal in distress which will make an easy meal for them. It is possible to purchase so-called 'hunter's calls' from gun shops which are designed to imitate particular species such as ducks, but even a blade of grass held between the thumbs and blown over will produce quite a convincing distress call after some practice.

Natural coniferous woodland

Native coniferous woodlands such as the Caledonian Pine Forests of Scotland, or the spruce woods of Scandinavia, have much richer shrub and ground layers than those of commercial plantations, and consequently their mammal populations are much richer. Deer browse on the shoots and fruits of bilberry and other shrubs, and the best way to see them is to search for their droppings and tracks on the woodland rides and then work out where their main feeding areas are. Having established the best feeding areas, visits can be made during the early morning or evening when they are likely to be most active. Remember that deer have a very good sense of smell and very good hearing, but eyesight is less well developed and they are not able to see stationary objects very clearly. When approaching them be very careful not to let your scent drift towards them. If you should accidentally snap a twig and alert the deer, keep absolutely still until they have relaxed again. As long as you do not repeat the mistake they should continue to behave normally. Your best chance of seeing deer without them seeing you is to use a high seat. In some woodlands these are provided for the benefit of the foresters when they wish to cull the deer, and it is normally possible to get permission to use them outside the shooting season. Alternatively you can just climb a suitable tree and wait. Deer do not look up very frequently and your scent will be carried away over their heads, and so you stand a much better chance of seeing them.

Typical animals: fieldbrief

Phylum Mollusca
Slugs can sometimes be found in mature pinewoods. Search under logs and bark. In wet weather slugs are active during daylight.

Phylum Arthropoda
Insects Few butterflies and moths are encountered in pinewoods. Where there is an understorey with grass and bramble, species such as speckled woods occur, frequently sunning themselves in the same spot. Search pine bark to find well-camouflaged moths during daylight. Some large moth species, such as the hawk moths, rest at eye level on bark in June and July. In autumn, look for larvae descending pines in order to pupate in soil.

Beetle larvae are often found in old decaying pine stumps and fallen timber. Adults occur under bark and logs, and among pine needles, and can be caught in pitfall traps. Longhorn beetles are a dominant group in pine forests.

One ant species, the wood ant, is extremely beneficial in forests since it destroys large numbers of harmful insects. Their colonies are contained within large mounds of pine needles and twigs. Sometimes over 1 m (3 ft) high, usually on the edge of woodland rides. Do not sit too close to the mound as wood ants are aggressive and have a painful 'bite'.

Phylum Chordata
Birds BIRDS OF PREY The goshawk is found in large, mature pinewoods. A pile of feathers on the woodland floor cut, rather than plucked from their victim, is a sign of a goshawk kill. Look for these birds in the skies above the pinewoods, especially in the spring, when they perform an aerial display flight. Hen harriers prefer young pine plantations, and have a low-level flight with slow, easy wing-beats.

OWLS As in other habitats, owls are not particularly numerous in coniferous woodlands, but betray their presence by several 'clues'. Their regurgitated pellets, consisting of inedible matter such as bones, teeth and feathers, differ in shape and texture from species to species – a good spot to look for these is at the base of large trees which the birds may have been using as a roost. Any droppings on the ground under a tree are a sign that an owl may have been using it as a daytime roost. The nocturnal habits of owls make them particularly difficult to watch, but it is probably worth a visit to the wood just as the dawn breaks in the hope of spotting a long-eared or Tengmalm's owl as it flies back to its roost.

GAMEBIRDS Gamebirds will often 'sit tight' in the forest until you flush them from cover, flying up noisily on whirring wings. The large size and strange 'popping' calls of the capercaillie make it a difficult bird to miss; the males are especially vocal and territorial in the breeding season. Pheasants are also found in pinewoods; listen for their characteristic calls and look for them on the edges of woodland rides.

WOODPECKERS The bark of mature pines and rotten stumps support many insects upon which woodpeckers feed. They are difficult birds to spot and are best located by their calls. Some species 'drum' by tapping trees with their bills; this forms part of their display and is most evident in the spring. Woodpecker holes are excavated in dead trees and stumps; when a hole has been located in the spring, find a suitable spot to watch behind cover and wait for the birds to return to the nest site.

PERCHING BIRDS In coniferous forests, most small birds keep high up in the tree tops where they can be located by their calls. Goldcrests and crested and coal tits flutter among the branches uttering a series of high-pitched notes; they can often be found in flocks, especially in the winter. The sounds of pine cones and seeds dropping to the ground may be a sign of crossbills feeding in the trees above. Due to their dry diet, these birds need to drink, and frequently visit woodland pools, as do other small birds; a vigil beside one of these pools can be rewarding for the nature watcher.

Mammals MICE AND VOLES Many species live in conifer plantations, particularly those with young trees. Turn over logs or listen for rustling among pine needles.

RED SQUIRREL Look for movements in the tree tops and on tree trunks. Gnawed pine cones will provide a clue to its whereabouts. This species is quite often encountered on the ground and sometimes frequents woodland car parks and camp sites where it can be baited with ripe pine cones.

PINE MARTEN Alarm calls in other woodland animals and birds may suggest the presence of this predator. It keeps mainly to the tree tops but sometimes raids litter bins in remote woodland care parks at night; try waiting in a suitable spot after dark in a car and then turn on your headlights.

WILD CAT Extremely wary of man, mainly nocturnal and hence difficult to see. Look for its tracks in mud, especially near standing water. Baiting with carrion, such as road casualty birds, is most likely to be successful in winter when natural food is scarce.

STOATS AND WEASELS sometimes hunt along the edges of pinewoods.

DEER are often seen in small parties on woodland rides. They have a keen sense of smell and hearing, so try to keep down wind of these animals and freeze when you see them (deer are not particularly adept at picking up movements). Walk along bare rides (without twigs, to cut down noise) and scan through the trees with binoculars. If there is a convenient tree or high seat, climb it and wait for the deer to show themselves; early morning is a good time for this. Deer may leave signs of their presence: bark stripped from young trees and nibbled branches, for instance.

Deciduous woodland

The natural vegetation of most of lowland Europe is deciduous woodland, though much of this has been cleared by man for agriculture, fuel and industrial development. Nevertheless it is still possible to find extensive tracts of native broadleaved woodland in many areas. Few, if any, woodlands are completely untouched by man, however, for there is a long history of woodland management throughout most of Europe. Some of the best remaining woodlands were once preserved as royal hunting grounds and these, which existed long before man's clearances began, have provided continuous tree cover for thousands of years. They are sometimes called primary woodland and can be very rich in both plant and animal life, having suffered far less from disturbance by agriculture, although grazing by domestic animals can be a problem.

Primary oak woodland

This can be recognized by the presence of large numbers of oak trees, together with certain indicator species (plants which are normally only associated with ancient oakwoods). An extensive ground cover of woodland flowers such as bluebells or wood anemones will indicate that the woodland soil has lain undisturbed for a long time. Deciduous woodlands are characterized by several distinct layers or zones of vegetation, and nowhere are these better shown than in an oakwood. A typical oakwood will have at least 50 per cent of the tree cover consisting of oaks, with a number of other species such as ash, elm, hornbeam and lime found less frequently among them. These make up the **canopy layer** of the wood and together they form an almost complete cover of leaves, in summer blocking out much of the light to the woodland floor.

Below the trees will be found a number of shrub species, and these include midland hawthorn, alder buckthorn, holly and wild service tree. These comprise the **shrub layer**, and in ungrazed woodlands provide an important habitat for birds and insects. Below the shrub layer is an interesting layer of herbaceous plants, known as the **field** or **herb layer**, The flowering plants here bloom early in the year so that they can make use of all the available light before the canopy layer comes into full leaf and blocks it out partially. Primroses, wood anemones, yellow archangel, wood sorrel and wood spurge all help to make spring in an oakwood one of nature's great spectacles. As well as flowering plants, this layer will also comprise ferns.

The lowest of the woodland's four layers is the **ground layer**, which contains mosses, liverworts, algae and, in the autumn, large numbers of

PHOTOKEY canopy layer shrub layer

field layer ground layer

The layers of a deciduous woodland, as described in the text. Woodland management is an important element, ensuring that clearings are provided for species like warblers.

fungi. These feed saprophytically or parasitically on the decaying leaf mould provided by the other three layers, and even on the trees themselves, and in turn provide food for molluscs and other invertebrates, as well as certain woodland mamals. Apart from the fungi, which need no light at all, the plants of the ground layer are very tolerant of shade but usually require a very damp environment – the same conditions which encourage many invertebrate animals, too.

Coppicing and pollarding

Oak was such a valuable tree in the past that many oakwoods were managed in such a way that a constant supply of timber of useable size was always available. Trees with tall, straight trunks were encouraged, and below them were planted shrubs such as hazel which could be coppiced to provide a supply of small timber for making hurdles and fences or for charcoal burning. This practice has largely died out, but it is still possible to see the signs of former coppicing by looking for multi-stemmed hazels, or stumps with many side-shoots growing from them.

Pollarding was a method of taking a crop from the tree, whilst leaving the main trunk still standing. The top branches were cut off, leaving a tall trunk which then sprouted again to produce many more smaller branches.

Pollarded trees have a typically top-heavy, bushy appearance, and the many branches provide excellent nesting sites for a variety of birds.

Beech woodland

This occurs naturally on chalk and limestone soils, but beech is also widely planted, and grows well on some more acid soils. As it is a valuable timber-producing tree, many beechwoods have been extensively managed, usually by pollarding. A noticeable feature of well-established beechwoods is a thick carpet of beech leaves which, as they decay only very slowly, accumulate year by year to build up a layer several centimetres deep. A further reason for the lack of ground vegetation is the very dense shade cast by the leaf canopy. Woodland floor plants here are often saprophytes, feeding on organic matter, rather than making food for themselves. The pale green-grey cushions of the grey cushion moss are often found around the bases of mature trees, where they can make use of the water and nutrients which run off the tree during rainy periods. If a mature tree falls, allowing some light on to the woodland floor, many beech seedlings will flourish, and so will a large number of flowers, but they disappear eventually when one of the saplings grows to maturity and closes the canopy again.

Birch woodland

The birches are very widely distributed trees, and are often found in association with other species, particularly oak or Scot's pine, but in upland areas, near the limit of the tree line, pure stands of birch can be found. The silver birch, with its very characteristic white, papery bark, is more common in lowland areas, but the common or downy birch is more associated with uplands. As the birches cast a very light shade they often have a rich shrub and ground layer beneath them, made up of rowan, juniper, bilberry and a number of grasses. Lowland birchwoods support many other broadleaved species. The silver birch is frequently associated with the red and white spotted toadstool, the fly agaric. The light, wind-dispersed seeds of the birch make it a very efficient colonizer of burnt heathlands, newly cleared forest plantations and moorland edge. Decaying birches support many fungi, notably the birch bracket, and as the decay continues they make very easy burrowing for beetle larvae. These in turn attract birds such as woodpeckers which can also construct their nest holes in the soft trunks of the tree. As the birch is a relatively short-lived tree, birchwoods usually have plenty of old, decaying trees falling down, providing opportunities for the younger saplings to reach the light and grow to maturity.

Ash woodland

The ash is a hardy tree, able to survive on thin soils in upland areas. Where it does not suffer competition from other species such as oak it forms a fairly open type of woodland. Ash comes into leaf later than other trees and loses its leaves earlier than most deciduous trees, so there is plenty of light reaching the floor of an ashwood, thus giving an especially rich ground flora. When an ashwood develops on limestone soils some of the rarer herbs such as baneberry are found. Wild garlic, dog's mercury, woodrushes and yellow archangel all flourish in the light shade cast by ash leaves. Some of the rarer subspecies of the whitebeam are also found in the understorey (the layer beneath the leaves). In more fertile lowland areas ash is sometimes succeeded by the more dominant species like oak or beech. Because of this succession by other species pure ashwoods are rare in lowlands. Ash does not support as many invertebrates as the oak, so bird life is less abundant, but many common woodland species are usually present.

The seasons of the year

In winter the deciduous trees will have shed their leaves and, apart from some species like the winter moths, most of the insects will be inactive, but woodland birds like the treecreeper still search for insects in bark or buds, whilst others forage among the leaf litter on the woodland floor where many other invertebrates can still be found. Small songbirds tend to form mixed flocks and move through the wood together in search of food. Winter nights are often filled with the screaming calls of female foxes, or vixens, making their calls to attract the dog foxes for mating.

With the onset of warmer weather and longer days the herb layer flourishes, and the woodlands are filled with a display of spring flowers which must make use of the light before the leaf canopy closes over. Hellebores, aconites and snowdrops are among the first to bloom, and they are followed by primroses, oxlips and, in Britain, carpets of bluebells. The first of the woodland butterflies will appear on warm spring days and seek the nectar-producing flowers. The brimstone is often first, but it is soon followed by the speckled wood and the orange tip.

In early summer the woodland birds will have commenced breeding. Many of the insectivorous species, such as the great tit, attempt to synchronize their egg-laying with the appearance of the first oak leaves. This means that by the time the eggs have hatched the oak leaves will be sufficiently advanced to support a large population of caterpillars. As the oak leaves mature the many galls which infest the oak will also be seen; oak apples are very obvious early in the summer, but the spangle galls and marble galls become larger as the summer progresses. By the time the leaf canopy is fully developed most of the spring flowers will be seen as leaves and fruits only. Many of the woodland herbs are food plants for caterpillars; the larvae of the fritillaries are usually found on violets for example.

With the first rains of autumn the woodland fungi begin to appear. Although the underground mycelium is present throughout the year the fruiting bodies, or toadstools, usually appear in the autumn. Old stumps and fallen trees frequently support a mixture of fungi, and these are food for many beetle and fly larvae. The fruits of the woodland trees attract many birds and mammals at this time of year and some, like the grey squirrel and jay, store hazel nuts and acorns in the soil, and then search for them later when food is scarce.

Nature watching in deciduous woodland

Although, for the purposes of nature watching, we can divide deciduous woodlands into a number of distinct zones, it should be remembered that not all animals recognize them, and many may move freely between two or more zones, exploiting the full range of the habitat.

Canopy in spring and summer

In full leaf, the uppermost parts of a deciduous tree are a haven for wildlife, and huge numbers of insects and other invertebrates feed upon the leaves, and on each other. The lower leaves of the tree can easily be examined for this invertebrate life: look on and under the leaves, around the leaf stems and on the twigs themselves. (Some species will be highly camouflaged, either by their colouring or by resembling part of the tree itself, so examine everything closely.)

One of the easiest ways to see canopy invertebrates is to use a beating tray. This is a square-shaped net which is held beneath the tree to catch creatures which fall on to it when the stems and branches are shaken and the leaves are beaten with a stick. An upturned umbrella makes an ideal beating tray for this purpose.

Larger animals are also a feature of the canopy layer. In spring the myriad invertebrates provide food for the adults and young of woodland birds. The canopy also provides nesting sites and territorial song posts. Good views of birds in a leafy canopy are hard to obtain, since the leaves provide excellent

A couple of sharp taps on the leaves or a branch using a stick will dislodge tree-dwelling insects and other invertebrates, which can be collected in an upturned umbrella.

A green woodpecker at its nest hole. Birds are frequently heard before they are seen in woodland, and a knowledge of bird calls is essential.

cover. Your best views will normally be had by sitting quietly behind shrubby cover and waiting for birds to fly to and from trees. Some may also drop to the ground to feed on the woodland floor if you are out of sight.

Try and choose a site for birdwatching away from the general woodland path. A clearing in a less accessible part of the wood is ideal, for here birds will feel safer and are more likely to show themselves. Song is an important clue for leading you to birds. Tread carefully and stealthily, avoiding stepping on dry twigs, since most birds stop singing if they hear a human

Deciduous woodland

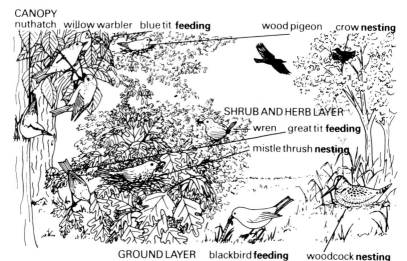

CANOPY
nuthatch willow warbler blue tit **feeding**   wood pigeon   crow **nesting**

SHRUB AND HERB LAYER
wren   great tit **feeding**

mistle thrush **nesting**

GROUND LAYER   blackbird **feeding**   woodcock **nesting**

(Above) A knowledge of which bird species exploits the various parts of the woodland is a useful aid to identification. The shrub layer in particular is important for nesting and roosting birds.

(Right) How to distinguish between a squirrel's drey and a wood pigeon's nest.

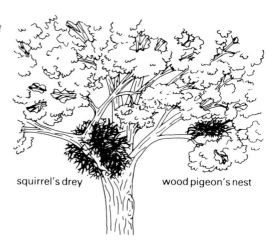

squirrel's drey   wood pigeon's nest

approaching. Look out particularly for wood pigeons and jays. They will burst from cover with, in the case of wood pigeons a loud clap of the wings or in the case of jays a cry of alarm, alerting all other wildlife to your presence.

Another useful clue to the presence of animal life in the trees is to look for branches moving in an unusual way. Squirrels leaping from tree to tree or large birds shifting about cause the branches to 'bounce' up and down – quite a different movement from the swaying action caused by the wind.

76

Canopy at dusk

The canopy layer at dusk presents an opportunity to study other species of wildlife. The woodcock – unusual in that it is a woodland wading bird – may be seen flying over the trees, owls may glide through the woodland, moths appear from their daytime hiding places to feed on honeysuckle and other flowers, and bats may now be seen flitting above the trees searching for insects. Bat identification by sight is notoriously difficult; for some species it is impossible. Although flight silhouettes, coupled with a knowledge of which species exploit this particular habitat, may help, a device called a bat detector is available, and is the best method for enabling identification of flying bats, for it analyzes the sonar 'clicks' emitted by them.

Canopy in autumn and winter

In autumn and winter, the canopy plays host to fewer invertebrates, but birds still search for food among its branches and settle to roost. There is a change round at this time of the year, with some of the spring and summer birds departing, to make way for birds which feed on buds and seeds. Squirrels are still active (contrary to popular belief, they do not hibernate) and their large, untidy nests of twigs and leaves – often lodged in the fork of a tree – are easy to see. The wood pigeon's nest, another untidy affair, has a flatter shape.

(Below left) During winter, many signs of nature – such as these oak galls – are easier to see. (Below right) In winter, birds often congregate in the denser parts of the woodland.

Deciduous woodland

The bark

The bark has its own array of wildlife, adapted to hide and feed under it, and among the fissures. Examine the bark with a hand-lens, and tiny spiders, mites and insects may be seen crawling about. Lift rotted or peeling bark carefully to reveal the galleries of boring insects and hidden pupae. Snails, woodlice and millipedes may also hide beneath the bark, and the adults and immature stages of certain species of butterflies and moths hibernate and rest on the bark.

Examining the trunk of a tree at night with the aid of a torch may reveal a teeming world of creeping life, as the denizens of the bark come out of the safety of their daytime hiding places to feed.

The bark may also reveal other signs of activity: some birds jam nuts into the crevices in order to lever them open, and rotted trunks may have holes inhabited by species such as woodpeckers, nuthatches, tits and owls.

(Below left) Tree holes like this should be investigated for signs of occupation by waiting out of sight close by. If the edges of the hole are worn, a bat is likely to be in residence.

(Below right) Carefully lifting birch bark for signs of animal life beneath.

Shrub layer

In some woodlands the shrub layer may include shade-tolerant species and can therefore be quite extensive, while in others it will only exist in areas where the trees do not cast strong shadows. The larger shrubs such as hawthorn, holly, bramble and hazel support a rich variety of woodland birds, as well as spiders, insects and other invertebrates. Here, too, may be found the ball-like honeysuckle, grass and leaf breeding nests of the

The fox dropping found on this mossy stump next to a woodland path (see close-up on right) indicated that it was being used as a territorial marking post.

nocturnal dormouse – the dormouse's summer nest is usually situated in a tree fork about 3 m (10 ft) off the ground, and the winter nest is usually on or under the ground, among tree roots and leaves. Search carefully among the shrub layer (gloves are useful to avoid prickles), for interesting insects and spiders, but do not disturb nests. Early autumn mornings are the best time to look for spiders' webs festooning the shrub layer. Gently agitating the web with a stick, or by some of the other methods described on page 102, may encourage the owner to come scuttling from its hiding place to investigate the source of the disturbance.

In sheltered sunny glades and rides the shrubs and attendant flowers such as bugle, violets and thistles play host to woodland butterflies. Once again, sitting quietly by some likely looking vegetation is often the best way to see these creatures, for even butterflies are aware of, and hide from, someone moving through their habitat.

Field layer and ground layer
Although, botanically, these are two distinct zones of a deciduous woodland, for the purposes of animal watching it is convenient to treat these low-level regions together.

Roe deer may be especially bold and easy to see in winter.

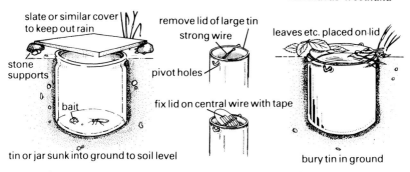

slate or similar cover to keep out rain

stone supports

bait

tin or jar sunk into ground to soil level

remove lid of large tin

strong wire

pivot holes

fix lid on central wire with tape

leaves etc. placed on lid

bury tin in ground

Two simple but effective traps: pitfall trap (left) and fliptop trap (right).

Ground flora

In spring, before the canopy layer shades out the light, many flower species are able to flourish. Attractive in themselves, they also provide the opportunity to see the small animals which come to the flowers for nectar, or which hide among their leaves and stems. In winter, the ground flora consists mainly of mosses and lichens, with autumnal flourishes of fungi. Investigate clumps of mosses for the small invertebrates seeking shelter among them at this time of year.

The way to investigate these small microhabitats is by getting down really low and looking very carefully, often best done with a hand-lens, under, over and among the vegetation. Sit quietly by clumps of woodland flowers and wait for insects to visit.

The tangled vegetation which forms when brambles, tree stumps, leaves and other plant debris accumulate is a particularly rewarding place to examine wildlife. Ground-nesting birds, as well as those just searching for insects and other food items, are commonly encountered (the greater the density of vegetation, the greater the number of insects and hence insect-eating birds), and can usually be heard rustling in the undergrowth. If you walk past, the culprit will usually 'freeze', but if you hide nearby the rustling will normally resume, and the inhabitant will soon show itself.

These patches also harbour small mammals. Settle down, as well concealed as possible, and listen for the tell-tale rustles of creatures such as wood mice, dormice and squirrels. This is an activity that will usually yield better results at dusk or when it is dark. Shrews are also commonly found among this kind of cover, and betray their presence by high-pitched, scolding squeaks. Glimpses of all these creatures are often fleeting, as they burst from cover and back. Baiting a likely spot with nuts, carrots, pieces of fruit, etc. may provide longer views – but be prepared for several fruitless 'watches' until your quarry finds the bait – or traps can be set (see page 103).

Rotting timber

This is an important microhabitat for many animals (and plants). Search beneath the wood for adult and larval invertebrates. Carefully peeling back the bark may also reveal creatures within. Old discarded planks of wood are also worth lifting for investigation: snails and hibernating reptiles and

Deciduous woodland

(Left) Never ignore any likely looking hiding place.

(Below) Feeding signs which are easy to spot: chewed hazelnuts on a mossy stump.

mammals may be hiding here. Tree stumps themselves are useful clues to woodland wildlife: thrushes' anvils, (stumps littered with shattered snails' shells) indicate not only the presence of thrushes, but also the types of woodland snail present.

Woodland floor

For the experienced naturalist, the woodland floor can provide fascinating nature watching, as well as indicating well-used runs, tracks, trails and other signs. By reading these signs, you can not only tell what animals are about, but can increase your chances of seeing them by 'staking out' their territory.

This dead wood mouse at least indicates the presence of the species in this woodland and, if fresh, can be used as bait for larger species.

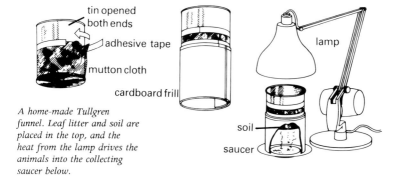

tin opened both ends

adhesive tape

mutton cloth

cardboard frill

lamp

soil

saucer

A home-made Tullgren funnel. Leaf litter and soil are placed in the top, and the heat from the lamp drives the animals into the collecting saucer below.

Feathers which appear to have been bitten off neatly at the base of the shaft (these are from a pigeon) indicate a sparrowhawk kill. Mammal predators usually leave skin and other remains behind.

In autumn and winter, listen for the sound of spiders as they hunt through the leaves, causing them to rustle. Gently disturbing the top layers of leaves reveals small animals seeking shelter from birds and the weather. You may also come across wood ants on their foraging expeditions.

Animal runs can usually be recognized by the fact that the vegetation has a flattened appearance, but is often too narrow, or too far from paths, for it to be made by humans. Further confirmation can be had by searching carefully for droppings, which may indicate the presence of foxes, deer or rabbits, for instance. Look for droppings also on prominent objects such as tree stumps and large boulders. Clearings are also good places to watch: these breaks in the denser woodland may be more heavily grassed than other areas, and

Some of the characteristic signs left by mammals. The bottom row are droppings; these may vary according to their age and the mammal's diet.

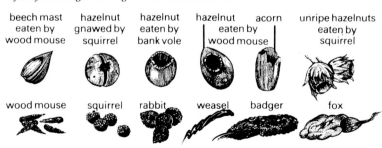

beech mast eaten by wood mouse	hazelnut gnawed by squirrel	hazelnut eaten by bank vole	hazelnut eaten by wood mouse	acorn	unripe hazelnuts eaten by squirrel

wood mouse	squirrel	rabbit	weasel	badger	fox

therefore frequented by browsing mammals like deer, as well as insect- and seed-eating birds.

Many woodland mammals build nest burrows, so search for these in banks, near tree roots and in quiet spots away from general footpaths. Many books give very precise sizes for badger, rabbit and fox holes. In reality, these are often much larger than the sizes stated, so do not be surprised to find rabbits using a burrow that you could almost climb down yourself! Be prepared also for the unexpected: amphibians such as toads are not averse to using woodland holes to rest in when not feeding. Much smaller holes in the woodland floor itself are likely to have been made by solitary wasps and other insects.

Investigating holes

1   Does it look used? Is the earth freshly dug, and are there signs of food remains or droppings nearby?
2   Smell hole for possible indication of animal life within;
3   Look down it with a torch. Does it end very abruptly or does it look likely that something lives within its depths?
4   Are there cobwebs over the hole (probably not in use if there are);
5   If you want confirmation that a hole is in use, place a few small sticks over the entrance. The next day, the sticks will have been pushed aside when the occupants came out to feed.

Having established that the hole is occupied, the fieldbrief on page 91 will indicate the likely sizes of holes produced by some woodland animals. Small mammals can be caught in a harmless mammal trap, baited and placed

Placing a few sticks over the entrance of a hole to determine whether or not it is occupied.

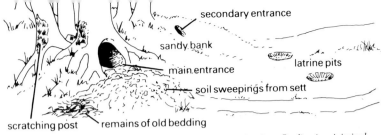

A badger's sett is often excavated in a sandy woodland bank where flooding is minimized.

entrance hole

droppings on prominent grassy tussock

food remains

The fox usually chooses a more open, grassy site – often taking over a rabbit burrow.

A hopeful badger watcher in position. Even when all the conditions seem ideal, you must be prepared for the occasional non-appearance of your quarry. Young naturalists should always be accompanied by adults during night watches.

nearby, or may be watched by hiding nearby and waiting patiently. Larger mammals like badgers and foxes are wary, and are best watched from a vantage point, off the ground, where your scent is unlikely to be carried to their hole. (Woodlands cause wind to eddy, so that it is difficult to be sure your scent won't carry when you are on the ground.) The ideal place to wait is in a conveniently placed tree, but you must be prepared for a possibly long vigil; wrap up warm, and resist the temptation to climb down to stretch your legs. You should be in position by dusk, even if nothing is expected to happen for several hours. A moonlit night will enable you to see any signs of activity quite clearly as the occupants emerge, but a torch with a red filter will help to illuminate the scene without alarming your quarry. To encourage events, try baiting near the entrance (see fieldbrief). Also, avoid the use of strong perfumes, after-shave lotions and insect repellents and – above all – don't light up a pipe or cigarette. These are alien smells which will cause shy animals to become even more wary.

Woodland edge

This is one of the most fruitful areas of woodlands for wildlife. The brighter conditions mean that flowers and other small plants can flourish even in high summer, resulting in more insect species. These in turn attract birds, bats and other animals which feed on them. Many woodlands are adjacent to farmland, heathland or moorland, and therefore this may increase the chances of seeing the wildlife which also exploits these habitats.

Sit quietly out of sight at dawn, during an afternoon or early evening, and await events. If the woodland edge is adjacent to farmland animals such as rabbits will come from their woodland burrows to feed on the crops. These in turn will be preyed upon by foxes. Badgers, mice and other mammals will also venture forth from the security of the woodland to forage on open land. Look for any obvious tracks leading from the woodland on to adjacent farmland.

Insects and other small invertebrates among the foliage can be caught with a beating tray or upturned umbrella (see page 74), or by baiting a tree or fence post with a syrupy mixture attractive to moths. This last method is best done on warm nights between June and August. The most productive times are the hour just after sunset, and again about an hour after midnight.

Recipe for moth attractant

2 tablespoons of treacle	2 tablespoons of sugar
1 tablespoon of beer	a little rum

Warm the mixture gently in a saucepan until it all dissolves. Keep it bottled until ready for use, and then smear it on.

Woodland edges are fruitful areas for nature watching. Learn the roosting times of birds using the woodland, and you may see a sparrowhawk attack as the roosting flock flies in.

An alternative method is to use either a proprietary or a home-made light trap (see page 97).

At dusk, on spring, summer and early autumn evenings – sometimes even in winter – look just above the trees for signs of bats. Species which nest in woods, under nearby bridges and in sheds, etc., emerge at this time to feed on the night-flying insects. Identification of bats in flight is beyond the scope of most amateur naturalists (although bat nets and bat detectors are among the equipment available to the avid bat-watcher), but they are still fascinating to observe as they dart about the sky. You may be able to narrow your subjects down to one of only a few species, however, if you can estimate their approximate size.

Birds provide some of the best opportunities for nature watching at the woodland edge. Species such as pheasants are seen most often on the ground, and elsewhere the bark and canopy feeding species are much in evidence. Here, too, are found species more often associated with open land – fieldfares, rooks, crows and magpies, for instance. Birds of prey, especially sparrowhawks, find the concentrations of potential food, together with the open space for manoeuvrability, well-suited to their feeding methods, and may be in evidence at any time of the year. Look upwards for other birds of prey as buzzards, which often wheel and soar above woodland edges.

Typical animals: fieldbrief

Phylum Mollusca

Mainly nocturnal, woodland snails and slugs hide by day under stones and logs, emerging at dusk to feed on fungi and other plants. In wet weather they may be active during the daytime; look under vegetation near woodland paths. At night, some species may be encountered climbing trees.

Phylum Arthropoda

Insects Extremely numerous everywhere. An oak tree may support several hundred different species. Although the warmer months may yield the best results, even in the depths of winter some species will seek the warmer conditions within the wood, and others will be found hibernating or resting in or under bark, logs, leaves, stones, mosses and other vegetation. Tullgren funnels, baiting, sieving soil and leaf litter, moth traps and beating trays are among the best methods for catching a wide variety of insects, but their sheer abundance means that even the casual observer will see plenty of species. In general, the greater the amount of foliage and vegetation, the more species there will be. Warm, humid weather encourages many species to take to the wing.

Moths are mainly active at night. Many are experts at daytime camouflage, so search carefully on bark, under leaves and on twigs, both for the adults and their caterpillars. Butterflies frequent woodland glades and woodland edges, where the conditions encourage the growth of nectar-producing flowers on which they can feed.

Flies of many types feed on fungi, dung, flowers and the corpses of animals. Beetles may be found on the bark of trees or on leaves, in leaf litter and in the soil. Baiting the ground with a small dead animal (a road casualty bird is ideal) will soon attract a small army of scavengers, burying beetles and other feeders. Bugs are found generally on leaves and stems, where they suck the sap of trees and bushes.

Wood ants are immediately recognizable by their large size. These purposeful creatures tend to swarm about the woodland floor as they go about their foraging expeditions. Their mound-like nest is often situated near the base of a tree.

Several species of bees inhabit woodland. Some use the discarded nests of small mammals, but any small hole in a woodland bank is the possible home of an insect and a short wait to see if it is occupied is worthwhile. Bees also frequent the woodland flowers of rides and edges. Old holes in trees may provide nests for hornets, or the branches of the tree itself may support a papery wasps' nest.

Other insects such as crickets, lacewings and scorpionflies may also be encountered among the vegetation.

Woodlice, centipedes and millipedes may be found by disturbing leaf litter or by searching under bark, rotting logs or in the soil.

Spiders Some are camouflaged and creep up on insects feeding on leaves, others spin webs over old bank holes and among the lower vegetation layers. Yet others, such as wolf spiders, actively hunt through the leaf litter and woodland floor debris for victims.

Phylum Chordata

Amphibians Several species of salamanders, newts, frogs and toads are found in woodland, especially near pools and marshy places. Generally nocturnal, they hide by day under stones, logs and debris, or in holes, but some are likely to be encountered during the day after rain. Tree frogs may be found in foliage rather than on the ground.

Reptiles A few species are found in European woodlands and, unlike amphibians, are generally diurnal and therefore easier to see.

TORTOISES AND TERRAPINS Prefer light woodlands with moist places and dense vegetation; often only the head and neck are visible when in water.

GECKOES Nocturnal, often found in olive groves. Look under the bark of dead trees.

LIZARDS Some species may be seen basking on trees and rocks in open, sunny woodland, and others in damper, lush areas by streams.

SNAKES Usually found near water or by woodland edges; sometimes sunning themselves on raised banks or stumps.

Birds The birdlife of deciduous woodlands is extremely complex. There are seasonal differences, with the arrival and departure of migrants, and with fluctuations of endemic species in response to changing food supplies.

The birdwatcher must also remember that different species are often adapted to a life in the various woodland layers – canopy, shrub, field and ground – and that the type of woodland, and its density and extent, are also crucial factors affecting the presence and abundance of certain birds.

There are several ways of birdwatching in woodlands: you may see or hear a bird or a flock and get closer by carefully advancing forward, or you can wait by a likely spot, concealed from view.

BIRDS OF PREY Buzzards, goshawks, sparrowhawks, kites and hobbies are the most commonly encountered woodland birds of prey, although other species may also build a nest in trees or copses even if they hunt elsewhere. Usually seen flying low or circling around the edges of woodland, species such as the sparrowhawk nevertheless hunt in the deeper parts of woodland, particularly where there are clearings. Watching and waiting is the best technique for seeing them, especially if you can locate a nest.

GAMEBIRDS Black grouse, pheasants and hazelhens are the most likely species to be encountered. They prefer dense woodland cover, from which they make foraging expeditions on to more open land.

WADERS The woodcock is found in boggy woods. Usually nocturnal, you may stumble across it during the day as it lies camouflaged against the woodland floor.

PIGEONS AND DOVES Wood pigeons and stock doves are common in woodland. The calls of these birds are a useful clue to their whereabouts, as is the clapping sound made by their wings as they fly. Although essentially birds of the trees, they often feed on the ground, and may be encountered in clearings.

OWLS Mainly nocturnal, many species of owl choose to nest in tree holes in woodland, although only a few, like the tawny owl, actually hunt within deciduous woodland. You may see owls perching on trees during the day, but the best method is to wait quietly by a tree hole, to see what emerges at dusk.

BEE-EATER, ROLLER, HOOPOE These colourful insect-eating birds may be encountered by woodland clearings and edges as they search for food, although they also inhabit open country with scattered trees. Rollers and hoopoes nest in tree cavities, and may be seen emerging.

GOLDEN ORIOLE Prefers tree canopy; best located by calls; hard to see in trees despite bright colours of male.

WOODPECKERS Nesting in tree holes and feeding on insects, various species of woodpeckers may be seen in woodlands. The calls and drumming sounds they make may lead you to them. Woodpeckers prefer mature trees and insect-ridden timber.

PERCHING BIRDS AND SONGBIRDS The families most commonly associated with deciduous woodland are larks, pipits, orioles, starlings, waxwings, crows, wrens, warblers (including flycatchers), thrushes, tits, nuthatches, treecreepers and finches. Many of these birds occur in flocks, and different species are adapted to exploit the habitat at varying times of the year. Overall, the perching birds and songbirds are found over a wide range of different types of deciduous woodland. The flying feeders such as flycatchers prefer open woodland since they must be able to manoeuvre easily in pursuit of their flying prey, whereas other species such as jays, wrens and nightingales all prefer denser shrubby woodland for their less aerial, more secretive lifestyles. Some of the species in this group build nests in the tree tops and some nest in natural cavities. There are also ground nesters, and species which built nests in low vegetation.

Mammals Generally speaking, mammals are shy creatures requiring not only a stealthy approach, but often a dusk, dawn or night vigil in order to see them. The many tracks, trails, feeding signs and other clues to their activity which they leave can be vital in locating the nests or favoured feeding areas of certain species. Banks, dense vegetation and tree roots are favoured sites for nests.

HEDGEHOG, SHREWS, MICE AND BANK VOLE These mammals all inhabit the woodland floor and may be encountered in undergrowth, although some are nocturnal and a red-filtered torch is necessary to see them. Small mammals may be caught in Longworth or other harmless traps placed near burrows.

BATS Look around woodland edges at dusk for species like the noctule, barbastelle, long-eared, Bechstein's and Daubenton's.

SQUIRREL Usually easy to see, although tends to 'hide' around the back of a tree if threatened. Late summer and autumn are among the best times to see these animals, when they often come to the ground to search for nuts.

DORMOUSE Builds several nests – hibernation, breeding and summer – in dense vegetation, especially with hazel and honeysuckle; nocturnal and mainly arboreal.

RABBIT Burrows – about 15 cm (6 in) in diameter – normally near the edge of woodland, with access to farmland.

STOAT, WEASEL Range widely over different habitats in search of prey such as rodents, rabbits and birds. Usually active by day as well as night, they can often be encouraged to likely spots by baiting pieces of piping.

GENET Hides by day under bushes in woodlands bisected by streams.

FOX Another wide-ranging predatory animal. Its den is usually in a grassy bank, often recognizable by the musty smell and discarded food remains near entrance. The entrance may be much larger than suggested in identification guides, but is often about 20 cm (8 in) minimum. Baiting the entrance with a carcase, and maintaining a quiet watch – preferably in a tree or elevated hide so that your scent does not betray your presence – will increase your chances of seeing a fox in woodland.

BEECH MARTEN Usually nests in buildings (like woodman's hut) or among rocky crags.

BADGER Typically, badgers' setts are excavated in quiet parts of woodland under tree roots in banks. The entrance has a minimum diameter of about 35 cm (14 in). Piles of soil spilling down the slope and shallow latrine holes nearby will confirm this as a badgers' sett. Fresh droppings, nest bedding in the form of straw, and fresh footprints all indicate that the sett is in use. A hide, above the level of the sett and about 10 m (30 ft) away, is the ideal watching site, and you must be in position, and quiet, by dusk. The badgers usually emerge shortly after dark. Peanuts placed near the entrance will often encourage them to come out. Badgers do not hibernate, and can be viewed in this way all year, although the cubs are active in late spring and early summer.

DEER Many woodlands have special reserves where these shy mammals are easier to see, but really wild deer are best viewed by searching first for their regular runs – identified by flattened ground vegetation, footprints and droppings – and then waiting quietly close by. Woodland clearings, where deer come to browse on the trees, are also fruitful areas for watching. Remember to keep downwind of deer, and avoid noise of any kind.

WILD BOAR Nocturnal, but may be heard snorting, or wallowing in woodland pools. Secluded glades should be watched for resting individuals.

Lowlands

Most lowlands are managed as farmland. This is usually either ploughed for crop sowing and harvesting, or is maintained as grassland for grazing by domestic stock such as cattle and sheep. Overall, the management of the lowlands has resulted in a patchwork mosaic of fields bordered by fences and hedges.

As little as a thousand years ago, lowland Britain and parts of Europe were covered in broadleaved woodland. These forests were gradually cleared and planted with crops. Modern arable farming methods have created large fields and there has been a tendency towards the planting of monocultures: single species such as wheat, barley, oats and corn.

There are several distinct types of grasslands which characterize the lowlands. For instance, grass may be grown as animal fodder and harvested as hay. Before modern farming methods were applied, hay meadows contained a large number of different grass and herb species and this floral diversity was reflected in the large number of animals which lived there. These areas of open grassland were usually found on the alluvial soils of river valleys where winter flooding was a regular feature. The normal pattern of use was for the grass to be allowed to grow without grazing until well past mid-summer when it was ready to be cut for hay. After hay-making cattle would be able to graze the meadow, enriching the soil with their manure, and then they would be moved off to feed on the hay crop during the winter period of flooding. This type of management allowed the flowering plants to set seed before they were cut down, whereas grazing throughout the year would prevent this. Few plants can tolerate constant removal of leaves and shoots and so only grasses, clovers and some distasteful species like buttercups and the snake's-head fritillary can survive constant grazing. Some hay meadows are still managed in this traditional manner and they are excellent sites for watching wildlife, being particularly rich in invertebrate species.

The economic demands of modern agriculture, however, have meant that hay is now often grown as a controlled mix of perhaps two or three species of grass, and all other species of 'field weeds' are excluded by the application of herbicides. Much of the lowlands are now covered with this relatively species-poor type of grassland.

Grasslands may also be grazed by stock such as cattle and sheep. The downlands are a particular type of grazed grassland which occurs on chalk soils, often on steep slopes, and are another example of a habitat originally created by man's clearance of the natural climax vegetation.

The shallow chalky soils formerly supported a woodland composed mainly of beech, but on very steep slopes yew, box, juniper and whitebeam also occurred. There are still a number of such woodlands which survived the clearances, but over most areas a type of grassland has developed which has a very characteristic flora supporting an interesting population of animals, especially insects.

Calcium carbonate, or chalk, is clearly the most abundant plant nutrient in chalky soils, but other essential nutrients are often very scarce, restricting the growth of some plant species. This tends to reduce the dominance of any single species, thus diversifying the flora. The type of management of the grassland is also important. Traditionally, permanent grassland was grazed by sheep, and sometimes rabbits as well, but recently there has been a tendency to allow cattle to graze the old downlands. The constant grazing prevents the colonization of the grassland by shrub species, thus maintaining the open nature of the habitat. Also, many of the plants show interesting adaptations to resist grazing. The characteristic aromatic nature of the chalk turf is a result of the scents produced by the plants to discourage grazing; some of them are even poisonous. Many of the chalk turf herbs have a prostrate form and are often prickly so that they are less attractive to grazing animals. South-facing slopes support species able to tolerate dry summer conditions, and they usually support the best butterfly populations. Ants also thrive in these conditions, and their ant hills are a striking feature of old chalk grasslands. Snails are also abundant on chalk grassland because of the availability of the calcium carbonate they need in order to build their shells. Grazed grasslands can occur on other types of soil, notably clays and loams, but in general these do not have the floral and faunal diversity of the chalk downlands.

Hedgerows

Hedgerows are very important features of the lowlands. In terms of their value to wildlife they are as vital as nature reserves for the shelter, protection and food which they provide. Many hedgerows were created in Saxon times to mark the boundaries between adjacent parishes. The normal practice was for a ditch to be dug on the actual boundary and the spoil used to make a bank which was then planted up with native shrubs and trees. Many other shrubs and herbs colonized the hedgerow from the surrounding woodland, and as the woodlands were gradually felled, the hedgerows became the only places where some woodland species could survive. Parish boundary hedges are usually wide and meandering, and because of their great age support the greatest variety of wildlife. In the eighteenth century when acts of parliament were passed permitting the enclosure of land a further set of hedgerows were created. These were usually symmetrical and planted with only one or two shrub species such as hawthorn and blackthorn. Elms were often planted along the hedgerows to provide timber and extra shelter, but sadly most of them have now gone as a result of Dutch elm disease. Many of the hedgerows have also gone, as modern farming practices demand larger and larger fields. This is a continuing process, so those which still survive are especially valuable.

Nature watching in meadow and grassland

For many people, this habitat epitomizes the countryside. Sadly, the gently rolling landscape, bordered by woods and streams and with its fields full of flowers, is a less common sight today as more and more land comes under the plough. Nevertheless the meadows which remain still support a wide-ranging selection of wildlife.

When to go

For the multitude of insects which are a major feature of this habitat, spring and summer are undoubtedly the best times to visit. At these times of the year many mammals and birds are much in evidence, too, making this a habitat with something to offer for everyone. Winter also has its attractions here, however, for although the insect life is much reduced, the mammals are still present and the birds display a change round, with many traditional winter-visiting species in evidence.

Starting at the edge

Before walking into the meadow, take stock of the landscape and its general features, and try to calculate how this will be reflected in the wildlife:

1   Is there a stream, and if so does it have sallows, willows or other trees growing in it?
2   Is the habitat bordered by woods, or is there a copse in the centre of the field?
3   Is it a dry, hilly meadow or a flat flood meadow?

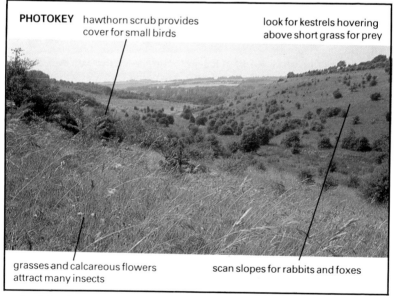

PHOTOKEY   hawthorn scrub provides cover for small birds

look for kestrels hovering above short grass for prey

grasses and calcareous flowers attract many insects

scan slopes for rabbits and foxes

Herb-rich downland.

94

The Adonis blue butterfly feeds on horseshoe vetch and other leguminous plants and has two broods: one in May-June and another in July-August.

4   Is there a hedgerow system which will afford natural pathways for wildlife to go from one place to another in safety?

Avoid, at this stage, letting your outline be seen. Stay in your car (if you have a view of the field from it) or keep behind any hedges or stone walls that may be present. Try to look through gaps in the hedges or around the sides – not over the top – for any birds or mammals in the meadow. Often you will see nothing for several moments for, although you may still be invisible, the animals may already have heard or even smelled you, so just sit quietly until they feel safe again. You may need to scan the meadow with your binoculars for if the vegetation is quite high, all you will see of, for instance, a fox, will be a muzzle and a pair of ears just above the vegetation. Look near the edges of the field for rabbits; they tend to move from their burrows to graze vegetation quite close by, and seldom venture into the middle of a field. A hare may be seen here, however. Although you may see such sights at any time, late afternoon and evening, or early morning, are the best times to watch.

Look upwards for birds flighting in from nearby trees and for kestrels and other birds of prey hovering overhead looking for prey. You may see the ghostly flapping of a barn owl, especially during spring when it has chicks to feed and is therefore less nocturnal. From your hidden vantage point you can also use your binoculars to scan the flowers for butterflies.

In the meadow

Having decided that you have seen all you want from your hiding place, it's now time to advance slowly into the meadow itself. The flowers, and hence the insects, will depend very much on the type of meadow – whether it is chalky or not, and whether it is damp or predominantly dry. Damp meadows often have a richer flora, and certainly are richer in animals such as amphibians, snails and grass snakes.

You can see many types of insect by simply moving quietly from flower to flower or by standing still, but the best views are often obtained by using a sweep net. (This method also catches many insects you didn't know were there!) Sweep the net through the vegetation, first one way and then the other. As you bring the net back, flick the handle over so that the net folds, enclosing any creatures. Gently remove them for identification. The humble

Lowlands

Satyridae
(graylings, ringlets, heaths, browns)

fluttering, undulating flight

Nymphalidae
(tortoiseshell, fritillary, comma, peacock, red admiral)

long, straight, low swoops

Pieridae
(whites, orange tips, brimstones, clouded yellows)

low, looping, zig-zag flight

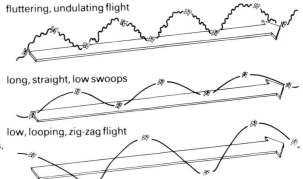

Many butterfly families can be recognized by their distinctive flight patterns.

cow pat, or any other dung heap, should also be investigated. Lift it with a stick, and look for carrion bettles and other scavengers feeding on it. An important point to remember is that many butterflies are only on the wing in sunny conditions; they will often drop into cover even if the sun just passes behind a cloud. Mole hills and ant hills are two obvious features of many meadows, although with completely different origins. Fresh mole hills means that the mole is nearby. You may be able to anticipate the emergence of the next mole hole and, in damp or dim conditions, even the mole itself may surface for a short while. Ant hills are also a feature of rich meadows,

(Below left) Mole hills. If they are very fresh, the mole may still be active, and you might glimpse its snout and forepaws as it carries more soil to the surface. (Below right) The fox may be seen hunting over lowlands.

96

and the ants themselves can normally be seen nearby.

In the early morning, examine the grass for the masses of tiny spiders' webs which will festoon the vegetation.

Getting off the ground

If there is a copse, or even a single tree, in the field, this will make an ideal substitute high seat from which to watch wildlife. Get into position by mid-afternoon, and avoid the temptation to climb down again. Since you are now out of view, and because your scent is carried above the noses of mammals, you should get good views of many birds and mammals in the field below you as the day wears on. If there are rabbit burrows nearby, you can try baiting them beforehand with rabbit pellets, and a carcase or road casualty bird may entice a fox from its den or attract a stoat. Incidentally, if you should encounter a stoat near, say, a hedge or stone wall, stay where you are for a few moments, even if it disappears. Its inquisitiveness will soon get the better of it and it will reappear briefly to take another look at you.

Holes in walls are not only the hunting places of predatory mammals, but may give shelter to mice and voles. Their runs may be clearly visible, and your high seat is again a good place to watch from. Alternatively you can lay a trap (see page 103) in a likely spot.

At night

The meadow at night plays host to many insects, spiders, snails, slugs as well

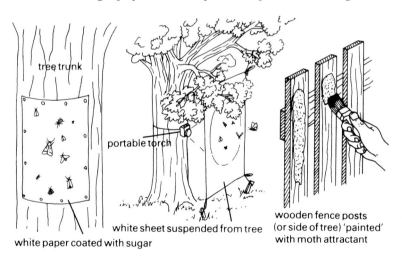

tree trunk

portable torch

white paper coated with sugar

white sheet suspended from tree

wooden fence posts (or side of tree) 'painted' with moth attractant

Three methods of attracting moths.

as, of course, mammals and birds such as owls. Shining a torch on the grass and looking carefully may reveal many creatures, and a pitfall trap (see page 81) will enable you to discover others. You can also set up a moth trap near to some trees or a hedgerow.

Any signs of mammal activity seen during the day, such as nibbled grass stems, gnawed tree bark or droppings, should be followed up by a night-time vigil nearby. You could perhaps sit by a hedge, or under a makeshift shelter of an anorak supported partly on the hedge and partly by sticks. A red-filtered torch will let you see whatever comes near without it being alarmed.

Investigate any clumps of corn, dry reeds or other tall, dense vegetation for signs of harvest mice. These nocturnal mammals may be seen darting about the stems, and their nests, built high up in the stems are round with no obvious entrance.

Nature watching on arable land

Arable land consists of fields in which various crops are grown, and sometimes this type of habitat is less productive for the naturalist than many others. A single species of plant covering a huge area will attract less wildlife than a more varied area such as a meadow. There are still some birds, mammals and insects which have adapted to life in a monoculture, however, and some of them are so successful that they have become serious pests. The changing seasons bring different creatures on to the land as crops are being planted or harvested, so for most of the year there will be something to watch. The type of crop growing in the field will have an important influence on the wildlife found in it. A seed-bearing crop like maize or barley will attract seed-eaters such as the harvest mouse or buntings, whilst root-crops like turnips or potatoes will be less attractive.

PHOTOKEY wheat interspersed with poppies, thistles and other weeds: feeding and cover for several animal species

hedgerow   look for droppings and other clues along field edge

A field of wheat, just before harvesting.

98

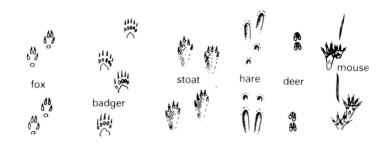

Snow tracks. Following fresh tracks may lead you to the animal's lair. (N.B. not to scale.)

When to go

In winter most arable land consists of bare open fields with little vegetation, except for some crops like winter wheat which are sown very early. If the ground is not actually frozen, invertebrates near the surface will provide food for birds such as starlings, lapwings and gulls which form large feeding flocks at this time of year. Rabbits may also venture out from woodlands in search of new growth, as will wood pigeons. In spring, as crops are planted or begin their first growth, a number of species move in to take advantage. Various insect species will be found, and ground-nesting birds like the skylark or lapwing betray their presence by displaying in the air over the wide open fields. More secretive species like the stone curlew display only at night. Common hares can be seen boxing in the open in early spring as the males take up territory and try to attract the females.

In summer, many species are difficult to see among the taller crops, but may betray their presence by calls or feeding signs such as nibbled leaves and stems. When the crop has been taken in after the autumn harvest flocks of seed-eating birds often congregate on the stubble to glean any leftovers. Large numbers of finches and buntings appear soon after the harvest, and the open field will provide a good hunting ground for predators like the barn owl. Later in the autumn many fields are ploughed so that when the winter frosts come the soil will be broken up into fine particles. Gulls and corvids (members of the crow family) follow close behind the plough feeding greedily on earthworms, leatherjackets and the other soil invertebrates brought to the surface.

Day and night activity

Remember that the growing crop is someone's livelihood so do not try to walk through it, but go round the edges or keep to paths. In any case, you are far less likely to see things if you appear out in the open yourself. If possible, keep to any available cover or squat down and scan the open field with your binoculars. Some species, aware of your presence at first, will crouch low on the ground and remain motionless, relying on their camouflage to protect them. If you keep still for long enough, and are well concealed, they may feel sufficiently safe to show themselves.

Very early mornings in spring are the best time for watching displaying birds. Hunting foxes or deer may also be seen out in the open then. Warm, sunny summer afternoons are ideal for watching butterflies and other insects. Dusk is another good time to watch birds, as they often gather in large flocks on open fields before flying off to roost in nearby trees. Owls begin hunting at dusk, and the little owl will begin making its cat-like calls whilst perched on fence posts. Look out also for foxes between the rows of standing crops as they hunt for small mammals, and for rabbits, badgers and other animals moving from their woodland retreats. It is still possible to watch birds and mammals on a moonlit night, but you should use binoculars with good light-gathering power. Woodcock will sometimes come out of the woods to feed, barn owls will quarter the ground for prey and stone curlews will be active during early summer. Many moths take to the wing on warm nights and these are hunted by bats which can also be seen. (See page 97 for methods of attracting moths.)

Nature watching in hedgerows

Hedgerows were originally planted to delineate boundaries, enclose livestock and to act as windbreaks, but they are also important and diverse habitats for many animals and plants. In addition, they often serve as vital pathways for animals, providing cover as they move from one place to another. The main hedgerow plants are usually deciduous – hawthorn, dogwood, elder, hazel, etc. – but these may be augmented with other shrubs

PHOTOKEY

emergent tree: used by roosting birds such as owls

gap in hedge may be used by foxes and other animals

ditch may provide moist living conditions for invertebrates

A hedgerow in summer.

Using this technique, nests will be seen silhouetted against the skyline. Harvest mice may also build nests in hedgerows.

such as honeysuckle, bramble and ivy, as well as the occasional tree. At the base of the hedge is usually a herbaceous layer of grasses, nettles, cuckoo-pint and other seasonal flowers. Another feature of hedges is the drainage ditch which is often constructed on one side. This is another microhabitat well worth exploration.

When to go

Although the hedgerow is likely to attract and support a wider variety of species during spring and summer, it also acts as an important food source and place of refuge in autumn and winter, and so there should be something to discover at any season. Hedgerows with plenty of nectar-producing flowers, berry-producing shrubs and thick vegetation will obviously be richer in animal species than sparse hedgerows.

Shrub layer

The bulk of the hedge provides nesting sites for a number of birds and mammals. In summer, nests can be most easily seen if you kneel near the base of the hedge and look upwards – the shape should be silhouetted against the skyline. Mammal nests, such as those of harvest mice and dormice, will usually be situated nearer to the ground, and resemble balls of grass and leaves.

101

Gaps in the hedge may have been made by animals using them as a regular route from one side of the hedge to the other. Examination of the hole may reveal tell-tale hairs, showing that the route is used by a fox or a stoat for instance, but in any event they indicate useful spots for you to lie in wait for the wildlife to pass through.

The shrub layer also supports a huge and varied invertebrate population. A close examination will reveal many species of insect flying among the vegetation or seeking refuge within it. By day, many flying insects can be collected by brushing a sweep net through the foliage (provided the hedge is not of the type that will snag the net). Other species can be collected by using a kite net or upturned umbrella and disturbing the foliage (see page 74). At night, the moth population can be identified by shining a torch among the foliage or by using a sugaring technique (see page 97). The best results, however, will be obtained by using a mercury vapour trap, or, a method which is cheaper although slightly less effective, a bright camping lamp placed on a large sheet of white paper or cloth. Choose warm nights for moth watching.

Hedgerow insects are themselves preyed upon by spiders, which spin webs among the foliage to trap them. Initially spiders can be difficult to see: they are often drab, and lurk quietly out of sight among the foliage. However, their webs are quite visible – especially in the morning when they are covered in dew, or after a light shower of rain. To entice spiders out of their hiding places you must simulate a small struggling insect trapped in the spider's web. There are several ways of doing this:

1   Touch the web with an oscillating tuning fork;
2   Touch the web gently several times in quick succession with a feathery grass head;
3   Squirt a little water on to the web with a house plant spray;
4   Blow gently on the web several times in rapid succession with a straw.

Some spider species will also fall into a beating tray, used as described above.

Hedgerows are of course important habitats for birds, and you should always approach a hedgerow with binoculars and field notebook at the ready. Several species may nest in the hedgerow or its emergent trees, and for others it is a useful song post from which to mark out territory. If the hedgerow links up with copses of trees or woods, try taking cover among the trees and birdwatching at the hedgerows from them.

Lower layers

Examining and identifying the flowering plants of the lower part of the hedgerow will provide a useful clue to the insects likely to be found; many butterflies, for instance, are quite specific in the foodplant requirements of their caterpillars. The moist conditions of the lower layers favour other invertebrates and should be closely examined (especially under leaves, etc.) for animals such as slugs, snails and centipedes. During damp weather or in the early morning snails especially are likely to be seen out in the open, browsing on the foliage.

In winter, the lower hedgerow provides safety for hibernating mammals, reptiles and, again, snails and other invertebrates and their pupae. Any

A Longworth mammal trap in position. The trap is now covered with more grass to make it less conspicuous. Check the law regarding the capture of species like shrews before you set traps.

creatures which are found should be left undisturbed and covered up again.

During the warmer months of the year small mammals such as hedgehogs, voles, shrews and dormice frequent the hedgerow, feeding on insects, worms, eggs and vegetation. A small mammal trap sited near the base of the hedge, or near a run – indicated by a path worn in the grass – will usually yield results.

If you do not wish to trap any animals but just wish to tempt them to bait instead, place a selection of greenstuffs (such as carrot and lettuce) in a suitable place. Bread dipped in aniseed is also an attractive bait for small animals.

Predators such as stoats and weasels also patrol the hedgerows for prey, and a piece of fresh meat, or a road casualty bird, may lure them. Place the bait somewhere where the animal will feel safe in securing it, and then hide nearby. Stoats and other sinuous predatory mammals often hunt for food in narrow places, such as burrows, so you could try placing the bait in a piece of pipework. The same techniques for mammal watching at hedgerows are those required for watching in woodlands: quietness, patience and an

103

Looking closely at the bottom of hedges may reveal nest entrances like this one; probably a fox's.

understanding of the animals' basic habits. As with any form of baiting, it is quite likely that you will have to carry it out regularly for several nights – perhaps without even attempting to await results – until animals become used to finding food in a particular place.

Look carefully in this part of the hedgerow for larger holes which may be occupied by foxes or rabbits.

Ditches

The damp conditions here are ideal for aquatic species such as amphibians which may lay their eggs to hatch in the water, and for dragonflies and other aquatic invertebrates. A small net, such as a child's shrimping net, is useful for securing the aquatic inhabitants of a ditch. A good time to look in a ditch is after heavy rain: snails and other invertebrates may have been washed in, and can be easily collected. Old bottles are worth investigating since they sometimes contain the corpse of a small animal which crawled in and then became trapped – you may even be able to rescue a live, recently interned victim!

Typical animals: fieldbrief

Phylum Annelida

Earthworms are abundant in downland soil and even in ploughed arable land. Worm 'casts' are clues to their presence. Found on the surface only after heavy rain and at night. Search at night with torch.

Phylum Mollusca

Slugs are numerous on downland turf. Search under logs and stones during day, or use a torch at night. Sometimes active during day after rain. Many slugs, such as species of *Arion*, seem to prefer dying or decaying plant material. Others eat living plants and can become arable pests.

Snails are common on chalk downland. Species such as the garden snail and the brown-lipped snail are often found under stones during dry weather. Snails' shells are frequently found smashed by song thrushes on favourite stones or 'anvils'. Search through mole hill soil for the minute white shell of the blind snail, and the glossy shell of the slippery snail.

Phylum Arthropoda

Insects Many different species of butterfly are on the wing from May to September, and most have particular species of larval food plant. It is therefore worth checking in an identification guide for the food plant before searching for caterpillars. The blue butterflies are the most commonly encountered group of downland. They are rather fast fliers and therefore are best caught for examination and identification when less active in the morning and evening. They roost on grass stems, sometimes in cornfields adjacent to downland. The skipper butterflies are also fast fliers and, with their rather drab colours, can easily be overlooked. Search the dry paths, for many of these small butterflies like to bask in the sun, wings flat, warming up on the stones and soil. The 'brown' butterflies are similar to the skippers, though larger, and their caterpillars are often difficult to find since they feed mainly at night. Search the grasses with a torch or try sweep netting for them.

Moths are mainly nocturnal species, and a night sample with a moth trap or baited post is the best way of seeing them. Very large numbers can be caught in this way and identified but it is important to remember not to release the captives in the same spot, for birds can take advantage of this unexpectedly abundant food supply. In the daytime, a sweep through the grass with a net can yield moths roosting in the vegetation.

Beetles are common on downland, but often secretive. Lift up stones during the day and set pitfall traps for them at night, when they are most active. Dung beetles are common on grasslands, collecting animal droppings which are buried as a source of food for the larvae. Look for the tell-tale holes in bare ground where adults have emerged. On warm summer nights, glow-worms light up the hedgerows and chalk banks, and a careful search for these fascinating insects can be rewarding.

Flies are common on downland and are attracted to carrion and animal dung, on which many species lay their eggs.

Bugs are often abundant among downland and hedgerow vegetation.

They can be beaten from bushes with a stick into an upturned umbrella or caught by sweep netting the grass.

Ants, wasps and bees are also a common sight on downland. The yellow meadow ant constructs conspicuous ant hills, especially in ancient pasture; ploughed arable fields support few ants. Bees and wasps include both social and solitary species, and holes in banks are worth investigating for the nests of these insects. On sunny days bees can be watched collecting pollen from the many species of downland flowers.

Grasshoppers and crickets often betray their presence by song; each species has a distinct song pattern. Grasshoppers tend to occur mainly in open grassy areas, whereas the related bush crickets prefer grassland bordered by scrub, into which they can dive for cover if disturbed. Some species, such as the wartbiter, only sing on warm days – in the wartbiter's case, when the air temperature is above 21°C/70°F. In general, you are more likely to find grasshoppers and bush crickets in sheltered, south-facing sites, out of the wind.

Centipedes, millipedes and pseudoscorpions are common soil invertebrates found by turning over stones and logs. The pseudoscorpions are most easily detected by laying soil out on a sheet or by using a Tullgren funnel.

Spiders Crab spiders are found on flower heads waiting for insects to land and be caught in their outstretched legs. They can be quite well camouflaged, so patient searching on the flowers is necessary. Other species live under stones and among dry grass. Web-spinning spiders are conspicuous, especially in the early morning, when the dew on their newly spun webs catches the sunlight. The purse-web spider lives in a silken tube, half buried in the ground. The spider is sensitive to any movements caused by an insect moving across the tube, and can be enticed above ground by tickling the tube with a grass stem.

Phylum Chordata

Reptiles Lizards and snakes like to bask on sunny banks. They are best approached in the early morning when they are more sluggish. Snakes such as the adder spend a great deal of the day coiled up on a bank or near an old tree stump. Avoid sudden movement when watching reptiles, and if you get close, make sure that your shadow does not fall over them; this is sure to scare them off.

Birds BIRDS OF PREY The high populations of small mammals on downland attract several species of birds of prey. Kestrels can be seen hovering over grassy banks and the rarer Montagu's harrier quarters the ground in search of its prey. Sparrowhawks hunt small birds on the downlands; it is worthwhile scanning with binoculars along hedgerows, as these are favourite spots – the birds fly rapidly along the line of the hedge and then swoop down on to their prey.

OWLS Barn owl pellets may be found near ruined buildings and outhouses, which these birds use as nest sites, or under tree roosts. This species is occasionaly seen at dawn and dusk and often uses a fence post as a look out. The little owl hunts by day, making it easy to detect; its cat-like calls are distinctive.

GAMEBIRDS Encouraged by man for shooting. Partridges appear as small dark objects in fields and are not obvious until they move; they prefer to run, rather than fly from danger.

Pheasants are much less wary outside the shooting season and can be approached quite closely. They do not as a rule stray very far from cover.

Quail are rather secretive but a tape recording of their call, when played back, may reveal them.

WADERS A few species of wader feed on downland. Watch for them feeding in flocks in grassland – lapwings in particular are easy to see due to their striking plumage and alarm calls.

PIGEONS AND DOVES Often feed together in fields. Best viewed through a suitable hedge, where your outline is not visible.

PERCHING BIRDS Also often in flocks. Mixed flocks of buntings, sparrows and finches feed together on downland, especially in winter. Avoid being seen, for once a single bird has detected your presence, the whole flock will be up in a matter of seconds. If this does happen, however, make a careful note of the wing and tail patterns of the birds, as these plumage differences are one of the best ways of distinguishing between them. Some warbler species are found on downland, particularly in scrubby areas. They do not often show themselves, and song is a good way of identifying them. Locate the bird first by the song and then by searching the bush or hedgerow for tell-tale movements and a closer view.

Mammals RABBITS Perhaps the most common and characteristic downland mammal. The colonial burrows or warrens are sited on grassy banks, often those covered with brambles. Look for tufts of fur clinging to the burrow entrance as a sign that it is in use. Entrance may be very large, but often 15 cm (6 in) across. As rabbits are very alert and have a good sense of hearing and smell they are best watched from cover in a downwind position. Early morning and evening are good times to watch them as they feed outside their burrow entrances.

VOLES, MICE AND SHREWS Downland supports high populations of these small mammals. Baiting small mammal traps along the sides of paths and at the bottom of hedgerow banks will reveal which species are present. If you sit down quietly in a likely grassy spot – a summer's evening is a good time – you may hear squeaks and rustlings and perhaps obtain a fleeting glimpse of a mouse or shrew. Harvest mice construct their spherical nests of dry grasses in reeds, cereals and other similar vegetation.

MOLE Mole hills are obvious features of downlands. Moles sometimes come above ground so a patient wait in a suitable field may be rewarded.

WEASEL AND STOAT Voracious predators of mice, voles and rabbits. Reasonably common but difficult to observe. Oblivious to observers if in pursuit of prey. Listen for screams of rabbit and a stoat is probably near at hand. Family parties also take little notice of man.

FOX AND BADGER Sometimes have their earths and setts on edge of arable and downland fields. Watch entrance at dusk with binoculars. Check wind direction and ensure you are downwind of hole. Badger setts generally have dry bedding material near entrance if occupied (see also page 86 for more details).

DEER Sometimes feed in open fields, most often at dawn and dusk. Very wary, they are best viewed from a distance through binoculars.

Freshwater habitats

Freshwater habitats are varied and widespread. Some support a great abundance and variety of life, and are among the most valuable of wildlife habitats, whilst others can be almost devoid of all living things.

Ponds and gravel pits

Ponds are small bodies of fresh water which, unlike lakes, rarely have rivers or streams flowing in or out of them; they are therefore stagnant, but can be very rich in invertebrates and fishes. They are usually highly eutrophic, and can sometimes be covered in floating vegetation such as duckweed. Small pools which dry up in the summer are difficult habitats for many species, notably fishes, but many invertebrates produce a dormant stage which is able to resist drought conditions.

Created by the extraction of sand and gravel, gravel pits are mostly of uniform depth, but some have shallow areas which attract migrant birds and are colonized by wetland species of plants. Dragonflies and other aquatic insects are common, since they can easily fly to, and colonize, other nearby pits. If the pits have small islands on them these will be exploited by ground-nesting birds such as common terns and ducks, which can nest safe from predators like rats or foxes.

Lakes

Upland lakes are among the most barren of all freshwater habitats, particularly those in areas of hard, igneous rocks and acid soils. Sometimes the water can be crystal clear, due to the lack of plankton and low levels of silt entering, but in others the water is stained brown with peat. The flora consists of plants such as shoreweed, the moss *Fontinalis* and some simple algae. More sheltered bays support a richer flora of species like bogbean and water-lily. The animal life is similarly impoverished, and comprises some invertebrates living in the bottom ooze or browsing on submerged rocks. Some birds may nest on upland lakes, however. Such barren lakes are termed oligotrophic.

Lowland lakes usually have a very rich flora comprising rooted, surface-floating and planktonic plant life supporting an abundant animal population, particularly larger invertebrates and fishes, and birds which feed or nest by water. The reason for the increased plant growth is the greater availability of nutrients. The softer rocks of lowland areas, agricultural fertilizers and sewage effluent all contribute to nutrient levels. Lakes which support such a wealth of life are called eutrophic. Where the lake is sufficiently shallow, rooted vegetation will appear and the emergent vegetation around the banks will lead to the deposition of silt, enabling other species, less suited to life in deep water, to colonize the shallower margins. The common reed is the best-known example, and is often seen fringing lowland lakes, eventually forming complete reed beds with little or no open water. The pattern of succession seen in lowland lakes therefore is a transition from open water to a community of rooted, submerged plants. At the margins is a community of emergent plants like the yellow iris. Soon the reed becomes dominant, forming a dense reed bed which, as it becomes drier, encourages trees and shrubs to grow in it. One of the latest stages in succession is a rather damp type of woodland known as alder carr.

Reservoirs

Usually constructed on upland sites where the deep valleys, high rainfall, impervious rocks and low levels of land use make building easy, reservoirs are very similar to oligotrophic lakes, but they may have even less vegetation on the shores due to the fluctuating water levels. Some provide winter refuge for huge numbers of birds, but in the summer recreational activities can cause disturbance; many water authorities are now setting aside areas to be maintained as sanctuaries.

Rivers, streams and canals

Rivers and streams can often be classified into a number of distinct zones according to the nature of the bed, the speed of the current and the types of fish present. The **headwaters** of a river rising in the hills are typically oligotrophic, supporting few species of plants or animals. The current is fast, providing plenty of oxygen as the water splashes over stones, but the temperature is usually low. The **troutbeck zone**, characterized by the presence of trout or similar species, has more plants and insects, and the current, although still fast, is reduced in places where deep pools form. The bed is usually stony, and from time to time floods may cause deep erosion. The **minnow reach** has the first rooted plants, such as water crowfoot. Grayling and minnow are among the fishes here, and where there is some silt many invertebrates may be found. The **lowland reach** is slow flowing, the waters carry much more silt, and the river meanders. More rooted vegetation grows here and the bottom mud supports many more invertebrates such as swan mussels and midge larvae. These are food for fishes like roach and bream which can survive lower oxygen levels and higher temperatures. The banks often support a rich plant life and so birds, mammals and insects will be much more abundant here.

Canals are similar to the lowland reaches of rivers and, although man-made, are soon colonized by invertebrates and fishes. Some canals in current use are prone to pollution and disturbance, but others are important wildlife habitats. Abandoned canals, or those used only casually for recreation, are excellent wildlife habitats, with access facilitated by means of the towpath. At intervals along some canals are large ponds or flashes, which are constructed to provide extra water for the locks. These can show all the features of lowland lakes, and usually have rich plant and animal life.

Wetlands

Low-lying areas around rivers and lakes may become waterlogged or flooded, resulting in marshes or fens. Unlike bogs, where the mineral content is usually very low, marshes and fens are often rich in alluvial deposits and support a diverse flora. This encourages a large variety of insects, spiders, molluscs and amphibians, and many birds (such as snipe and redshank) also come to feed in these areas. Wetlands are important sites for overwintering wildfowl.

Nature watching in ponds

For many people this is one of the most endearing and interesting places to watch nature. Many of the techniques and items of equipment used here can be applied to other freshwater habitats. A pair of wellingtons are essential footwear, and a hand towel is an often overlooked non-essential but useful piece of equipment. More specialized items include a long-handled net, sieves, a plastic sheet for laying out samples and weed, a rake or dredge, various dishes and jars, and a hand-lens.

PHOTOKEY

bankside vegetation harbours dragonflies and damselflies

look around lilies and other aquatic vegetation for basking fishes

look for signs of rising fishes and surface insects

A rich lowland lake in summer – ideal for nature watching.

(Above) Damselflies are commonly seen resting on waterside vegetation.

(Right) During spring you can identify the presence of many amphibians by their eggs. Some newts and salamanders also lay their eggs on stones. Salamandra and Pleurodeles lay clumps of eggs.

frog spawn

newt egg

toad spawn

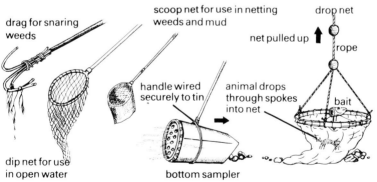

drag for snaring weeds

scoop net for use in netting weeds and mud

drop net

net pulled up ↑

rope

handle wired securely to tin

animal drops through spokes into net

bait

dip net for use in open water

bottom sampler

Nets, a bottom sampler and a grapnel for use when investigating ponds and other freshwater habitats.

When to go

Whenever you choose to visit a pond you are sure to see something of interest. However, if you wish to search for specific animals the timing of the visit should be considered.

In the morning, you are more likely to encounter recently emerged insects in the waterside vegetation. Also, most insects, and especially dragonflies, do not become active until the sun has warmed them up. Therefore, you can watch or photograph them at close range at this time. This is also the best time for observing frogs and toads mating, partly because of the lack of disturbance. Birds are also more active at first light.

The heat of the day causes insects to become more active. Dragonflies can be seen feeding and engaging in territorial disputes. You may also be lucky enough to see them mating and egg laying if you are quiet and patient. Some aquatic insects breathe oxygen from the air and, as the water temperature rises during the day, their metabolic rate speeds up and they must make more frequent visits to the water's surface. Midday is, therefore, a good time to watch for water beetles and bugs at the surface.

As the evening draws on, the daytime insects are replaced by swarms of mosquitoes and midges, and, over streams and rivers, mayflies. Because of the numbers of insects in these swarms, birds such as swallows and swifts congregate to feed on them at dusk. These may be joined by bats which continue feeding throughout the night. Other mammals may now start to make an appearance, too.

Many insects emerge as adults from larval forms at night, partly because predators such as birds are less active then. A torchlight search of the water's edge and associated plants may reveal a variety of organisms including dragonflies and mayflies.

The time of year is also important in determining what animals will occur. Spring is the time to search for mating frogs and toads and to look for their spawn. The aquatic plants will not have grown, and so it is relatively easy to observe animals in the water. Most insects are at their most obvious during the summer months. Adult insects such as dragonflies can be seen above the water's surface, whilst below the surface adult and larval forms of many other groups can be found. This is the best time of year to see family parties of waterbirds, and a patient watch from a hidden vantage point should be rewarded. By the time autumn comes, the aquatic vegetation will be extremely dense, making observation relatively difficult. Adult bugs and beetles are most numerous now and will be encountered near the surface of the water. During the winter months, the water plants die back and many of the animals hibernate. However, the larvae of many species of insect may still be found by netting, and hungry birds and mammals can still be encountered also.

Pond edge

Many fascinating aspects of pond life can be seen simply by waiting patiently and quietly by the pond's edge. Approach the water stealthily and try to remain at least partly concealed among bushes and reeds. Keep your eyes open for the many species of waterbird that nest and skulk in the emergent vegetation. If you hear the alarm calls of these birds, move quietly away to avoid disturbing their nests or alerting predators to their whereabouts.

Many insects rest and spend much of their lives among waterside vegetation. Dragonflies use regular perches from which to keep a look out

(Above left) With a sturdy, fine-mesh net you can sample both the water and the mud at the bottom. (Above right) Empty the contents of the net into a dish containing a little water to discover what you have caught. Examining the water itself with a hand-lens will reveal other, much smaller creatures not visible to the naked eye.

both for prey and rivals of the same species, and some insects emerge as adults from their aquatic larval stages. The adults, and the cast skins of the larvae, can be found by close scrutiny of the plants or by sweep netting.

Some aquatic animals will also be visible from the pond's edge. Frogs often congregate in the margins of ponds and, although wary, will return to bask in their favourite spots if you are patient. During the summer, many of the large species of fish shoal in the shallows in order to spawn, and are generally oblivious to the quiet onlooker. Aquatic bugs and snails are also readily visible from the edge of the water. Water voles, weasels – even deer – will often be seen near the water's edge providing you are concealed, perhaps among some nearby trees or in a hide, by late afternoon.

Open water

The open water is an extremely productive region for the pond watcher. Scan the surface carefully for water bugs and other insects. Some species skate across the surface, whilst others are submerged and cling to the surface film. Look for signs of fish activity. Sometimes you will see several small fishes leap out of the water. This is usually an indication that a predator is on the hunt below the surface.

In the water itself, the many species of pond weeds provide both food and shelter for larval and adult insects, water snails and many other creatures. The best way to observe these animals is to net a sample of weed and place it in a tray. Try to slip the net gently into the water and then vigorously sweep it up towards the surface taking some weed with it. If you want to sample weed from the centre of the pond, this can be done from a boat or with the aid of a dredge to haul in samples. As an alternative, the head of a garden rake tied to a rope will serve the same purpose. Remember that the sampling may disturb many of the animals, and they may not be immediately visible in your catch. Given time to recover in a bucket you may find many more animals than you first imagined.

Mud and silt

Despite its apparently unpleasant nature, many animals find sanctuary in the mud and leaf litter that collects on the bottom of ponds. Many are microscopic, others are often well camouflaged and covered in silt, and are, therefore, difficult to spot. If you place a sample of mud in a tray and patiently leave it, the animals will eventually betray their presence by movements. As an alternative you could try washing the sample through a small-mesh sieve. After a little perseverance you should end up with a varied collection of small creatures.

Nature watching on lakes and reservoirs

Upland lakes, and reservoirs, are low in nutrients and therefore support less plant and animal life than lowland lakes, but they are also usually remote and suffer less from disturbance. For this reason they provide safe nesting areas for more wary birds such as divers and grebes, and overwintering quarters for other species. Many of the techniques for nature watching on rivers and ponds can also be applied to lakes and reservoirs.

When to go

Winter is ideal for birdwatching, as flocks of wildfowl gather then to feed on submerged vegetation and invertebrates; during the breeding season they are more dispersed and, in any case, you should not visit areas where sensitive species are nesting. Spring and autumn are good times to look for migrant species such as waders which might spend a short time on the stony shores of large lakes before continuing on their journeys. During summer the resident breeding species will be active, and the few invertebrates which inhabit these larger lakes will be easier to see; hatches of mayflies, for example, can be quite spectacular on some evenings.

Shorelines and margins

The strong wave action on large lakes prevents much vegetation from growing on the shores, which are often very stony. On reservoirs, as a result of the fluctuating water levels, they can also be very barren. Before walking along the shores scan them carefully for feeding or roosting waders. Having checked the shore for waders the partly submerged stones at the water's edge can be examined for invertebrates like the tiny lake limpet. Be very careful, however, for a steeply shelving shore can drop away into very deep water. Look for signs of predatory mammals on the shore such as droppings or fish remains. If these are present it is probably best to return at dusk to watch for the mammals themselves from a concealed place.

Where there is less wave action some vegetation may grow, and this will provide more food and shelter than on the stony shores. Pond-dipping

The red-throated diver nests by upland lakes.

techniques (see page 113) can be applied here but, as before, caution is necessary. There may be more cover here in the form of bankside vegetation, so this should be made use of before moving out into the open. Nesting birds will use the vegetation in these sheltered spots, so it is important to avoid disturbance in the breeding season. Examine any log or prominent stone for the spraints of otters, or bird droppings. This will indicate a regularly visited place which will be worth watching for a longer period. Examine the vegetation for aquatic insects such as dragonflies.

As on the seashore, large lakes often have a strandline of debris blown ashore by the prevailing winds. Look along the strandline for feeding birds before walking along it. Examining the debris closely will give some pointers to the aquatic inhabitants of the lake. Plenty of plant debris will be found, but mollusc shells also get washed ashore. Lakes with a fairly high calcium carbonate content will support swan mussels, whose empty shells sometimes litter the shore. Look closely at these to see if they have been

115

In winter, signs of animal activity such as footprints and droppings will still be much in evidence around the lake margins. Look for bird activity in the reed beds.

opened by a predator; if they have a large chip out of one margin a heron may well have been involved. Dead fishes sometimes drift ashore, and are an attraction to scavengers like the black kite or even a fox. Some lakes are artificially stocked with trout, but many other fish species can be encountered, and if not too decomposed can be fairly easily identified.

Islands and sandbanks

Small stony islands sometimes appear where a river enters a lake and deposits shingle. These make safe roosting places for birds which will fly to them if disturbed from the shore. In very windy conditions look on the downwind side where roosting waders might be sheltering. Divers and grebes often nest on low grassy islands but should never be approached when sitting as they are extremely sensitive to disturbance.

Open water

Binoculars or a telescope are essential here, and on large bodies of water it is important to sweep across the water several times in order not to miss anything. Some diving birds can stay under water for about a minute, so you might easily miss them first time round. Diving birds are normally found over the deeper water, but dabbling ducks like the teal can only feed on the shallower margins. Take note of the wind direction and look for any debris on the water blown there by the wind. This debris, consisting of leaves, waterweed, dead insects and other organic matter, is a source of food for fishes – you may see a trout breaking the surface to take floating insects – but the debris also attracts many birds, such as gulls. Insectivorous birds such as wagtails and pipits often feed along the edge of dams, and may also nest there. Look along reed-fringed margins for fishes such as rudd and carp lazing near the surface. A piece of bread thrown on to the surface here may attract some species.

It is not practicable to apply pond-dipping techniques over most of the surface of a large lake or reservoir – although you can do this in the shallows – but if a boat is available some sampling of the invertebrates can be carried out. Towing a plankton net behind the boat will trap free-swimming species, including small fishes, whilst a baited drop-net will catch deep-water species.

Special conservation areas

On large bodies of water there is frequently a high level of recreational use by man; angling, water-skiing and sailing all add to the disturbance, thus many waters now have sanctuary areas where these pursuits are prohibited. Before entering a nature reserve check carefully about rights of access, and try to keep all disturbance to a minimum. Very early in the morning, before the water-skiers and sailors have appeared, many of the birds are likely to be dispersed over the lake, but as the disturbance increases they will retreat to the quieter zone. A good plan is to get into a concealed position, possibly a hide, and watch from there as the birds return. These sanctuary areas are sometimes in more sheltered places and so, in addition to birds, more insects will probably be present.

Nature watching on rivers, streams and canals

Moving fresh water is a diverse habitat, providing many interesting opportunities for nature watching. From source to sea, a river's character changes dramatically and the plants and animals which colonize it vary at

PHOTOKEY   waterbirds hide in bankside vegetation
fishes lie beneath overhanging trees

weed provides cover and food for fishes and aquatic invertebrates

Rivers which flow over chalk have clear waters.

different stages of its course. A river may have its flow interrupted by weirs, and it may also be associated with pools and small tributaries, dykes and ditches. The few items of equipment which are useful for investigating this habitat are described on pages 110 and 111.

When to go

Although the seasons play an important part in determining the species present, moving water always has something to offer the naturalist. In spring and summer there is perhaps a greater number of species to be seen; the birds for instance are swelled by visiting warblers and others, and insects are also in 'much greater abundance. However, winter has many compensations: rivers may be the only places where unfrozen water offers suitable conditions for ducks and other water birds; mammals will be hungrier and perhaps bolder, and of course fishes – the major inhabitants of rivers – can be watched equally well in winter or summer. Early morning and early evening are often the most rewarding times to visit this habitat.

Approaching water

Try and make your approach to the water as stealthy as possible. If there are trees nearby – perhaps a wood – take cover behind these and train your binoculars on the water from there. Many waterside birds will take flight or melt into the reeds at your approach, and herons will just flap lazily off, too. Watch for birds by scanning reed beds, as well as the open water. Also look for species such as kingfishers flying from nearby trees, and for any bird movements on the bank itself. Predatory mammals may also be patrolling the bank looking for unwary victims.

If there are no trees nearby use whatever cover is available: stone walls, bridges, hedges – even your car. You can watch the river from a hidden vantage point for as long as you wish of course, but there is still plenty more to see by getting closer to the water.

River bank

The river bank itself can provide many clues for the naturalist. In places where the bank shelves gently to the water – the sort of area in which cattle often come to drink – look for footprints of birds and other signs such as feathers. Mammal footprints may also be present here. Around the bank you may well find other items: deer droppings, or the droppings of weasels, otters and foxes; perhaps even the signs of a struggle where a mink surprised a resting duck and carried it off. It's just a matter of getting down on your hands and knees and looking.

Now find a quiet place in amongst the reed beds or some other thick riverside vegetation and just sit quietly. (Try and resist the temptation to swat the midges that may descend on you!) One of the reasons why anglers are such successful waterside naturalists is that their sport demands hours of patiently sitting still. Many an angler has had a kingfisher perch on his rod end or voles investigating his lunch box! If you move, try to do so in unison with the wind moving the vegetation. In this way you will become part of the scenery. Listen for the sound of birds: you may only have limited vision from your hiding place and so must let the birds advertize their presence.

Erecting a temporary hide to watch water birds and mammals such as voles. Once secure, viewing holes must be cut in the material.

Birds on the water will probably be the easiest to see, but if the light is poor you can at least distinguish between ducks, and coots and moorhens if you remember that ducks have straight backs while those of coots and moorhens are more rounded. Mammals make characteristic V-shaped ripple patterns as they swim in the water. At dusk, bats will appear, making swooping flights over the water to catch insects.

If the stream or river is lined with trees, forming an arch, you will find that birds often use this as a safe flightway, instead of flying outside, in open country.

Bridges form an interesting microhabitat: bats and birds may nest on ledges underneath them, and the piers and supports are favoured places for otters to deposit their oily droppings or spraints. (Shingle islands are also worth investigation: birds often use them for nesting and roosting.)

Bankside vegetation

The vegetation of river sides supports large populations of animals, particularly insects, although birds such as reed warblers may nest here, and mammals such as water shrews may inhabit the lower layers. Search carefully among reed stems for emerging dragonflies and other insects. Sit quietly by tangled waterside vegetation and you may hear the scolding squeaks of the water shrews. These little creatures seldom keep still, and appear and disappear again into the undergrowth very quickly.

Holes in the bank

Look for holes in the bank. They may be inhabited by water voles, kingfishers or even crayfish (if under water). Water voles' nests can easily be identified by the close-cropped vegetation surrounding them, and the runs, or paths, leading to the water. The first clue of a water vole in the vicinity is often the 'plop' it makes as it enters the water.

(Above) The otter: a rare waterside mammal which requires skill and patience to spot.

(Right) Several different nests may be found in reed beds and other similar nearby vegetation.

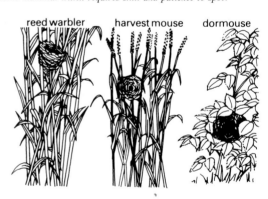

In the water

The techniques needed for investigating the invertebrate life of rivers are similar in many ways to those needed for ponds and lakes. If the water is too deep for you to reach the bottom easily, you must use a small shrimping or, better, dip net to take a sample of the aquatic life. You can sweep the net

120

(Above) The first attempt at sifting the weed in the shallows of this river revealed a leech.

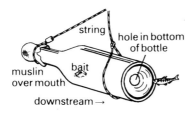

string

hole in bottom of bottle

bait

muslin over mouth

downstream →

(Left) Small fishes such as minnows can easily be caught in a bottle trap.

121

through open water, but sweeping it beneath lily pads, and by reeds or other bankside vegetation will often yield the best results. A plastic dish filled with river water is useful for examining your finds. A sample of the mud dredged up from the bottom – either with a strong net or with a bottom sampler (see illustration) – can also be examined in this way. Where the water is shallow, particularly in fast upland streams, the small aquatic life comes to terms with the conditions in a variety of ways. Some larvae cling to stones with powerful feet and others hide under stones away from the flow. Therefore the best way to find these creatures is to lift stones and examine them carefully. You should also investigate any aquatic vegetation for creatures seeking shelter there.

Fish watching

This can be a fascinating form of nature watching. The most rewarding places are streams or shallow waters with good visibility. Whereas airborne noises are the ones to avoid when watching birds or mammals, fish are highly sensitive to vibrations transmitted through the ground, and to shadows cast over the water or the sudden appearance of the human form. Therefore begin your fish watching about 10 m (30 ft) from the water at least. Tread extremely softly and, as you near the water, complete the last 5 m (15 ft) on your hands and knees, moving forward slowly. At no time should your outline be visible against the skyline. Now peer through any available bankside cover into the water. Polarized sunglasses will help to reduce glare, allowing you to see much more clearly. Look for any movement: it may be the flash of silver as a fish rolls to snatch at an insect, or just a white diamond shape suddenly appearing as a trout opens its mouth to

Typical fish lies in a river.

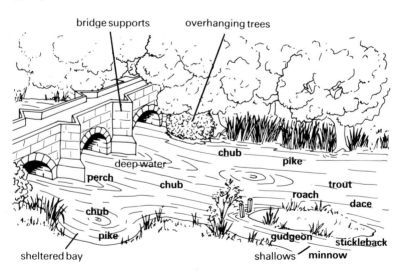

(Above) When fish watching, keep low when approaching the water.

(Below) At the water's edge, remain as still as possible, and do not lean over the edge any more than is necessary.

Fish watching from a bridge enables you to view the water in mid-stream, and from a different angle.

breathe. Once your sight is accustomed to the medium, you will be able to make out the dark shapes of the fishes' backs.

Bridges are also good vantage points from which to watch fish. You can encourage less shy species to come to the surface by dropping pieces of bread on to the water. Next, squeeze a small piece of bread into a ball. If you drop it into the water and watch it sink, you may see a larger fish appear from the shadows to take it.

Quiet pools, especially if trees overhang them, are favoured places for fishes to lie in wait for natural food to fall into the water and are good places for you to try looking for fish. Some greedy small fry can be 'angled' for by dangling a piece of meat tied to string in the shallows. Leave it for half a minute or so and then gently pull it from the water. A fish may be hanging on to the meat and can be scooped up with a small net. Minnow traps, available from most angling shops but easily constructed from a bottle with a hole knocked in the bottom, are also successful for catching small fish species.

Nature watching on wetlands

Wetlands support a great variety of species which require water at some stage in their life-cycles, but are not dependent on large expanses of very deep water. Many marshy areas are also dissected by streams and ditches which provide a habitat for truly aquatic species. In addition, many terrestrial species visit wetlands to nest or feed on the rich pickings.

124

When to go

Winter floods turn marshes into shallow lakes, thus attracting many wetland birds. At times of extensive flooding the birds can be dispersed over a wide area, but as the waters subside the feeding wildfowl will concentrate into a smaller area. In spring the resident bird species will take up territory prior to breeding, and amphibians will congregate in the ditches for spawning. During summer many of the drainage ditches will become choked with vegetation, making some species difficult to see, but many insects will be on the wing, and birds such as swallows, martins and swifts fly low over the marshes to feed on them.

As with most other habitats, early mornings are best for seeing and hearing birds, and in spring many waders will be displaying from the early hours. (Wildfowl often fly in from their roosting areas to begin feeding at dawn during the winter.) During the day, especially during very warm weather, many insects will be on the wing, and dragonflies can be seen hunting up and down the ditches. Dusk brings a further burst of bird song; the eerie calls of the water rail may be heard in ditches and dense reeds, and the hirundines (members of the swallow family) gather in large flocks over the marshes before flying off to roost. Many amphibians start calling at dusk in spring and early summer, and herons may still be stalking the ditches in search of prey.

PHOTOKEY

bogs are often characterized by cotton-grass

dragonflies and damselflies hawk over vegetation

look for sundews around the margins

Permanent boggy pools are small-scale wetland habitats.

125

Where to look
Drainage ditches and permanent pools are important features of marshy areas, and the techniques of pond-dipping can be applied here. Take note also of any logs or stones scattered around the marsh and inspect these carefully for creatures hiding beneath them. Marshes used for grazing sometimes have open-sided cattle shelters to provide some cover for livestock in bad weather. These buildings, known as 'hovels', are an obvious attraction for birds and should prove interesting if watched for a time. Do not enter them if any birds are nesting, and try not to disturb any livestock which might be sheltering there. Fence posts scattered around a marsh are used by birds of prey as roosting and low-level prey spotting points. Scan around them carefully through binoculars before going out on to the marsh. If cattle are grazing on the marsh, their feet will disturb insects, and these attract feeding birds. The lack of cover means that concealment may be a problem. You can reduce your own outline by crouching down, or can use a car as a hide. Better still is to erect a proper hide and watch from it over several days.

Typical animals: fieldbrief
Phylum Porifera
Freshwater sponges are found encrusting stones and plant stems in still or flowing water.

Phylum Cnidaria
Hydra hangs from stones and water plants, and contracts into a blob if disturbed. Collect sample of weed and place in jar of water. Leave for an hour or so and *Hydra* will have moved to the glass, thus easier to see.

Phylum Platyhelminthes
Planarian flatworms mainly found in flowing water. Feed on detritus, so often found by sampling the bottom of streams.

Phylum Annelida
Oligochaete worms generally feed on detritus, so found among mud and stones. Some species live in mud tubes visible from above the water.

Leeches are flattened worms which sometimes swim with an undulating motion, but are usually found attached to plants and stones, unless actively feeding on host, to which they are attached by suckers.

Phylum Mollusca
Molluscs are abundant in calcium-rich waters where this is used in construction of their shells. Familiar freshwater snails can be numerous in still and slow-flowing water, often attached to rocks and weeds. Species such as the great pond snail often move across surface film and obtain air supply at surface. Snails can be examined by netting samples of the vegetation and studying it in a tray.

Freshwater limpet is a miniature version of its marine counterpart. Found attached to stones and weirs in fast-flowing streams and rivers.

Freshwater bivalves such as the swan mussel are common in slow-flowing, silty rivers. Lie buried in mud with siphons protruding for filter feeding. In rivers where common, numerous empty shells washed up on bank edge. Smaller pea mussels are found in range of habitats from ponds to rivers.

Phylum Arthropoda

Crustaceans Some species are microscopic. Water fleas and copepods occur in vast numbers. Note jerky movements through water. Ostracods scurry over surface of the mud and feed on detritus.

Many larger species found in still and flowing water. Fairy shrimps breed in temporary pools and puddles. Isopods such as the water louse are found among mud and roots in streams and ponds. Freshwater shrimps also found among detritus of stream beds. Crayfishes are found in fast-flowing streams. During the day they hide under stones. Best caught by holding net downstream of boulder and lifting edge nearest net. Crayfish should shoot into net.

Insects Stonefly larvae found under stones in flowing water. Adults hide among streamside vegetation.

Mayfly larvae live in or on mud. Generally found in flowing water. Adults exhibit mass emergence. Huge swarms of males can be seen on warm May evenings beside rivers. Adults can be netted from waterside vegetation.

Some species of bugs are carnivorous, others feed on plant juices. Most species breathe aerial oxygen so return to water surface at frequent intervals. Pond skaters live on water surface. Respond to movements of insects trapped in surface film on which they feed. Water boatman hangs from underside of surface film and has a similar diet. When swimming, looks silvery due to trapped air bubble. Other species such as water scorpion and water stick insect remain motionless and camouflaged among vegetation waiting for prey. Both have long breathing tubes which break the water surface.

Beetles: many species found as larvae and adults in all freshwater habitats. *Dytiscus* and related diving beetles are active swimmers and fierce predators. Frequently return to water surface to replenish air supply which is held under wing cases. Larvae are also highly carnivorous. Whirligig beetles are common sight on surface of pools. Large numbers can be seen spinning around. Disappear into depths when disturbed but return quickly.

Adults and larval beetles are best collected by netting samples of weed and detritus.

Flies: larval forms of many species found in all freshwater habitats. Mosquito and midge larvae live at surface of still and stagnant pools. Adults emerge in vast numbers forming swarms over water. Larvae of other species such as craneflies live among decaying vegetation at the bottom of pools. Blackfly larvae are found in fast-flowing streams. They live inside a 'tent' attached to stones.

Dragonflies: larvae of dragonflies (and related damselflies) are carnivorous. Many species actively stalk prey among water plants. Others live buried in mud and detritus and wait for passing prey. In spring, larvae emerge from water and climb up waterside vegetation prior to emergence as adults. Examine vegetation at night during May and June with a torch to witness the emergence process. Adult dragonflies sometimes remain near cast nymphal skin until morning so a search at dawn might be fruitful. Adult dragonflies and damselflies catch insects on the wing. Some species return to a regular perch to eat the meal and watch for potential prey, and rivals.

Alderflies: adults are poor fliers. Can be disturbed and netted from waterside vegetation. Larvae live in mud and are active predators.

Moths: a few species have aquatic larvae which live inside 'tents' constructed from portions of plant leaf. They pupate under water. Adult moths flutter low over surface of water.

Caddis flies are rather secretive, remaining hidden among vegetation during the day. Can be disturbed and netted from low waterside plants. Larvae found in a wide range of freshwater habitats. Most species build cases from stones, plant fibres and shells for protection. Material with which cases are built, and shape, are exclusive to each species.

Spiders and mites The water spider is a truly aquatic species, often visible from above surface of water. Look for silvery appearance of abdomen due to film of air. Constructs air-tents among pond weeds.

Adult mites can be seen scurrying over surface of detritus in ponds and streams. Larvae are parasitic, particularly on water bugs.

Phylum Chordata

Fishes Large number of species in European waters, but are seldom observed under natural conditions. Many of the fishes which can be observed naturally in ponds, lakes and rivers by following the fish watching techniques described on pages 122 to 124 are illustrated in the identification section.

Reptiles Grass snake is an expert swimmer. Catches frogs and fishes. Head held high above water. Other snakes such as adders are found near water.

Amphibians FROGS Numerous species occur throughout Europe. Croaking males often heard from a distance. A stealthy approach to water's edge may reveal numerous males competing for females, pairs in amplexus and spawn masses.

NEWTS Look around shallow edges of ponds and lakes in spring for courting newts.

TOADS Only return to water to mate and spawn in early spring. Common toad is widespread and found in small pools, but other species of toad have more specific European distributions and habitat requirements.

Birds DIVERS Swim low in water. Breed on upland lakes but may be encountered on lowland lakes in winter.

GREBES Expert swimmers, reluctant to fly. Great crested grebe breeds on lowland lakes. Other species breed on rivers and upland lakes.

HERONS Grey heron encountered in wide range of freshwater habitats. Remains motionless waiting for movements of fishes and amphibians. Purple heron and bittern found in extensive reed beds on Continent. Best seen at dawn or dusk as they fly to nesting and feeding areas.

DUCKS AND SWANS Numerous species breed in all European freshwater habitats. Easiest to see in winter on large unfrozen lakes.

BIRDS OF PREY Osprey favours large lakes and catches fishes by plunging into water. Breeds near well-wooded upland lakes but encountered in any suitable habitat in Europe on migration. Marsh harrier slowly quarters reed beds in search of birds and amphibians. Black kite has similar flight to marsh harrier.

WATER RAIL Best located by squealing and grunting calls, especially at dusk. Can be lured by tape recording of its own voice. Feeds in open during winter.

COOT AND MOORHEN Found on variety of lakes and ponds especially where there is cover around edge. Sit quietly and wait for them to swim from cover.

WADERS Variety of species found feeding around muddy edges of lakes and ponds, particularly during migration periods. Redshank and snipe breed in marshy fields. Both species keep look out from fence posts and perform flight displays over territories. Green sandpiper is often found in watercress beds and sewage farms.

GULLS Some species breed in noisy colonies around upland lakes. Mixed species flocks feed and roost on freshwater lakes outside breeding season.

SWIFTS AND SWALLOWS Huge numbers feed on insects over lakes and reed beds during summer months. Best seen at dawn and dusk when insects are low over water.

PERCHING BIRDS Reed beds and reed margins of lakes are productive for small passerines. Bearded tits easiest to see in winter when they are more active. Most reed bed warblers are summer visitors. Reed warbler has characteristic song. Look for movements in reed which do not follow swaying due to wind. Scan reed bed at dawn and dusk for Savi's warbler singing from top of reeds. Sedge warbler and reed bunting found in marshy areas especially where bushes present. Yellow wagtail breeds in marshy fields often among grazing cattle. Often perches on fence posts and barbed wire.

Mammals SHREWS Water shrew common in many freshwater habitats, especially small, shallow streams. Looks silvery when swimming due to air trapped in fur. Extremely active, never seeming to remain still; listen for squeaking calls.

BATS Seen feeding at dusk on insects over lakes and rivers, often in company of birds such as sand martins and swallows. Difficult to identify in flight except with aid of specialist 'bat detector' which brings high-pitched calls into range of human hearing.

WATER VOLE is often found on river banks. Look for waterside entrances to burrows and 'vole-gardens' – areas where vegetation is nibbled. Droppings much in evidence. Can be tempted with apples as bait. HARVEST MOUSE may also build nest in tall vegetation. COYPU is best located by muddy, flattened vegetation at waterside, with droppings. OTTERS are scarce and shy. Look for signs such as droppings (spraints) left on prominent riverside stones, webbed footprints in mud, mudslides and half-eaten remains of fish. Difficult to see except by chance encounter. Less secretive in spring, at start of breeding season. MINK is an introduced predator often escaped from fur farms. Look for tracks, trails and signs. Less secretive than otter. Other predators such as FOX and WEASEL may also be seen.

DEER Species such as roe deer, and the introduced Chinese water deer, often visit lakes, especially when surrounded by woodland. Look for footprints in the mud near water's edge.

Estuaries

An estuary is the mouth of a river at the point where it reaches the sea. Along the length of the estuary the shoreline is subject not only to the effect of the tides, but also to the influence of fresh water. The salinity at the mouth of the estuary can be very close to that of sea water, which is 35‰, but further up it can be as low as 5‰, with a concentration gradient between the two points. As the tide advances up an estuary a wedge of denser salt water pushes along the floor of the estuary, whilst the less dense fresh water moves down above it, thus creating brackish conditions between the two layers.

A strong current is normally found in the middle of the estuary where the fresh water flows down to the sea, but the current can be very slack along the shores and in sheltered inlets, and it is here that silt is deposited to form mudflats. The silt is full of nutrients and suspended organic matter, and is very fertile. Phenomenal numbers of molluscs, crustaceans, worms and other invertebrates are able to live in this estuarine mud, and in turn support very high populations of fishes, birds and, ultimately, man.

PHOTOKEY
cover for naturalists beneath trees

main water channel – last refuge for truly aquatic species at low tide

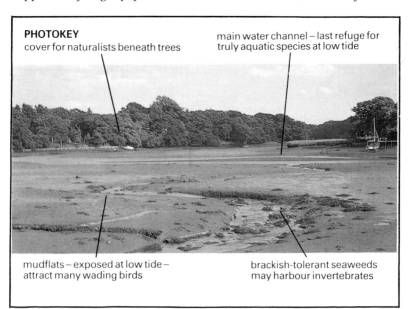

mudflats – exposed at low tide – attract many wading birds

brackish-tolerant seaweeds may harbour invertebrates

An estuary at low tide. Note the birds feeding near the water.

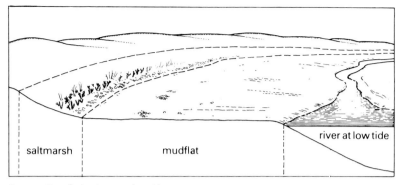

Cross-section of an estuary at low tide.

Extensive mudflats and sandbanks are therefore very worthwhile habitats for the naturalist to study. The size of the sand grains has some bearing on the types of organisms found in the sand: very fine sands and muds retain most water between the particles, whereas coarser sands tend to drain more quickly. Most burrowing invertebrates will therefore be found in the finer sands where there is plenty of water and the burrowing is easy. Very fine mud particles adhere closely together and restrict the movements of some invertebrates, and are usually coated with a film of bacteria thriving on the organic debris which settles on the surface of the mud. Often the bacteria are so numerous that they seriously deplete the oxygen supply, producing anaerobic conditions. This can be recognized by the black colour about 4 cm (1½ in) below the surface and the evil smell resulting from the presence of iron sulphide which the bacteria produce as a waste product. Few organisms can survive in these conditions.

The outer edges of the mudflats and the upper reaches of estuaries become colonized by salt-tolerant flowering plants to form saltmarshes. Glasswort, seablite and sea purslane are all able to survive the daily covering of their roots by salt water due to the high level of salts in their own cells. They also have a number of other adaptations enabling them to exist in these conditions. Eventually the saltmarshes become drier, due to the increased accumulation of silt around the roots of the plants, and a number of grasses and other flowering plants with less salt tolerance are able to become established.

Species which live in the sea but breed in fresh water, such as the salmon, or others which live in fresh water and breed in the sea, like the eel, are able to move through estuaries, but there are very few exclusively estuarine species: most of the inhabitants are marine or freshwater species which are able to tolerate brackish conditions. The tiny mollusc *Hydrobia*, or the small crustacean *Corophium*, are often present in vast numbers, providing an important source of food for other estuarine species.

Estuaries also provide a link between land and sea for man, and many major ports are located on estuaries, often with extensive industrial development associated with them. This creates many problems, particularly of pollution, but there is also an element of disturbance to overwintering

131

or breeding species. Further threats to estuaries today are the siting of nuclear and conventional power stations on their shores. Some estuaries have been designated sites for tidal barrages in order to use the energy of the tides to produce electricity. Other schemes involve turning estuaries into huge reservoirs to provide drinking water by a desalination process. These schemes would cancel out the effect of the tides, thus preventing birds from feeding on the mud. Many other organisms which are adapted to life in intertidal mud would be unable to cope with the changed conditions, and the unique variety of species would cease to exist.

Nature watching on estuaries

Estuaries are the interface between two similar, yet paradoxically different, habitats – the sea and a river. The animal life must not only deal with the traditional hazards of seashore life – alternate inundation and exposure – but must also face the problems presented by brackish conditions. Brackish water is a mixture of salt water and fresh water, yet many animals are remarkably tolerant of it, as witnessed by the wealth of creatures awaiting discovery by the naturalist.

Apart from the gradual change in conditions from sea to fresh water, a change is also discernible when an estuary is viewed in cross-section. Low tide reveals a wide expanse of fertile yet fluid mud – the mudflats – flanked on either side by areas of firmer ground colonized by plants showing varying degrees of tolerance to the conditions. This vegetated region, bisected by creeks and channels, is known as the saltmarsh.

When to go

An estuary and its associated saltmarsh and mudflats are best visited at low tide. For, with the retreating tide, comes an army of specialist feeders: the wading birds, probing into the ooze for molluscs and other invertebrates or flicking over the vegetation for food with their investigating beaks; and the crawlers – the predatory crabs and worms hidden safely when the tide was in, but now slithering for cover before they, too, end up as prey. The birdwatcher can gain most from this habitat from autumn through to spring, but for general interest there is something to see at any time of the year.

A car can make an excellent hide for bird or mammal watching.

Avocets are specialized mud feeders.

Although early morning, as the mist clears from the water, can be a productive time to visit, your arrival will be governed by the state of the tides, and the local tide tables should be consulted beforehand. It is also important to remember that at low tide the birds you are looking at may be some distance away, and if the sun is directly in your face they will be no more than silhouettes.

Birdwatching

If you should arrive before low tide, don't worry. Look for any islands or raised sandbanks not covered by the sea. These areas are important high-tide roosts for seabirds. Train your binoculars on to them and you are likely to see oystercatchers, sanderling, knot, dunlin, and other species huddled together patiently awaiting the retreating tide. Other birds may be swimming, so again scan the sea carefully with binoculars for gulls and ducks.

At low tide, the birdwatcher can really come into his or her own. But the sheer expanse of the habitat – especially at the seaward end – can mean that views of birds are quite distant. Therefore it might be worth investing in a

The stages in building a hide. Alternatively, you can buy one from specialist suppliers.

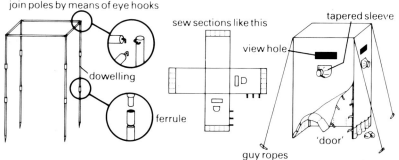

join poles by means of eye hooks

sew sections like this

tapered sleeve

view hole

dowelling

ferrule

view hole

'door'

guy ropes

telescope, mounted on a tripod. Whether you use a telescope or a pair of binoculars, the essential rules of birdwatching remain the same: avoid letting your quarry see you if possible. On the open expanse of an estuary or saltmarsh this can be difficult, but sitting down in front of sea walls, constructing makeshift cover by the mudbanks of rivers, using your car, or even just crouching low to disguise the dreaded human form as you get into position, will all help to reduce the birds' anxiety and therefore encourage them to feed closer to you than they otherwise would. For many birdwatchers a hide is the answer to the problem of cover, and it is well worth considering either purchasing or making one. The hide must be situated safely on dry ground, preferably before dawn. If you set up the hide in view of the birds, get an accomplice to enter the hide with you and then leave. The birds will then assume the hide is empty, even though you are still inside. A hide can, of course, be used to watch not only birds but also mammals in almost every type of habitat where natural cover is unavailable or unsuitable.

Few birds nest on the saltmarshes, since flooding is a frequent hazard, but apart from those which just come and feed, estuaries are important staging posts for many migrant species. Therefore you should visit this habitat as often as you can, for there is always the chance of seeing different species.

Mammals
The techniques of birdwatching mentioned above will invariably offer you glimpses of mammals such as foxes and otters which patrol across the mudflats at dawn in search of dead animals to scavenge. The foreshore of the river at low tide is a particularly good place to lie in wait for mammals. The presence of mammals will usually be indicated by droppings, but the soft mud is the ideal medium for leaving footprints, and should be carefully examined for such signs. They may suggest random wanderings, but they may also indicate the regular beat of some prowling mammal. The soft mud also leaves perfect impressions of bird footprints, some of which are quite diagnostic: many guides to tracks and trails illustrate these.

Footprints will help you identify many species present on the estuary.

Saltmarsh

The region where plants begin to colonize the mudflats is also colonized by species of dependent animals. Browsing molluscs feed on the seaweeds, attracting birds which feed on them. Look among the sea aster, sea lavender, thrift and other flowering plants for visiting insects and predatory spiders. Between the colonies of plants scavenging crabs can be found.

The saltmarsh is characterized by species such as sea lavender and glasswort.

Look for small pools like this one left at low tide: they may contain grazing Hydrobia *and crabs. Note how small the* Hydrobia *are; many of the creatures you seek are smaller than you might imagine.*

Bridges, piers and other man-made structures projecting into the mud are colonized by many of the same creatures which festoon the rocky shore. If you look carefully you can find sponges, bivalve molluscs, barnacles, hydroids and other animals, all exhibiting the pattern of zonation imposed upon them by the rigours of a life spent partly submerged and partly exposed to the air.

Mudflats

Towards the seaward end the mudflats are often a mixture of sand and mud, but at the landward end they tend to have more of a silty, muddy character. Most of the species living on and below the mudflats can tolerate brackish conditions, but there is also a gradual zonation of species which prefer either marine, or freshwater, conditions. Just before low tide you can often still see the tentacles of buried worms waving in the current, sifting the last few items of food before the tide retreats. Crabs, echinoderms and other predators may be hunting on the surface of the mud, and the occasional

Sieving the mud and water will reveal burrowing species such as cockles.

flatfish may flap to safety at your approach. A dip net dragged through the water against the flowing current will often catch small floating creatures.

At low tide there is an opportunity to see the crabs, ragworms, *Hydrobia* snails and other creatures which still remain on the surface. As the tide recedes they become covered with fine mud, and soon disappear beneath the surface, so look for any unusual movements among the ooze which might indicate animal life. Use a small trowel to lift them gently from the mud for identification.

Soon, most of the animal life retires beneath the surface, but you can still

A lugworm's burrow lies between the feeding depression and waste cast.

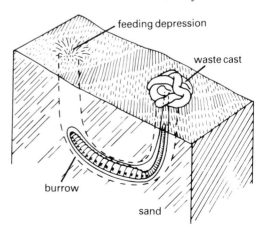

137

see signs of the presence of worms, echinoderms and molluscs. Every hole, hump or furrow is an indication of something beneath the surface. Dig up a spadeful of mud and then sift through this with your fingers – it is often useful to smooth a handful on the palm of your hand and look for any signs of movement. Alternatively, you can dig up a spadeful of wet mud and wash this through a fine-mesh sieve. The animal life collects in the sieve, and the contents can then be turned out into a plastic dish and examined with a hand-lens.

Typical animals: fieldbrief

Although a few species of lowly marine invertebrates such as sponges and hydroids may be encountered on estuaries – usually attached to piers and pilings – they are never as numerous as on a rocky shore. However, several groups of animals are well represented on estuaries.

Phylum Nemertina
Near the seaward end of estuaries some species of ribbon worms may be found by digging in sand or mud or by looking under stones.

Phylum Annelida
Bristle worms Several species are adapted to estuarine conditions. Ragworms are predatory creatures which can be found in and on the estuarine mud, where they lie in burrows at low tide, but hunt actively at high tide. Lugworms are sedentary, but can be located at low tide by searching for their burrows. These are indicated by a waste cast a few centimetres from a depression in the mud (the feeding end of the burrow). Digging down with a spade parallel to the suspected burrow will usually reveal the worm. Fan worms build their protective tubes in the mud and at low tide, especially near the seaward end, these may be seen just projecting above the surface of the mud.

Phylum Mollusca
Gastropods are represented especially by the small (6 mm long) snail *Hydrobia*. This animal may be found in huge numbers, covering the surface of the mud. The presence of *Hydrobia* will indicate rich feeding grounds for many birds. Bivalve molluscs include oysters, tellins and cockles, all of which burrow into the mud; and piddocks, which burrow into soft rock, firm sand or wood. Normally, digging into mud will bring many of these to the surface, but the tell-tale depressions many species leave in the mud's surface are a useful indication of their presence. Watching where waders and other birds are feeding in numbers will also lead you to likely spots.

Phylum Arthropoda
Barnacles Encrusting species will be found on rocks and piers, but stalked barnacles may be found on driftwood.
Shrimps, prawns, isopods and amphipods *Corophium* is a common species. It lives in a burrow or under stones at low tide, but may also be seen just as the tide recedes still crawling over the mud. Other species may also be

encountered by searching under stones and seaweeds.

Crabs Like their counterparts on seashores, these tend to remain hidden under rocks and seaweeds or in the mud, waiting for the return of the tide to bring food. Some species live in holes in the banks of estuaries. A few species, like the common shore crab, are able to find food at high and low tide, and can be seen most easily by crouching down and looking for movements in the mud.

Insects and spiders The flowering plants of estuaries attract several species of butterflies, true flies and other insects such as beetles. The general techniques for insect spotting should be applied here. A few species of spiders, including the wolf spider, also hunt on estuaries.

Phylum Chordata

Fishes Species such as the grey mullet may be seen nosing among the vegetation when the tide is in. Various species of flatfishes also live in estuaries.

Amphibians Certain species of frogs may be seen on estuaries, feeding on the invertebrates uncovered at low tide. They will normally try and stay near cover, such as by banksides, to avoid predators.

Reptiles Occasionally snakes can be found among the flowering vegetation of estuaries.

Birds Estuaries form important feeding areas for birds. Waders, gulls, ducks and geese gather in often huge numbers on estuaries, exploiting the rich food reserves. At low tide, the birds may be some considerable distance from the observer and so a telescope is a useful piece of equipment. Avoid letting your outline stand out against the sky; crouching down with your back to the sea wall is a good idea, keeping out of the wind.

WADERS Several species are commonly seen, including oystercatchers, knot, redshank curlew and dunlin. (See page 153 for more detailed information on watching waders.)

DUCKS AND GEESE Rafts of sea duck such as eider and scoter can be seen and some freshwater duck, including mallard and wigeon, occur also. Many species of geese feed on the saltmarshes bordering estuaries, and Brent geese feed near the waterline on eel grass.

CORMORANTS AND SHAGS Sometimes these birds fish in estuaries, venturing far up the river into fresh water.

BIRDS OF PREY AND OWLS Barn owls and short-eared owls hunt over estuaries, as do marsh harriers and even the occasional peregrine falcon.

PERCHING BIRDS A few species like the rock pipit feed on the shoreline, and meadow pipits and yellow wagtails occur on saltmarshes.

Mammals Most species will be scavengers, usually seen during evening, night or early morning. OTTERS, although rare, favour this habitat and their oily droppings and webbed footprints may be seen on banksides. More casual visitors such as FOXES, MINK and WEASELS may also leave tell-tale signs. WATER VOLES and RABBITS may be seen wherever grassy areas provide cover. Truly marine mammals such as SEALS and DOLPHINS can also be seen making their way up or down an estuary. For the more terrestrial mammals, discovery – unless by chance – is usually a matter of concealment and patient waiting.

Seashores

The seashore supports a greater abundance and variety of life than any comparable area on land. Organisms which are completely unrepresented on land will be encountered, such as echinoderms, whilst other groups, like the molluscs and crustaceans, have far more representatives on the seashore than on land or in fresh water.

The most striking feature of the seashore habitat is the rise and fall of the tide. Governed by the gravitational pull of the moon and the rotation of the earth, the mass of water in the oceans surges upwards to cover the shore and then retreats again twice daily in an approximately twelve-hour cycle. When the sun, moon and earth are in an approximately straight line the tidal effect is greater, and a larger area of shore is exposed at low water. These spring tides alternate with neap tides on a monthly cycle.

The range of the tides determines to some extent the abundance of shore life; a vast tidal range will provide a great expanse of shore for colonization by shore-dwellers such as some of the brown algae and the periwinkles, whilst the smaller tidal range of the Mediterranean means that these species are almost absent. A striking result of tidal action is that of zonation, in which seaweeds and marine animals arrange themselves according to their tolerance to exposure.

In addition to the fluctuating tide levels, seashore creatures must also adapt to changing currents and exposure to wave action. Some stretches of shore, especially the Atlantic shores of north-west Europe, face an almost constant severe battering from the waves due to the prevailing westerly winds. The inhabitants of these rocky shores must adapt to this constant pounding; for this reason many of them are small and encrusting, or live in crevices, feeding on particles carried to them by the currents. An exposed shore can be recognized by the lack of brown seaweeds, the almost complete cover of barnacles and the extensive bands of black and orange encrusting lichens in the splash zone, where drenching by salt water is a not infrequent occurrence. Above the splash zone grow some salt-tolerant flowering plants.

Although many external factors may be variable – such as exposure to the air, currents, wave action and the physical nature of the shore – one factor remains remarkably constant: sea water has a concentration of dissolved salts of 35‰ and most marine organisms are unable to cope with any changes in salinity. The concentration of dissolved salts in the Mediterranean is somewhat higher at 37‰ due to the increased evaporation and the low levels of fresh water entering it. The northern limits of the Baltic, on the other hand, have a much lower salinity at about 5‰. A few creatures like the shore crab and the flounder are able to adjust to changes in salinity, however, and these are typical of the species found in estuaries where brackish conditions occur. Others, like the starfishes and sea urchins, are quite unable to cope with low salt levels, and so they are never found away from the open sea.

Rocky shores

Rocky shores make up the largest proportion of the coastline of north-west Europe. A great range of ecological niches is available for colonization by marine species, and so both the variety of species and the number of individual organisms can be very high. The dense carpet of algae found on the sheltered rocky shore, the most profitable of all habitats for the marine biologist to work in, will hide a wealth of invertebrates making good use of the cool, damp conditions and the protection from predators. Crevices, rocky overhangs, gulleys, caves and boulders all provide scope for colonization by a variety of species.

Some stretches of rocky shore are particularly interesting because of the number of rock pools they contain. Certain types of rock, for example chalk, erode in such a way that rock pools do not form, but in areas where harder rocks are present deep pools can form and creatures which normally live below the low-water mark are able to survive higher up on the shore. Small, shallow rock pools high up on the shore are less suitable for colonization than deeper pools low down on the shore. When exposed to the sun the shallow pools will heat up, lose oxygen and, because of the increased evaporation, become much more saline. Large, partially shaded pools on the other hand, offer conditions similar to those encountered in the sea. Deep gulleys which connect with the sea also support many species which are normally found in much deeper water.

Sandy beaches

Sandy beaches often form in sheltered bays, but some magnificent beaches also occur on very exposed shores where there are no rocks or cliffs. No firm anchorage can be found on sand, so the inhabitants of these beaches must dig a secure home beneath the sand. Some emerge when the tide comes in to feed on the surface, whilst others remain concealed, feeding and breathing through long tubes or siphons which extend to the surface. There are other species which can burrow through the sand searching for their prey.

Shingle beaches

Shingle beaches are the most inhospitable of all marine habitats, as the constantly shifting pebbles can crush all types of marine organisms. There is no scope for colonization until the shingle has become stabilized, when a few very hardy plant species such as sea sandwort or yellow-horned poppy can grow above the high-tide mark. Most of the creatures found on a shingle beach will have been cast up by the tide and will also probably be dead. Piles of decaying seaweed provide temporary homes for sandhoppers and these attract birds like turnstones which feed on them.

Sand dunes

On exposed sandy shores the wind-blown sand accumulates around objects such as stones to form low hills known as dunes which eventually become colonized by an interesting community of highly specialized plants. One of the first colonizers is the sand couch grass, and this is soon followed by the much larger marram grass. This important grass has a very extensive root system which penetrates the sand to a great depth.

Once the marram grass has become established and has stabilized the sand many other flowering plants are able to grow in the dunes. The oldest dunes are those furthest away from the sea and they will have the most varied flora growing on them. If the sand has a high proportion of shell debris in it, it will be calcareous in nature and a plant community similar to that growing on chalk grassland will develop. The hollows between the dunes are known as dune slacks and are often very damp. A fen-type flora can develop here: marsh orchids, adder's tongue fern and other species associated with damp grassland flourish in these damp hollows and a rich invertebrate population can be supported. Butterflies appreciate the shelter and the great abundance of food plants, but there are also many species of burrowing insects like sand wasps which can make use of the sandy soil for constructing their underground nesting chambers. Larger animals are also attracted to the conditions offered by wet slacks.

Nature watching on rocky shores

Most rocky shores are rewarding places for the naturalist, for they are one of the few habitats where at least some wildlife is almost guaranteed to be on view. The more exposed rocky shores are less productive than those which lie in sheltered spots, but one of the characteristics of rocky shore life in general is the hardiness of its inhabitants, and so even in harsh conditions some animal life is likely to be found sheltering in suitable crevices.

The animal life, although in part seasonal and even nocturnal, is mainly determined by its ability both to withstand the battering it receives from the waves, and to undergo a twice daily inundation by sea water and exposure to drying winds, as the tide flows and ebbs. Since all the marine invertebrates (and the fishes) are adapted to taking oxygen from sea water, it follows that when the tide recedes those left exposed will most likely be encountered in places which are at least still moist, if not in rock pools themselves, although species such as limpets avoid desiccation by clamping tightly to the rocks, thus reducing water loss.

The stealthy approach to nature watching is still necessary, however, even on a seashore with its somewhat 'captive' fauna, for many invertebrates quickly hide, or take up a defensive posture, when shadows are cast over them, and of course the birds of rocky shores are as wary of humans as their counterparts in other habitats.

When to go

Rocky shores are worth visiting at any time, and periodic visits throughout

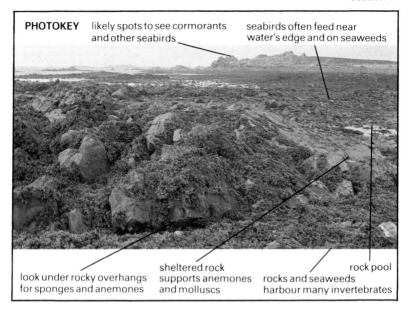

PHOTOKEY   likely spots to see cormorants
and other seabirds

seabirds often feed near
water's edge and on seaweeds

look under rocky overhangs
for sponges and anemones

sheltered rock
supports anemones
and molluscs

rocks and seaweeds
harbour many invertebrates

rock pool

The tolerance to inundation and exposure determines the regions of a rocky shore colonized by different animals.

the year will help to indicate seasonal species. Time your visits to coincide with the period just before low-water (tide tables or the local coastguard office will provide this information), and before strolling down the beach look for any birds sitting on the rocks waiting for the tide to recede fully. Always begin at the bottom of the beach and work upwards, to avoid being cut off by the incoming tide. Beware the incoming tide also if you round a headland to gain access to another beach; you may become stranded if the tide cuts off your route back to the original beach.

Rocky shore zonation; animals as well as plants exist at different levels on the beach.

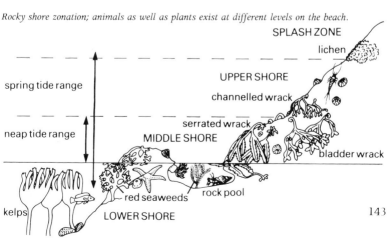

SPLASH ZONE

lichen

spring tide range

UPPER SHORE

channelled wrack

serrated wrack

neap tide range

MIDDLE SHORE

bladder wrack

red seaweeds

rock pool

kelps   LOWER SHORE

143

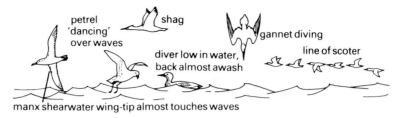

petrel 'dancing' over waves

shag

gannet diving

diver low in water, back almost awash

line of scoter

manx shearwater wing-tip almost touches waves

Birds at sea can often be identified by their flight patterns or the way in which they sit on the water.

At sea

The seashore and the sea itself are so intimately joined together that a visit to any shore must automatically take in some 'sea watching'. Apart from birds such as gulls feeding on the water or wheeling overhead (especially near cliffs), scan the water at or just above sea level for low-flying birds such as mergansers, scoters, oystercatchers and cormorants.

In many areas seals haul themselves out to sunbathe or to give birth on sheltered beaches, and can often be seen in the surrounding seas, especially as the tide draws in and the human population makes its way to other pursuits. In the water, the heads of seals can be identified as they resemble footballs (or sometimes large bottles) bobbing up and down, sometimes disappearing as they dive for food. Many offshore islands are important breeding grounds for seals, and boat trips to view these are usually available.

It is also worth inspecting the sea close to the lower shore for drifting jellyfishes, wind-blown hydroids such as the Portuguese man o'war and the by-the-wind sailor, or any small fish species which may be probing the rocks for food. Sit quietly and look into the water, using polaroid type sunglasses, if possible, to reduce glare. Next, with a stick, lift some of the seaweed from the water and pull it towards you. Several species of animals

(Below left) A stick will help you reach those seaweeds and their attendant animals which are seldom exposed by the tide. (Below right) Most marine animals will hide beneath seaweed when the tide is out.

which cannot tolerate exposure may be found clinging to the fronds of permanently submerged seaweeds. Search carefully among the fronds.

Rocks and seaweeds

Now work your way slowly up the beach, examining the seaweeds and rock crevices as you go. Most of the invertebrate life will be under the seaweed, since this is the moistest place, so lift the fronds and look carefully beneath before replacing them. Some of the worms and small crabs are well camouflaged; when you lift the seaweed just pause for a few moments in case the movement of some cunningly camouflaged animal gives itself away.

Rock crevices, and the tiny pools which remain where the base of the rocks meets the sandy part of the beach, are other areas to be investigated. Many molluscs often congregate together in rock crevices, and the shallow water at the base of the rocks often supports anemones and echinoderms. The small blobs of 'jelly' often seen when the tide is out are in fact anemones which have retracted their feeding tentacles to await the return of the tide.

Many small creatures hide safely under stones, so lift these (slowly, to avoid sucking sand into the water and reducing visibility), but be prepared to catch any inhabitants before they dig or scuttle from view.

(Above) Scan the rocks in a crouched position when looking for bird movements.

(Below) Lift rocks slowly and carefully, and wait a few seconds for any signs of movement. Replace the rocks afterwards.

(Below) Cast-up holdfasts such as this one from a laminarian seaweed often harbour a variety of life among the 'roots'. Wash the contents into a dish with sea water and examine with a hand-lens.

145

Higher up the shore, the molluscs dominate the rocks, and species such as limpets and periwinkles will probably be the most commonly encountered species, but mussels and barnacles (the latter are in fact crustaceans) are often present in large numbers, too. At the upper part of the beach, squat low on the rocks, and scan the view with binoculars for shore birds. Oystercatchers, turnstones and dunlins are among the many species which probe and pick among the sand and seaweed for tiny invertebrates. Often, their movement among the rocks is the best way of spotting them, for their camouflage is superb. Many beachcombers are unaware of the birds on a beach until, forced towards the water's edge by advancing humans, they suddenly take off and fly over the sea.

Rock pools

Rock pools can often represent the sea in microcosm. Each tide brings potential new inhabitants, making the pools a constantly changing environment. In addition to their fixed populations of seaweeds and slower-moving molluscs, they may harbour various creatures such as worms, echinoderms, crabs and fishes – all stranded when the tide receded.

To examine a rock pool, sit with your face to the sun (to avoid casting a shadow) and wait quietly. Polarized sunglasses will again prove invaluable here. After a few minutes, the inhabitants will have accepted your face peering in, and will start to creep and dart into view. Avoid any sudden movements which will send them scurrying back to cover. If you wish to catch and briefly examine any of these creatures, a dark coloured net baited with meat (a piece from your sandwich will do) must first be rested on the bottom of the pool. Even after this is accepted by the inhabitants, it still requires skill and patience to capture timid, fast-moving species such as fishes or prawns. Try using a minnow trap also, as described on page 121.

Cliffs

The cliffs which girt our rocky coastlines can provide, in spring and early summer, a superb spectacle in the form of feeding and nesting seabirds. The sea cliffs of Britain and western Europe support large and important populations of many species, such as fulmars, kittiwakes, gannets, gulls, puffins, razorbills, cormorants and shags.

The best views are obtained by climbing to the top of one cliff or headland and then looking across to the next with binoculars, but avoid breaking the skyline by keeping low when you reach the top of the cliff. The windy conditions usually encountered mean that you will need to steady the binoculars to prevent buffeting. Do this by lying flat, or sitting with your elbows supported by your knees. Different species of birds exploit different regions of a cliff face, thus utilizing all the available ledges and crevices. Offshore stacks and small islands are also colonized by many species, and boat trips are often arranged to view the best of these colonies.

In certain areas cliff tops provide superb vantage points from which to watch migrant species, particularly in stormy weather during autumn and winter. Some of these are resident species, but others are species on passage, so here is an opportunity to see birds which are not necessarily native to the country in which they are seen.

Cliffs and offshore stacks can be exciting places for birdwatching, especially at nesting time.

At night

The seashore also has something to offer the nocturnal naturalist. Browsing species of molluscs such as limpets are active at night, creeping over the rocks in search of seaweeds, and also returning miraculously to exactly the same piece of rock. Shine a torch in a rock pool and, indeed, in any of the places where a search is usually made by day, to see how many other species are active. Crabs in particular are highly active at night, scavenging near the strandline among the dead bodies of cast-up animals.

Nature watching on sandy beaches

Compared with rocky shores, sandy or muddy shores may at first appear almost devoid of life, but the correct techniques can uncover a varied and interesting community of animals.

Strandline

The strandline is the highest part of a beach reached by the tide, and is usually marked by a motley collection of cast-up seaweed, shells, and – too often – plastic bottles, tin cans and other human flotsam and jetsam. The investigation of strandline debris can be very rewarding, however, especially when freshly cast up, and particularly after storms. When fresh, many of the marine animals will still be alive; they can provide an insight into the animal life usually seen only by divers. Look carefully among the seaweed and on the sand beneath it. Also look in empty shells and the net-like holdfasts of seaweeds for any animals sheltering there.

147

The strandline is best investigated when the tide is receding.

Sandy beaches

Most of the animals here actually live beneath the sand, to escape predators and desiccation, but many betray their presence by leaving feeding casts or depressions on the surface.

Near the low-tide mark look for irregular star-shaped holes less than 1 cm across; these are left by the sea potato, a burrowing echinoderm. The low tide mark is also the best place to search for the projecting tubes of mason worms, constructed of sand grains, and for signs of lugworms, which leave characteristic coiled casts. Many molluscs also choose this part of the beach in which to burrow. At very low tides walk backwards down the beach and look for tiny jets of water spurting through the sand; these are made by the siphons of razor shells.

In general, any hole, depression or hump in the sand is likely to have been caused by the activity of an animal, and rapid digging should enable you to

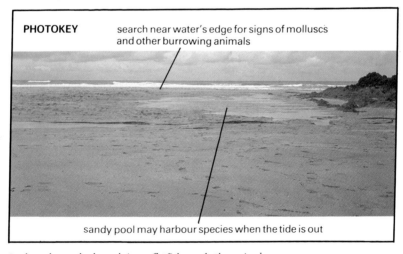

PHOTOKEY — search near water's edge for signs of molluscs and other burrowing animals

sandy pool may harbour species when the tide is out

Sandy pools may harbour shrimps, flatfishes and other animals.

bring the creature to the surface for closer examination (see fieldbrief). Molluscs such as cockles can often be revealed just by scuffing the surface with your feet.

Footprints betray the activity of many species of shore birds, as well as scavenging mammals such as rats, foxes and otters. An early morning vigil, perhaps from a parked car, may reveal some of these mammals. The gulls, waders and other shore birds can be seen probing into the sand or sifting among the strandline debris for invertebrates. You need to conceal yourself in order to watch many of these species, so look for likely 'hides' such as beached boats, dunes, etc., and adopt the typical birdwatcher's approach.

Sandy pools

Sandy pools represent similar conditions to those of a sea-covered beach, and are worthy of special investigation. Fishes, burrowing anemones, molluscs, worms and prawns are among the creatures which seek safety here. Moving a small stick vigorously through the top centimetre of sand will dislodge anything lurking just beneath the surface; watch closely to see what swims away. Another technique is just to sit quietly and see what stirs.

Sand dunes

Sand dunes provide a hinterland to many sandy beaches, and where they are colonized by marram grass and other flowering plants, then insects and spiders are worth searching for. Birds such as terns and oystercatchers nest near the high-tide mark, and skylarks and meadow pipits nest in the dunes. Rabbits often burrow extensively through the dunes, leaving their characteristic droppings and excavations, and may be preyed upon by foxes, stoats and weasels, which also seek the eggs and young of the nesting birds.

Nature watching on shingle beaches

Some beaches are composed almost entirely of various-sized pebbles, and are known as shingle beaches. This shifting, grinding world is a difficult environment for burrowing animals, and only the parts of the beach where the pebbles have become stabilized in sand or mud, and consequently colonized by plants, are suitable for most wildlife.

The strandline may be worth examining (see page 142) for sand hoppers, insects and other invertebrates. Certain species of birds nest or feed among the stabilized parts of the beach, their nests often camouflaged superbly among the debris. In winter, flocks of snow buntings, feeding on seeds and insects, appear as a flash of white along the shoreline.

Any seaweeds which have colonized the beach should be investigated for gastropod molluscs, sea urchins, crustaceans and the like, as described for investigating rocky shores (see page 145). Look carefully on the pebbles for the chalky tubes of certain polychaete worms, and for barnacles. Similarly, the flowering plants should be examined for any interesting species of visiting insects.

Seals may haul themselves on to quiet shingle beaches, and hares, rabbits and foxes may be encountered moving among the vegetation.

Typical animals: fieldbrief

Phylum Porifera

Found on the lower shore down to deep water, sponges are easily overlooked, so search carefully; attached to seaweeds, shells, under stones, rocks and overhangs.

Phylum Cnidaria

Hydroids Found on the middle and lower shore down to deep water. Two main groups: sessile species usually attached to rock pool sides, weeds and stones; second group pelagic, usually encountered only when washed ashore.

Jellyfishes Mostly pelagic, usually encountered only when washed ashore. Exception is the tiny, stalked jellyfishes which may be encountered by lifting and examining seaweeds from the low-water mark or from rock pools.

Sea anemones Those that can withstand desiccation appear as blobs of jelly at low tide, attached to rocky overhangs, crevices and other sheltered spots. Some cannot retract tentacles and usually live in rock pools or similar wet places. A few species burrow in sand, and are best encountered in sandy pools.

Corals Usually found in water from depths of 1 m (3 ft) downwards, but a few may be attached to rocks and stones at extreme lower shore.

Phylum Platyhelminthes

Flatworms are found from the middle shore downward under stones and seaweeds. They need careful searching for, since most species are less than 1 cm long.

Phylum Nemertina

Found from the upper to the lower shore and in deep water, depending on the species. Most ribbon worms burrow in mud and sand, but some may be found under stones.

Phylum Annelida

Bristle worms Depending on the species, these are found usually from the lower shore downward. Two main groups: errant forms, such as the ragworm, burrow under stones, in sand and mud and among seaweeds, searching actively for food: some may also be found in pools. Sieving bucketfuls of sand from the low water mark may reveal burrowing species. Sedentary forms, such as the lugworm, are characteristic of sandy beaches; the worm lies in a burrow, the tail end of which is characterized by a waste 'cast', and the head end of which is characterized by a depression in the sand. Digging close to a parallel line between the cast and depression may reveal the worm. Other sedentary worms build protective tubes of sand grains attached to stones or projecting from the substrate. Serpulid and spirorbid worms are sedentary species which attach their chalky tubes to stones and seaweeds. (A few other minor worm groups may also be encountered.)

Phylum Mollusca

Of the 7 classes of molluscs, 5 are commonly encountered on the seashore. Chitons occur mainly on rocks and under stones on the lower shore.

Gastropods – the most numerous class in terms of species – are found mainly on rocky shores from the upper shore to the lower shore, creeping among seaweeds, attached to the tops of rocks or hidden among crevices. Among the most obvious of the invertebrate seashore animals, the discovery of most gastropods is simply a matter of careful searching. A few gastropods have reduced shells or lack shells altogether; these species burrow into the sand near the low-water mark and a few are found only in rock pools and shallow water – these slug-like molluscs are characterized by gills and other appendages and bright coloured bodies. Scaphopods (tusk shells) burrow in deeper water, but their shells may be cast up.

With few exceptions, such as mussels, living bivalve molluscs are only encountered in any numbers on sandy shores or the sandy element of rocky shores, and here they burrow into the substrate. Since they communicate with the sea by means of tubes (siphons), they are best located at low tide, near the low-water mark, by examining the beach carefully for holes, jets of water or unusual humps or depressions. Species such as cockles may be uncovered by scuffing the sand with your foot. A few bivalves bore into rock and wood, and an examination of groynes, old pier supports and the softer rocks and clays may reveal some species.

Most cephalopods (cuttlefishes, squids and octopuses) are usually only encountered by divers, but occasionally you may discover cuttlefishes burrowing in sand at the extreme low-water mark, or an octopus in a lower shore rock pool.

Phylum Arthropoda

Barnacles Encrusting barnacles festoon rocks, piers, breakwaters and boats. Stalked barnacles may occur on driftwood washed ashore.

Shrimps and prawns This large and varied group of crustaceans occupy a variety of niches on the seashore and in the sea. The best places to look for species are rock pools and sandy pools. They are extremely sensitive to shadows cast over them, and will quickly retire from view if disturbed; wait quietly for signs of movement.

Isopods and amphipods These creatures inhabit crevices in rocks or live under stones and among seaweed; some species bore into wood or burrow into sand. Many are almost colourless, and so careful searching is necessary; careful sifting of wet sand from the middle shore downwards may reveal species.

Lobster and squat lobsters Lobsters tend to inhabit cracks, crevices and rock pools, usually near low water. Search among rocks and stones, especially where they are grouped together to form miniature 'caves'. Apart from lobsters, the division Anomura also contains other crab-like crustaceans and the hermit crabs. Hermit crabs are easily recognized, since they occupy the cast-off shells of molluscs. They usually inhabit shallow water, but may be encountered among rocks and stones at the lower shore.

Crabs The true crabs are a varied group. Those that occur on the seashore can be found in a variety of niches: among seaweed (often well camouflaged, so turn the seaweed and wait for a give-away movement), under stones, in sand or in rock pools. Many crabs are more commonly encountered at night, when they scavenge among the lower shore debris. Dangling a piece of dead fish on the end of a piece of string may entice a crab from its hiding place in a rock pool.

Centipedes, insects, spiders, false scorpions and sea-spiders Sea-spiders may be found among seaweeds, under stones and in crevices, from the upper shore to the lower shore. The splash zone, and the flowers of shingle beaches, may attract true spiders, centipedes and insects, and spiders may be found in sand dunes.

Phylum Bryozoa

Bryozoans are often encountered on rocks, seaweeds and other objects. Typically, many species resemble a whitish gauze, especially those which encrust seaweeds from the middle shore downwards.

Phylum Echinodermata

Feather stars These can sometimes be found attached to the rocks in pools and in shallow water.

Starfishes Various species may be found on or among rocks, or burrowing into sand.

Brittle stars These mainly occur among rocks, stones and seaweeds on the lower shores, especially where sea water still covers them.

Sea urchins, sand-dollars and heart urchins These bristly or spiny forms mostly live in deep water but may be cast up after storms, although a few live among rocks and seaweeds from the lower shore downwards. Sand-dollars and heart-urchins burrow in soft substrates such as mud and sand, and may be identified beneath the surface from the small, distinctive star-shaped depressions they leave.

Sea-cucumbers Some of these distinctive, worm-like echinoderms are found among seaweeds and under rocks and stones from the lower shore downward, or burrowing into sand.

Phylum Chaetognatha, Hemichordata and Chordata

Members of the Phylum Chaetognatha are generally transparent, elongated creatures which may be found in rock pools. Members of the Phylum Hemichordata are worm-like creatures which may be encountered burrowing into sand or mud near low water. (See bibliography for identification guides to these groups.) The phylum Chordata includes some small, colonial, jelly-like creatures (known as sea-squirts and salps) which may be found attached to rocks, piers and seaweeds near low water. This phylum also includes the largest and most highly advanced creatures – the vertebrates. All the vertebrate groups are represented on the seashore.

Fishes Most fishes lives either in the open sea or in rock pools, but a few live buried in the sand in shallow water. These include the weever, which projects its venomous fins above the sand, and various flatfishes such as the flounder and sole. The weever is a fish to be avoided, but you may encounter flatfishes by gently disturbing the sand in shallow water and sandy pools. Rock pool fishes can be found by gently disturbing the seaweed or by waiting for any species to swim into view.

Amphibians Frogs and toads are sometimes found on sandy beaches.

Reptiles You may rarely encounter a stranded turtle on a beach.

Birds Seashores are important feeding grounds for many groups of birds, which gather in large numbers on their way to and from their breeding sites. Therefore both the state of the tide and the time of year are crucial if you are to see the many bird species the seashore has to offer. Just before high tide is a good time to see shore birds as they are brought to feed close to you. Some of the most important types are listed below.

WADERS The most numerous of all the seashore birds. You will often see them in large flocks on estuaries and mudflats. Flocks of dunlin and knot can appear as whisps of smoke, changing from dark to light as the birds change direction simultaneously. Some species of waders form mixed flocks: oystercatchers, knot and redshank often associate with each other. Look for waders as they congregate in a roost on the last available patch of exposed mud or shingle at high tide. Some waders are found only on certain types of shore – purple sandpipers for example, are confined to rocky shores. Waders can also be distinguished by their particular feeding habits. Sanderling and ringed plovers run close to the advancing waves; redshank walk deliberately across the mud, pausing to stab their prey, and avocets sieve the water with a side-to-side motion of their beaks. Waders are shy birds, wary of close approach and so a knowledge of their calls is an invaluable aid to identification, especially when the light is poor.

GULLS AND TERNS Gulls are large, noisy, mainly white seabirds which frequent estuaries and seashores, sometimes feeding in the company of waders. Terns feed close offshore, diving from a height after small fishes. Their forked tails distinguish them from the larger, stockier gulls. Gulls are expert fliers; watch for them soaring on rising air currents near sea cliffs where some species rest.

SEA DUCKS, DIVERS AND GREBES All these birds dive from the water surface. Look for them in silhouette out to sea, the basic head and body shape rather than colour distinguishing the main groups. Divers and the smaller grebes sit lower in the water than the ducks, backs almost awash.

CORMORANTS AND SHAGS Are often seen on rocks, holding their wings open.

AUKS Auks only come ashore to breed on sea cliffs. At sea these black and white birds are usually seen in small flocks which fly in lines low above the water with whirring wing-beats.

PERCHING BIRDS A few species of perching birds occur on shores, such as rock pipits and shorelarks, mainly feeding among the seaweed on the strandline.

Mammals Most typical are COMMON and GREY SEALS. At high tide both species may be seen bobbing about in the water. Grey seals more often seen on rocky shores, and common more likely on sandy shores. Both species may haul up on to quiet beaches. Boat trips to seal sanctuaries and islands are a good way to see seals. Other mammals, like FOXES and STOATS, may scavenge during evening, night and early morning. Look for footprints and droppings. In many places OTTERS have been forced to feed on rocky shores. Look for them at dawn and dusk on sheltered, seaweed-covered rocks where they hunt in the gulleys for slow-moving fishes.

Identification section

Sponge (Halichondria panicea)

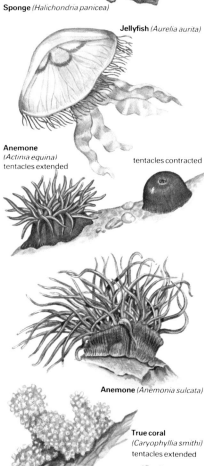

Jellyfish (Aurelia aurita)

Anemone
(Actinia equina)
tentacles extended

tentacles contracted

Anemone (Anemonia sulcata)

True coral
(Caryophyllia smithi)
tentacles extended

Soft coral
(Alcyonium digitatum)

skeleton

Invertebrates

Space does not permit illustrations of the majority of invertebrate species likely to be encountered: instead, we have concentrated on illustrating usually one typical representative of each group and describing the features of the group as a whole.

Sponges
Sponge
Height usually up to 5 cm (2 in); few may be taller. Primitive sessile animals occurring in a wide variety of sizes and shapes – usually encrusting, branched or globular; many colours; occur attached to rocks, etc. in suitable places throughout Britain and Europe. ▤, ▨

Coelenterates
Jellyfish
Body diameter about 10–90 cm (4–35 in). Body consists of umbrella- or bell-shaped dome with dangling tentacles possessing stinging cells; often washed into coastal waters, sometimes in considerable numbers; occur on British and European coasts. ▤

Anemone
Height about 3–10 cm (1–4 in) according to species; few much bigger. Squat hollow body with ring of stinging tentacles around mouth; usually attached to rocks; occur on rocky shores and in pools on coasts of Britain and Europe. ▤

Soft coral
Height about 30–50 cm (12–20 in). Colonies consist of tough, branched processes attached to rocks; numerous individual polyps within colony have 8 feathery tentacles which appear when submerged; occur on sheltered rocky shores on British and European coasts. ▤

True coral
Height usually up to 5 cm (2 in); some colonial growths larger. Solitary animals living inside hard, cup-shaped skeleton; normally body expands outside cup, but contracts within if disturbed; attached to rocks, often in crevices, on lower shores of British and European coasts. ▤

Flatworms
Planarian worm
Length usually about 2 cm ($\frac{3}{4}$ in). Numerous eye spots at head end; glide over surfaces by ciliary action, occur in slow-moving streams in Britain and Europe. ✉

Nemertine worms
Ribbon worm
Length about 10 cm (4 in); few much longer. Unsegmented body with head possessing numerous eyes; found under stones on rocky and gravelly British and European coasts. ✉

Annelid worms
Earthworm
Length about 10 cm (4 in); few much longer. Segmented body; occur throughout Britain and Europe. ✎

Scale worm
Length 2 – 20 cm ($\frac{3}{4}$ – 8 in). Body covered by scales or hairs on back and hairs on sides; found in pools at extreme low water; occur on sandy shores of British and European coasts. ✉

Leech
Length 5 cm (2 in). Body flattened dorso-ventrally; suckers at either end; occur in streams, canals and ponds throughout Britain and Europe. ✉

Ragworm
Length 12 cm ($4\frac{1}{2}$ in). Body with lateral bristles; has large jaws; found under stones and in sand and gravel; occur on British and European estuaries and coasts. ✉

Lugworm
Length 20 cm (8 in). Lives in U-shaped burrow in sand; leaves characteristic cast in sand; occurs on sandy shores and estuaries on British and European coasts. ✉

Fan worm
Length 25 cm (10 in). Constructs tube of fine sand for protection; when covered by tide, fan of feeding tentacles protrudes; found on sandy shores at low-tide level on British and European coasts. ✉

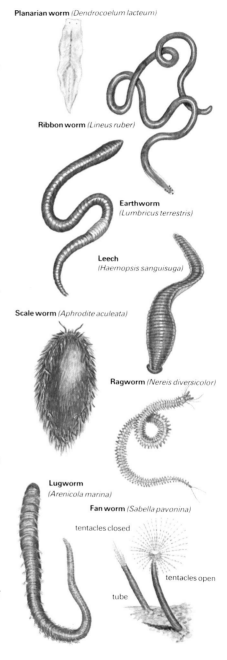

Planarian worm *(Dendrocoelum lacteum)*

Ribbon worm *(Lineus ruber)*

Earthworm
(Lumbricus terrestris)

Leech
(Haemopsis sanguisuga)

Scale worm *(Aphrodite aculeata)*

Ragworm *(Nereis diversicolor)*

Lugworm
(Arenicola marina)

Fan worm *(Sabella pavonina)*

tentacles closed

tentacles open

tube

Chiton *(Lepidopleurus asellus)*

Limpet *(Patella vulgaris)*

Periwinkle *(Littorina littorea)*

Periwinkle *(Littorina littoralis)*

Hydrobia *(Hydrobia ulvae)*

Cowrie *(Trivia monacha)*

Sea slug *(Aeolidia papillosa)*

Slug *(Limax maximus)*

Molluscs

Chiton

Length 2 cm (¾ in). Atypical molluscs superficially resembling wood louse; flat body protected by 8 dorsal shell plates; found clamped to rocks; body colour resembles that of rocks; occur on rocky shores in Britain and Europe. ⊟

Limpet

Length 7 cm (3 in). Conical shell clamped tightly to rocks by muscular foot; at night and high tide move over rocks grazing algae; leave conspicuous tracks; occur on rocky shores in Britain and Europe. ⊟

Periwinkle

Height up to 2.5 cm (1 in). Many colour forms, particularly yellow; remain concealed at low tide, except in damp weather; occur on rocky shores in Britain and Europe. ⊟

Hydrobia

Height 6 mm. Spire-shaped shell; in tidal waters, often adheres to vegetation at low tide; extremely numerous in suitable conditions; occurs on muddy estuaries and rivers in Britain and Europe. ⊠, ⊟

Cowrie

Length up to 5 cm (2 in). When alive, mantle tissue covers shell; siphon projects forward when moving; found among sea squirts on which they feed, or in rock pools; shells sometimes washed up on sandy shores; occur on lower shores of Britain and Europe. ⊟

Sea slug

Length up to 14 cm (5½ in); many smaller. Shell reduced or absent; external gills visible near posterior end; often abundant but difficult to find; occur on lower rocky shore and rock pools of Britain and Europe. ⊟

Slug

Length 10 cm (4 in). Lack external shell; most obvious at night or after wet weather; lay eggs in soil or under stones; feed on vegetation; occur throughout Britain and Europe. ◼, ◙, ▨

Terrestrial snail
Maximum height 4.5 cm (1¾ in); many
smaller. Often seen at night and after
wet weather; hide under stones during
daytime; hibernate in walls, ditches
and underground; occur throughout
Britain and Europe, ▨, ▣, ▬, ▣

Ramshorn snail
Shell diameter 3 cm (1¼ in). Shell coiled
and flattened into spiral; grazes algae
growing on pond weeds; one of several
freshwater gastropod mollusc species;
occurs throughout Britain and Europe.
▨

Garden snail (Helix aspersa)

Tusk shell
Length 5 cm (2 in). Often found washed
up on beach; living animals burrow in
sand but seldom seen as found at
considerable depth; occur in Britain
and Europe. ▤

Ramshorn snail (Planorbarius corneus)

Tusk shell (Dentalium entalis)

Swan mussel (Anodonta cygnaea)

Mussel
Usually up to 10 cm (4 in) long.
Bivalves with shell of 2 equal halves;
in life, many lie half buried in silt or
sand; some marine species attached to
rocks, often in dense colonies; occur
(according to species) on shores and
silty rivers and streams throughout
Britain and Europe. ▤, ▨

Cockle
Length up to 6.5 cm (2½ in). Ridged
shell in 2 halves; found buried on
sandy beaches and estuaries; many
species exist; occur on sandy shores
throughout Britain and Europe. ▤

Mussel (Mytilus edulis)

Tellin
Length up to 6.5 cm (2½ in). Two shell
halves thin and flattened; living
animals found buried in sand; empty
shells of some species resemble
butterfly wings; occur on sandy shores
of Britain and Europe. ▤

Cockle
(Cerastoderma edule)

Tellin (Tellina tenuis)

Razor shell
Length up to 20 cm (8 in). Unusual
bivalves with long thin shell valves;
live buried in sand; muscular foot
allows rapid escape when disturbed;
occur on low levels of sandy shores in
Britain and Europe. ▤

Razorshell (Ensis siliqua)

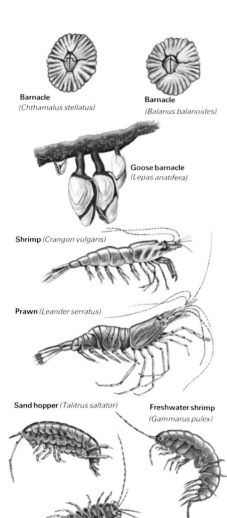

Barnacle
(Chthamalus stellatus)

Barnacle
(Balanus balanoides)

Goose barnacle
(Lepas anatifera)

Shrimp *(Crangon vulgaris)*

Prawn *(Leander serratus)*

Sand hopper *(Talitrus saltator)*

Freshwater shrimp
(Gammarus pulex)

Water louse *(Asellus aquaticus)*

Cyclops *(Microcyclops minutus)*

Water flea *(Daphnia magna)*

Arthropods
Barnacle
Diameter up to 3 cm ($1\frac{1}{4}$ in) –
encrusting; length 25 cm (10 in) –
stalked. Encrusting types have body
protected by conical shell composed of
overlapping plates fixed to rocks; at
low tide, shell opening covered by
protective plates which form shape of
kite; occur on rocky shores of Britain
and western Europe; **goose barnacle** is
found washed up on beaches; attached
by stalk to floating debris; body plates
thin and translucent; occur on
strandline of British and western
European coasts. ▣

Shrimp
Length up to 5 cm (2 in). Greyish body
well camouflaged against sand; outer
antennae almost as long as body; body
has appendages on each segment; first
pair of legs form stout, tweezer-like
pincers; occur on sandy estuaries of
Britain and Europe. ▣

Prawn
Length up to 6 cm ($2\frac{1}{2}$ in). Carapace
extends forward between stalked eyes;
body virtually transparent; outer
antennae longer than body; when
disturbed, shoots through water by
flicking action of tip of abdomen; occur
in rock pools and among seaweed in
Britain and Europe. ▣

Sand hopper
Length about 2 cm ($\frac{3}{4}$ in). Body laterally
compressed; has arched appearance;
when disturbed jumps by flicking end
of abdomen; found among rotting
seaweed and under stones near high
tide on rocky shores of Britain and
Europe. ▣

Freshwater shrimp
Length 2 cm ($\frac{3}{4}$ in). Body laterally
compressed; scavenges in silt and
among aquatic plant roots; swims
upside down by fanning movements of
legs; occur in streams and ponds,
especially on chalk in Britain and
Europe. ▣

Water louse (see page 158)
Length 2 cm ($\frac{3}{4}$ in). Body dorso-ventrally compressed; resembles wood louse; 1 pair of legs per segment on underside of body; occur all year round in debris on bottom of streams and ponds in Britain and Europe. ✉

Cyclops (see page 158)
Length 1 mm. Microscopic, forming major part of freshwater plankton; single, dark eye at front of body; jerky swimming movements through water; females carry paired egg-sacs; occur in standing freshwater throughout Britain and Europe. ✉

Water flea (see page 158)
Length 1 – 3 mm. Laterally compressed body is virtually transparent; single eye at head end; antennae used for swimming; occur in ponds and lakes in Britain and Europe. ✉

Squat lobster
Length 4 – 6 cm ($1\frac{1}{2}$ – $2\frac{1}{4}$ in). Flattened body; with tail end carried underneath; pincers held in front of body; found under stones on lower parts of rocky shores in Britain and Europe. ✉

Hermit crab
Body length 2 – 5 cm ($\frac{3}{4}$ – 2 in). Lives inside empty shells of winkles, whelks, etc; often found in pools on rocky and sandy shores of Britain and Europe. ✉

True crab
Length up to 18 cm (7 in); many smaller. Body protected by flattened, oval shell; feed and defend themselves with aid of 2 large pincers; 4 pairs of legs behind these; eyes on stalks; occur under stones and seaweed at low tide, especially on rocky shores of Britain and Europe. ✉

Crayfish
Length 4 – 8 cm ($1\frac{1}{2}$ – 3 in). Resembles miniature lobster; hides under stones and in holes in stream bed; two large pincers brandished if angry; occurs in streams and rivers in Britain and Europe. ✉

Squat lobster *(Galathea squamifera)*

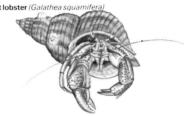

Hermit crab *(Eupagurus bernhardus)*

Edible crab *(Cancer pagurus)*

Shore crab *(Carcinus maenas)*

Crayfish *(Astacus pallipes)*

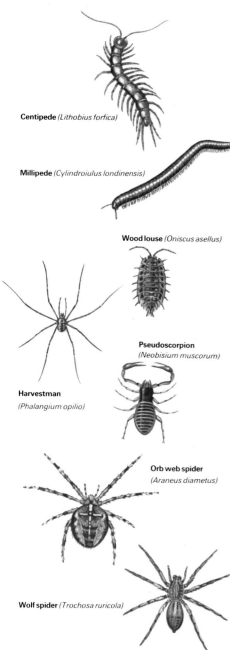

Centipede *(Lithobius forfica)*

Millipede *(Cylindroiulus londinensis)*

Wood louse *(Oniscus asellus)*

Pseudoscorpion
(Neobisium muscorum)

Harvestman
(Phalangium opilio)

Orb web spider
(Araneus diametus)

Wolf spider *(Trochosa ruricola)*

Centipede
Length up to 4 cm (1½ in). Long, shiny body flattened dorso-ventrally; 1 pair of legs per segment; moves rapidly when disturbed; active carnivore with large 'fangs'; catches soil invertebrates; found in soil and under stones during daytime; occur in Britain and Europe. ◨, ◪

Millipede
Length up to 3 cm (1¼ in). Long, dark, segmented body; each segment has 2 pairs of legs; found in soil and under stones; coil into spiral if disturbed; occur mainly in calcareous areas in Britain and Europe. ◨, ◪

Harvestman
Length: body 0.5 – 1 cm (½ in), legs 4 – 5 cm (2 in). Tiny body in relation to long legs; slow, deliberate movements; often hangs upside down as it moves among vegetation; feeds on small invertebrates; found throughout summer in Britain and Europe. ◨, ◨, ◪

Wood louse
Length 2 cm (¾ in). Dorsal surface of body armoured with horny plates; 1 pair of legs per segment, only visible from beneath; mainly nocturnal, hiding under stones during day; often congregates in large numbers in suitable refuges; occur in Britain and Europe. ◨, ◪

Pseudoscorpion
Length 2 mm. Superficial resemblance to scorpion, but lacks the 'sting'; first pair of appendages bear stout pincers; 4 pairs of legs behind these; scuttling movement when disturbed; found in soil and leaf litter in Britain and Europe. ◨, ◪

Spider
Length varies according to species: largest may have legs 5 cm (2 in) long. Body separated into cephalothorax and abdomen; 4 pairs of legs; mouth bears biting mouthparts; many species exist, but all are predatory, some building webs to ensnare prey, others hiding in wait or actively pursuing victims; occur throughout Britain and Europe. ◪, ◨, ◨, ◧, ◨, ◪

Wingless insects

Length usually up to 1 cm ($\frac{1}{2}$ in), according to species. Primitive, inconspicuous creatures usually found feeding on debris and minute organisms in soil, under bark and – particularly bristle tails – in houses; occur throughout Britain and Europe. ▨, ▣, ⊕

Mayfly

Wingspan up to 4.5 cm ($1\frac{3}{4}$ in). Nymphs aquatic, living in tunnels or under stones; they have 2 or 3 'tails' and external gills; adults have 2 pairs of unequal wings and often occur in large swarms in May and live for only a few hours; usually found near fresh water in Britain and Europe. ▨

Dragonfly

Wingspan up to 10 cm (4 in). Adult has 2 pairs of unequal wings held flat at rest; powerful fliers, patrolling particular stretches of water; solitary except when courting; on wing June – August; nymphs are fierce predators; stalk prey among pond weeds; large flattened eyes; use 'jet propulsion' when disturbed by shooting water from rectum; occur throughout Britain and Europe. ▨

Damselfly

Wingspan 4 cm ($1\frac{1}{2}$ in). Adult has 2 pairs of similar wings folded over body at rest; weak flapping flight compared with dragonfly; compound eyes relatively large but widely separated; nymphs have long, thin body and legs; prominent antennae; 3 projections from end of abdomen (caudal gills); predatory; movements slow and deliberate; found among pond weeds, or buried in sediments; occur in Britain and Europe. ▨

Stonefly

Wingspan up to 3 cm ($1\frac{1}{4}$ in). Adults have 2 pairs of wings folded flat over body; secretive, crawling among waterside vegetation and stones; larvae have flattened body with 2 long antennae and 2 cerci projecting from tail end; live in well-oxygenated rivers, clinging to stones; carnivorous; occur in Britain and Europe. ▨

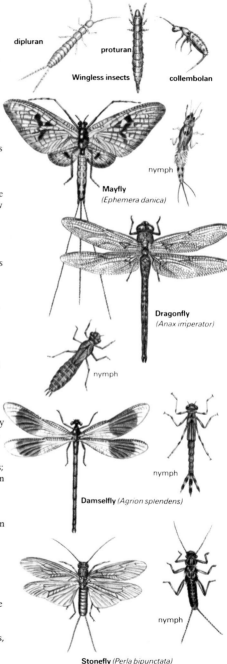

dipluran

proturan

Wingless insects

collembolan

nymph

Mayfly
(Ephemera danica)

Dragonfly
(Anax imperator)

nymph

nymph

Damselfly *(Agrion splendens)*

nymph

Stonefly *(Perla bipunctata)*

161

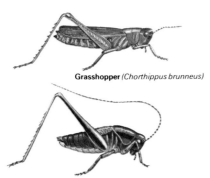

Grasshopper *(Chorthippus brunneus)*

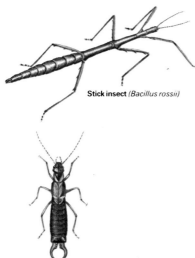

Bush cricket *(Leptophyes punctatissima)*

True cricket *(Gryllus campestris)*

Stick insect *(Bacillus rossii)*

Earwig *(Forficula auricularia)*

Cockroach *(Ectobius pallidus)*

Grasshopper
Length up to 5 cm (2 in). Hop well using powerful hind legs; winged species fly readily; nymphal stages appear June; adults occur until September; males 'sing', often in small groups, by rubbing hind legs against wings; occur in Britain and Europe. ▣, ▦

Bush cricket
Length up to 5 cm (2 in). Antennae longer than body; legs long and thin; hop well; female has long ovipositor; males 'sing' by rubbing wings together; adults appear from July to September; occur in scrub and woodland rides throughout Britain and Europe. ▣, ▦

True cricket
Length up to 2 cm ($\frac{3}{4}$ in). Live in burrows in sandy soil; males chirp from entrance to attract females; present as adults or nymphs throughout most of year; nymphs resemble adults but lack wings; wings held flat over body; occur in sandy soil in Britain (rarely) and Europe. ▣, ▣, ▦

Stick insect
Length 7.5 cm ($2\frac{3}{4}$ in). Long thin body and legs; lack wings; well camouflaged among vegetation; sometimes 'rock' when disturbed; young are miniature versions of adults; occur in bushes and trees in southern Europe. ▣, ▦

Earwig
Length 2 cm ($\frac{3}{4}$ in). Long, flattened body with short pale wings; pincers at rear end strongly incurved in male; nocturnal habits, found under stones and in soil during daytime; present throughout the year; occur in gardens, woods and soil in Britain and Europe. ▣, ▦

Cockroach
Length up to 3 cm ($1\frac{1}{4}$ in). Usually associated with man's food and rubbish; run rapidly when disturbed; body flattened dorso-ventrally; long antennae used as sense organs; females carry egg-cases at tail end; occur (according to species) throughout Britain and Europe. ▦

Praying mantis

Length up to 6 cm (2½ in). Elongated insects; front pair of legs held in position of prayer; head possesses large eyes; fierce carnivores, sit motionless on flowers and twigs awaiting insect prey; abdomen of female becomes swollen with eggs which are laid in protective cases on twigs; occur in southern Europe only.

Termite

Length 1 cm (½ in). Live in colonies of about 500 individuals in dry, dead wood; colonies consist of a royal pair, numerous young, and wingless soldiers; soldier has large dark head and mandibles; rest of body rather soft; occur in areas with dead timber around Mediterranean.

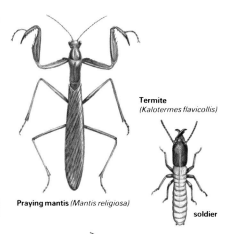

Termite
(Kalotermes flavicollis)

Praying mantis *(Mantis religiosa)*

soldier

Shield bug

Length 1 cm (½ in). Flattened, shield-shaped body; wings held folded over abdomen; well camouflaged among leaves; mouthparts adapted for piercing plant tissue and sucking sap; hibernate under logs and among leaf litter; occur in scrub and hedges in Britain and Europe.

Shield bug *(Acanthosoma haemarroidale)*

Pond skater

Length about 1 cm (½ in). Thin body and long legs supported on water surface; skate over surface propelled by middle legs; jerky changes in direction; often congregate to feed on insects trapped in surface film; occur in ponds and lakes in Britain and Europe.

Pond skater *(Gerris lacustris)*

Water boatman

Length about 1 cm (½ in). Swims upside down, often seen hanging from surface film; hind pair of legs form long paddles for swimming; looks silvery under water due to air trapped on body; feeds on insects trapped in surface film; occurs in ponds and lakes in Britain and Europe.

Water boatman *(Notonecta glauca)*

Water scorpion *(Nepa cinerea)*

Saucer bug *(Ilyocoris cimicoides)*

Froghopper *(Cercopis vulnerata)*

cuckoo spit on grass stem

Cicada *(Cicadetta montana)*

Aphid *(Aphis fabae)*

Water scorpion

Length 3 cm (1¼ in). Body flattened and leaf-shaped with long air-tube at posterior end; front legs held ready to grasp prey; well-developed tubular mouthparts; lies motionless among pond weeds; occur in ponds and lakes in Britain and Europe. ▨

Saucer bug

Length 1 cm (½ in). Body flattened and saucer shaped; found among pond weeds near water's surface; swims rapidly if disturbed when it looks silvery due to trapped air; active predator; occurs on ponds and lakes in Britain and Europe. ▨

Froghopper

Length up to 1 cm (⅓ in). Name derived from characteristic frog-like leaping ability; specialized mouthparts adapted for piercing and sucking plant juices. Small green nymphal stage exudes froth around itself (cuckoo-spit) and is commonly found among long grass and plant stems; occur in Britain and Europe. ▨, ▣

Cicada

Length 2.5 cm (1 in). Squat body with 2 pairs of large transparent wings held angled over body at rest; males produce characteristic reeling cicada song which is difficult to locate; nymphs are subterranean; adults found in June; occur in Britain (rare) and Europe. ▣

Aphid

Length up to 2 mm. Wingless summer generations feed on plant sap; reproduce rapidly, so often found in vast numbers on suitable plants; winged parthenogenetic females produced in autumn; occur throughout Britain and Europe. ▣, ▨

Lacewing

Wingspan up to 4.5 cm (1¾ in). Elongated body with 2 pairs of transparent wings with prominent veins; wings held angled over body at rest; adults found from July to May; often hibernate indoors in winter; occur throughout Britain and Europe. ◧, ◿

Lacewing *(Chrysopa carnea)*

Scorpionfly

Wingspan 2.5 cm (1 in). Wings mottled brown, held flat at rest; head has downward-pointing 'beak'; feed on dead insects – sometimes from spiders' webs; common in summer months on bramble bushes; occur throughout Britain and Europe. ◿, ◧

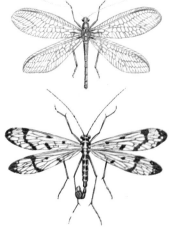

Scorpionfly *(Panorpa communis)*

Butterfly

Wingspan up to 8 cm (3 in); often less. Butterflies have 2 pairs of wings, generally folded together above body when at rest; wings covered in coloured scales; fly during day, often seen feeding on nectar using long coiled proboscis; antennae often knobbed at ends; larvae (caterpillars) have soft, segmented bodies; 3 pairs of true legs on first 3 segments; 5 pairs of fleshy prolegs at rear end; occur throughout Britain and Europe. ◿, ◧, ◧, ◧, ▭, ◪

Butterfly *(Aglais urticae)*

caterpillar

Moth

Wingspan up to 9 cm (3½ in); often less. Most adults are nocturnal fliers; 2 pairs of wings covered in minute coloured scales; at rest, wings either held flat or arched over body with upper wing visible; feed on nectar using long proboscis; antennae often 'feathery'; most species well camouflaged during daytime; larvae (caterpillars) with soft, segmented bodies, often having elaborate false eyes or resembling other creatures; occur throughout Britain and Europe. ◿, ◧, ◧, ◧, ▭

Hawk moth *(Mimas tiliae)*

Noctuid moth *(Noctua pronuba)*

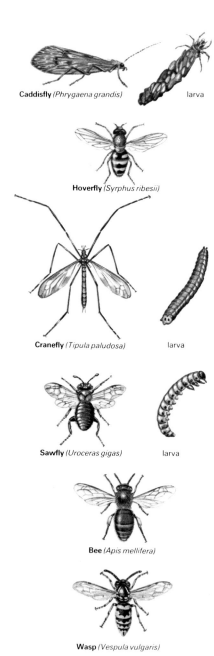

Caddisfly *(Phrygaena grandis)*   larva

Hoverfly *(Syrphus ribesii)*

Cranefly *(Tipula paludosa)*   larva

Sawfly *(Uroceras gigas)*   larva

Bee *(Apis mellifera)*

Wasp *(Vespula vulgaris)*

Caddisfly

Wingspan up to 6.5 cm (2½ in). 2 pairs of wings held angled over body when at rest; hide in vegetation during daytime; weak flight, mainly active at night; aquatic larvae construct protective cases from vegetation and pebbles; occur near still waters in Britain and Europe. ▨

Hoverfly

Body length 1 cm (½ in). Superficial resemblance to bees, but possess 1 pair of transparent wings; active in autumn; occur in gardens and woodland rides in Britain and Europe. ▣, ▨

Cranefly

Body length 3 cm (1¼ in). 1 pair of wings; ungainly flight; larvae are tube-like, without obvious head end, and live underground, eating plant roots; occur in grassland and on farms in Britain and Europe. ▨

Sawfly

Body length up to 2 cm (¾ in). Sawflies have 2 pairs of wings but lack constricted 'waist' of true wasps; females have saw-like ovipositor; larvae bear superficial resemblance to caterpillars of butterflies, most feed on leaves but some bore into wood and plant stems; occur in woodland and grassland throughout Britain and Europe. ▣, ▣, ▨

Bee

Body length up to 2 cm (¾ in). Often colonial insects constructing nest in cavities or aided by man as in honey bee; all species collect pollen; 2 pairs of smoky transparent wings; buzzing in flight; occur in gardens and grassland throughout Britain and Europe. ▨

Wasp

Body length up to 2½ cm (1 in). Wasps have 2 pairs of transparent wings and constricted 'waist'; 'sting' is modified ovipositor; some species are solitary, but colonial species construct nests in holes in ground and buildings; young fed on insects; adults fond of rotting fruit in autumn; occur in gardens and open country throughout Britain and Europe. ▨, ▣, ▣, ▣

Ichneumon wasp
Body length (including ovipositor)
6.5 cm (2½ in). Adults have 2 pairs of
wings and elongated body; long
ovipositor in female is used to
parasitize insect larvae with eggs;
females encountered stealthily
searching vegetation and bark for
hosts; occur in woodland and grassland
in Britain and Europe. ▣, ▣, ▣

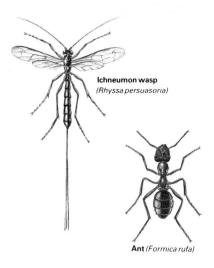

Ichneumon wasp
(Rhyssa persuasoria)

Ant
Length up to 1 cm (½ in). Wingless,
except for certain stages; constricted
'waist' between thorax and abdomen;
colonial, with foraging parties often
seen radiating from nests; occur in
woodland and grassland in Britain and
Europe. ▣, ▣, ▣, ▣

Ant *(Formica rufa)*

Terrestrial beetle
Length up to 5 cm (2 in); many smaller.
Characterized by having 2 pairs of
wings, the first pair of which are
hardened and form wing cases or
elytra; second membranous pair lie
folded underneath at rest; occupy wide
variety of habitats; generally very
active, predatory animals; larvae
usually live in soil or rotting wood;
occur throughout Britain and Europe.
▣, ▣, ▣, ▣, ▣

Terrestrial beetle *(Cicindela campestris)*

Aquatic beetle
Length up to 5 cm (2 in). Several species
occur, such as **great diving beetle**:
active, and swims well using hind legs
which form paddles; fierce predator;
often seen at water's surface
replenishing air supply stored under
wing cases; and **whirligig beetle**:
middle and hind legs used as paddles;
spins wildly on surface of water, often
in large groups; most obvious in late
autumn; dives at slightest danger;
aquatic insects occur in ponds and
streams throughout Britain and Europe.
▣

Whirligig beetle
(Gyrinus natator)

Great diving beetle *(Dytiscus marginalis)*

Weevil
Length 1 cm (½ in). Head extends
forward to form pronounced snout
which bears antennae and mouth parts
at tip; slow movements; most species
feed on bark and plants, including
nuts, sometimes becoming serious
pests; active May to October; occur
throughout Britain and Europe. ▣, ▣,
▣

Weevil *(Hylobius abietus)*

Bryozoan (Electra pilosa)
on seaweed

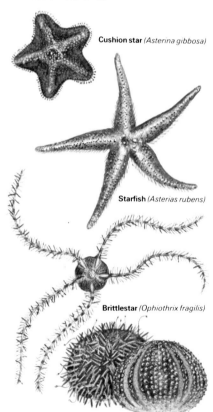

Feather star (Antedon bifida)

Cushion star (Asterina gibbosa)

Starfish (Asterias rubens)

Brittlestar (Ophiothrix fragilis)

Sea urchin (Echinus esculentus)

Bryozoans
Bryozoan
Height of colony 5 – 20 cm (2 – 8 in).
Minute, sessile, colonial animals
forming mat or branching tufts over
rocks or seaweeds; individual animals
live inside a protective case; occur on
rocks and seaweeds throughout Britain
and Europe. ▱

Echinoderms
Feather star
Diameter up to 20 cm (8 in). Body
consists of small central disc and 5
paired long feathery arms; variety of
colour forms; found by turning over
stones on lower shore; occur on
Mediterranean and Atlantic coasts. ▱

Cushion star
Diameter up to 15 cm (6 in). Body is
flattened disc generally with 5 short
arms; tips of arms turn up when
removed from water; found under
stones and in crevices on lower rocky
shore of Atlantic and Mediterranean
coasts. ▱

Starfish
Diameter up to 80 cm (30 in); many
species smaller. Body generally divided
into 5 radiating arms; upper surface
rough and spiny; lower surface covered
with large numbers of tube feet; slow-
moving, generally feeding on sedentary
molluscs; occur on lower rocky shores
and pools in Britain and Europe. ▱

Brittle star
Diameter of central disc up to 3 cm
(1 in). Small central disc with 5
radiating slender arms; arms possess
spines, and are extremely fragile; occur
under boulders and in crevices on
lower rocky shores of Britain and
Europe. ▱

Sea urchin
Diameter up to 10 cm (4 in), excluding
arms. Outer casing or 'test' almost
spherical; in life, shell is covered with
spines for protection, and tube feet for
movement; spines catch debris such as
seaweed, providing camouflage; occur
on lower shore, sometimes in pools, in
Britain and Europe. ▱

Heart urchin
Length up to 13 cm (5 in). Rounded, heart-shaped body; in life, covered in mat of brittle spines which accumulate silt; live buried in sand; empty 'test' is white, often washed up on beaches; occur on sandy shores in Britain and Europe. ▦

test (spines removed)

Heart urchin *(Echinocardium cordatum)*

Sea-cucumber
Length up to 30 cm (12 in). Sausage-shaped body; 5 rows of tube feet on underside; retractile tentacles at head end; some species produce sticky white threads from rear end if disturbed. Habitat: lower rocky shores. ▦

Sea cucumber *(Holothuria forskali)*

Hemichordates
Acorn worm
Length up to 30 cm (12 in). Burrowing in sand or mud in shallow and deeper water; body divided into 3 zones with a distinctive anterior proboscis, occur on Atlantic and Mediterranean coasts. ▦

Acorn worm *(Balanoglossus clavigerus)*

Chordates
Salp
Length up to 1 cm ($\frac{1}{2}$ in). Pelagic, barrel-shaped filter-feeders; mostly solitary but some colonial; confined to Mediterranean and adjacent waters. ▦

Salp *(Salpa maxima)*

Ascidian
Colony up to 40 cm (16 in) across. Form encrusting jelly-like colonies on rocks, holdfasts of seaweeds, etc; variety of colour forms, orange and blue are most frequent; particularly noticeable in summer; occur on lower rocky shores of Britain and Europe. ▦

Ascidian *(Ciona intestinalis)*

169

Fishes

Atlantic salmon *Salmo salar*
Length 1.2 m (47 in). Large size, adipose fin and (in breeding males) hooked lower jaw distinctive; spawns in upper reaches of large rivers, October–January; may be seen leaping from water to clear weirs and waterfalls; occurs in Britain, Scandinavia and countries bordering Baltic, North Sea and Atlantic. ▦, ▤

Trout *Salmo trutta*
Length 70 cm (28 in). Two forms: resident freshwater, and migratory sea form; found in both running and still water; note adipose fin; may be seen rising to aquatic insects on water surface; occurs throughout Britain and Europe. ▦, ▤

Pike *Esox lucius*
Length 1.2 m (47 in). Streamlined fish with forward facing eyes; dorsal fin set far back; found in still and running water; highly predatory: may be seen lurking beneath floating vegetation and in backwaters; takes fishes, young birds and mammals; occurs in Britain, and most of Europe except south-west. ▦

Chub *Leuciscus leuciscus*
Length 80 cm (32 in). Brassy body; back green-black; head large with whitish lips; found in running water; often shoals near surface taking insects, but larger individuals solitary; prefers water with overhanging trees and other sheltered spots; occurs in most of Britain and Europe. ▦

Roach *Rutilus rutilus*
Length 35 cm (14 in). Small roach especially may shoal near the surface or in shallow water, away from predators; slimmer, more silvery flanks and overhanging top lip distinguish it from rudd; found in still and running water; occurs in Britain, and most of Europe except south-west. ▦

Atlantic salmon

Trout

Pike

Chub

Roach

Minnow *Phoxinus phoxinus*
Length 14 cm (5½ in), usually smaller.
Large fins, striped dorsal parts and
silvery undersides; body narrows near
tail; usually found shoaling in shallows
of gravelly water; occurs in most of
Britain and Europe. ✉

Rudd *Scardinius erythrophthalmus*
Length 45 cm (18 in). Deeper, bronzy
body, redder fins and protruding lower
lip distinguish it from roach; prefers
reed-fringed lowland lakes where it
often feeds close to the surface; occurs
in much of Britain, and Europe except
extreme north and south-west. ✉

Gudgeon *Gobio gobio*
Length 20 cm (8 in). Elongate, rounded,
tapering body; mouth bears 2 sensory
barbels; back mottled grey-green;
bottom-feeding fish often found
shoaling in the shallows of gravelly
streams and rivers; occurs in Britain,
and Europe except south-west and
extreme north. ✉

Bleak *Alburnus alburnus*
Length 25 cm (10 in). Slim-bodied with
silvery sides and blue-green back;
usually seen shoaling in the shallows or
near the surface of gravelly streams
and rivers; often swims with darting
movements; occurs in most of Britain,
and Europe except extreme north and
south-west. ✉

Carp *Cyprinus carpio*
Length 1 m (39 in). Well-built fish with
large dorsal fin; mouth bears 4 sensory
barbels; usually feeds on the bottom of
lakes and slow-moving rivers, but may
be seen basking under lily pads; enters
shallow water to spawn; occurs in most
of Britain and Europe. ✉

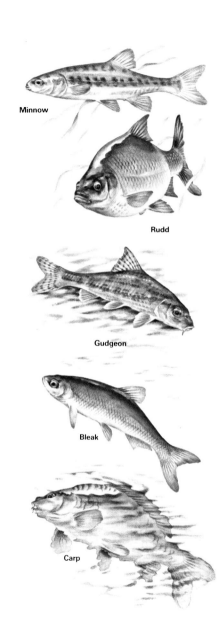

Minnow

Rudd

Gudgeon

Bleak

Carp

171

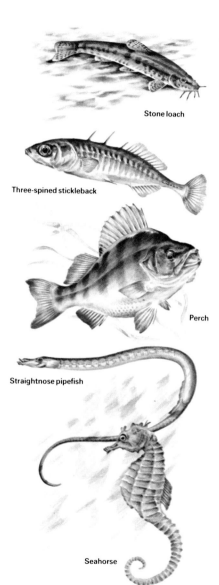

Stone loach *Noemacheilus barbatulus*
Length 18 cm (7 in). Long, thin body
with large tail fin; mouth bears 6
sensory barbels; found in clear running
water, especially with stones and
gravel; often hides under stones by
day; occurs in most of Britain and
Europe. ⊠

Stone loach

Three-spined stickleback
Gasterosteus aculeatus
Length 11 cm (4½ in). Active fish; body
has 3 dorsal spines and is covered with
bony plates; male in breeding season
has red throat; found mainly in rivers
and lakes, but also in brackish
conditions; occurs in Britain, and most
of Europe except central and some
southern areas. ⊠, ⊟

Three-spined stickleback

Perch *Perca fluviatilis*
Length 50 cm (20 in). Coarse body with
spiny first dorsal fin and gill covers;
huge mouth; vertical body stripes
distinctive; predatory, often feeds in
shoals in lakes and rivers, especially
near bridges, piles, etc; occurs in most
of Britain and Europe. ⊠

Perch

Straightnose pipefish

Straightnose pipefish
Nerophis ophidion
Length 30 cm (12 in). Long, thin body
with elongated snout; lacks pectoral
and tail fins; found among seaweeds in
shallow water and rock pools; occurs
around coasts of Britain and Europe. ⊟

Seahorse *Hippocampus hippocampus*
Length 15 cm (6 in). Unmistakeable
horse-like body with reduced fins;
often clings to marine vegetation with
tail; found among seaweeds in shallow
water and rock pools; occurs around
Mediterranean and Atlantic coasts to
English Channel. ⊟

Seahorse

Golden mullet *Mugil auratus*
Length 50 cm (20 in). Two dorsal fins,
anterior with 4 spiny rays; often enters
harbours and lower reaches of rivers
where it can be seen nosing at the
bottom in shallow water; occurs around
Britain, Mediterranean, Atlantic and
North Sea areas. ▤, ▨

Golden mullet

Sand eel *Ammodytes tobianus*
Length 20 cm (8 in). Lies buried in the
sand from low-water mark downwards
during the day: shoals in the shallows
at night; occurs around Atlantic,
English Channel, North Sea and Baltic
coasts. ▤

Sand eel

Corkwing wrasse *Crenilabrus melops*
Length 20 cm (8 in). One of several,
usually brightly coloured wrasses
which may be encountered; long dorsal
fin characteristic; found in shallow
water among rocks and seaweeds, and
in rock pools; occurs around coasts of
Britain and Europe. ▤

Corkwing wrasse

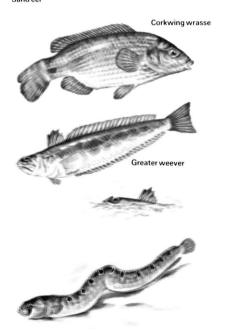

Greater weever

Greater weever *Trachinus draco*
Length 35 cm (14 in). Usually lies
buried in sand with just top of body
and eyes visible; beware venomous
spines on dorsal fin and gill cover;
found in shallow water; occurs around
Mediterranean, Atlantic, English
Channel and North Sea coasts. ▤

Butterfish *Pholis gunnellus*
Length 20 cm (8 in). Flattened, eel-like
body with long dorsal fin; found in
mud, sand and among rocks on lower
shore; occurs around Atlantic (North of
English Channel), Channel, North Sea
and Baltic coasts. ▤

Butterfish

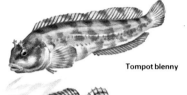

Tompot blenny *Blennius gattorugine*
Length 25 cm (10 in). One of several
similar species which may be
encountered; most characterized by
elongate fins and appendages above the
eyes; found in rock pools and among
seaweeds and mud; occurs around
Mediterranean, Atlantic and English
Channel coasts. ▱

Tompot blenny

Rock goby *Gobius paganellus*
Length 12 cm (4½ in). One of several
similar species which may be
encountered, most characterized by
double dorsal fins and bulging eyes;
found in rock pools, and among
seaweeds on lower shore; occurs
around Mediterranean, Atlantic and
English Channel. ▱

Rock goby

Lumpsucker *Cyclopterus lumpus*
Length 55 cm (22 in). Thickset scaleless
body; pelvic fins form a ventral sucker;
found on rocky substrates in shallow
water and rock pools; occurs around
Atlantic, English Channel and North
Sea coasts. ▱

Lumpsucker

Clingfish *Lepadogaster lepadogaster*
Length 7 cm (2½ in). Pointed snout and
long jaws; pelvic fins form a sucker;
usually found in rock pools and among
seaweeds in shallow water; occurs
around Mediterranean, Atlantic and
English Channel coasts. ▱

Clingfish

Flounder *Platichthys flesus*
Length 20 cm (8 in). One of several
flatfishes which may be encountered in
sandy pools or in sand in shallow
water; may also be found in estuaries;
occurs around the coasts of Britain and
Europe. ▱

Flounder

174

Amphibians

Fire salamander
Salamandra salamandra
Length 28 cm (11 in). Sturdy,
distinctively marked body and short
tail characteristic; inhabits damp woods
in hilly areas; slow-moving; often seen
after rain; nocturnal; occurs throughout
most of Europe, except extreme north.
🖼, ⬆, ⬇

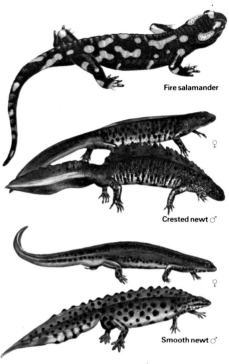

Fire salamander

Crested newt *Triturus cristatus*
Length: males 14 cm (5½ in); females
18 cm (7 in). Males develop large, spiky
crest in breeding season; skin feels
coarse; found in still or slow-moving
water, on land hides under stones, etc;
occurs throughout Britain and Europe,
except south-west and Ireland. 🖼, ⬇

Crested newt ♂

Smooth newt *Triturus vulgaris*
Length 11 cm (4½ in). Common; smooth
skin; belly usually orange with black
blotches; breeding males have large
crest and spots; breeds in still water,
but also found in damp terrestrial
habitats; occurs throughout Britain and
Europe, except south-west. 🖼, 🖼, ⬆,
⬇

Smooth newt ♂

Palmate newt *Triturus helveticus*
Length 9 cm (3½ in). Skin dry and
smooth in terrestrial animals; breeding
males develop a low crest and wide,
flat tail; breeds in pools (occasionally
running water), but otherwise quite
terrestrial; occurs in parts of Britain
and western Europe. 🖼, 🖼, ⬛, ⬇

Palmate newt ♂

Common spadefoot toad
Pelobates fuscus
Length 8 cm (3 in). Dumpy, with
smooth skin; large eyes have vertical
pupils; prominent spade on hind foot;
nocturnal; reacts by jumping about on
hind legs if threatened; breeds in pools,
but also found in cultivated areas;
occurs in many parts of Europe, except
extreme north and south-west. 🖼, 🖼

Common spadefoot toad

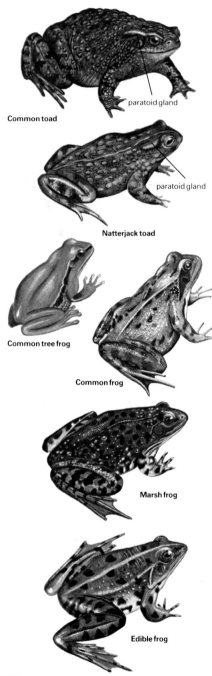

Common toad *Bufo bufo*
Length 15 cm (6 in). Heavily built, with warty skin; eyes have horizontal pupils; parotid glands distinctive behind eyes; mainly nocturnal; often found in dry habitats, hiding by day in holes and crevices, etc., occurs throughout Britain and Europe, except Ireland. ▱, ▱

Common toad

paratoid gland

Natterjack toad *Bufo calamita*
Length 8 cm (3 in). Sturdy and short-legged with distinctive parotid glands; usually has a bright yellow dorsal stripe; horizontal pupil; nocturnal; ratchet-like song; occurs in Britain, western and central Europe. ▱, ▱, ▱

Natterjack toad

paratoid gland

Common tree frog *Hyla arborea*
Length 5 cm (2 in). Small, neat frog with disc-like pads on fingers and toes; colour variable: green, yellow or brown; mainly nocturnal, often seen on foliage; duck-like call; occurs throughout much of Europe (introduced to Britain), except extreme north. ▱, ▱, ▱

Common tree frog

Common frog

Common frog *Rana temporaria*
Length 10 cm (4 in). Very common; sturdy with quite short hind legs; colour variable: grey, pink, brown, yellow or olive; breeds in water but otherwise largely terrestrial; occurs throughout Britain and Europe, except extreme south and west. ▱, ▱, ▱, ▱, ▱

Marsh frog

Marsh frog *Rana ridibunda*
Length 15 cm (6 in). Largest native European frog; sturdy with often pointed snout; very vocal, especially in breeding season; diurnal; usually found in or near pools and streams; occurs in south-west and eastern Europe, and introduced to Britain. ▱

Edible frog *Rana esculenta*
Length 12 cm (4½ in). Colour variable: green through brown with dark spots and marks; vocal sacs whitish; diurnal, may be found in full sun; usually very aquatic, found in various freshwater habitats; occurs in many parts of Europe, except south-west and extreme north; introduced to Britain. ▱

Edible frog

Reptiles

European pond terrapin
Emys orbicularis
Length 20–30 cm (8–12 in). Flatter shell distinguishes it from tortoises; lacks neck stripes of similar striped-necked terrapin; usually found in ditches and swamps, but basks at waterside; occurs in most of Europe except north, and some central areas. ▨

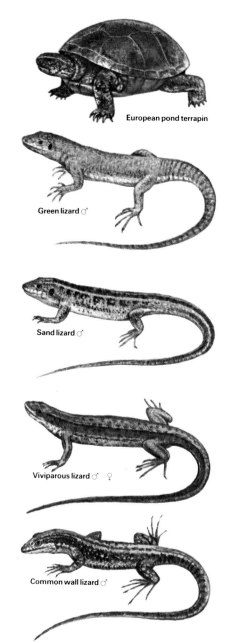

European pond terrapin

Green lizard *Lacerta viridis*
Body length 12 cm (4½ in): tail may be twice as long. Males all green with dark stippling, females green or brown with blotches; adult males (and some females) have blue throat; often found basking; occurs in much of central and southern Europe. ▣, ▨, ▣

Green lizard ♂

Sand lizard *Lacerta agilis*
Body length 9 cm (3½ in): tail about 1½ times as long. Male's head comparatively large; band of narrow scales discernible along back; colour variable: patterning often a mixture of green, brown, grey and black; occurs in much of central and northern Europe, including Britain. ▨, ▣, ▤, ▲

Sand lizard ♂

Viviparous lizard *Lacerta vivipara*
Body length 6 cm (2½ in): tail up to twice as long. Short-legged, long-bodied and with small head separated by distinct collar; colour variable: mainly brown; prefers damp areas but habitat varies with range; occurs in most of Britain and Europe, except Mediterranean and south-west. ▨, ▲, ▬, ▣, ▨, ▤

Viviparous lizard ♂ ♀

Common wall lizard *Podarcis muralis*
Body length 6 cm (2½ in): tail about twice as long. Colour very variable: usually patterns of brown and grey, but in parts of range green also; often seen on walls, rocky outcrops and trees; occurs in much of Europe, except north and south-west. ▨, ▣, ▣

Common wall lizard ♂

177

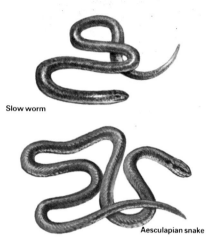
Slow worm

Slow worm *Anguis fragilis*
Length 50 cm (20 in), often smaller.
Smooth scaled body; males often have
blue spots, females often have vertebral
stripe; prefers damp places; secretive,
usually hides under stones, although
may be seen basking after rain; occurs
in most of Britain and Europe. ▨, ◙,
▣

Aesculapian snake

Aesculapian snake *Elaphe longissima*
Length 2 m (6½ ft), usually smaller. Long
thin snake; eyes with round pupils;
scales of adults often have white mark
on edge; often climbs trees, but also
encountered among rocks, ruins, etc;
likes sunny sites; occurs in much of
Europe except north and south-west.
◙, ▣, ▨

Grass snake

Grass snake *Natrix natrix*
Length 2 m (6½ ft), usually smaller.
Thick-bodied with rounded head;
round pupils; colour variable: usually
with black-bordered collar behind
head, rest of body grey, green or
brownish with blotches and stripes
according to range; may feign death;
occurs in most of Britain and Europe,
except extreme north and Ireland.
▨, ◙, ▨

Smooth snake

Smooth snake *Coronella austriaca*
Length 80 cm (32 in). Small, pointed
head and indistinct neck; round pupils;
colours variable: grey, pinkish or
brown – may be more intensive on
sides; diurnal but rather secretive,
preferring sunny sites; occurs in parts
of Britain and much of Europe, except
extreme south-west. ▣, ▨, ◙, ▣, ▣

Adder

Adder *Vipera berus*
Length 90 cm (36 in). Thick-bodied
with flat snout; several large scales on
head; in some regions may be confused
with other vipers: zig-zag dorsal stripe
usually distinctive; colours variable:
grey, brown, reddish or black; habitat
varies according to range; diurnal;
venomous; occurs in most of Britain and
Europe, except Ireland, south-west and
Mediterranean. ▣, ▭, ◙, ▨, ◙, ▣,
▨, ▤

Birds

Black-throated diver *Gavia arctica*
Length 63 cm (25 in). Breeds on
secluded lakes, especially in upland
regions; seen in winter along seashores,
sometimes in small flocks; bill thin and
straight; breeding call plaintive cry;
breeds in Scandinavia eastwards,
winters in Britain and western Europe.
🖼, 🖼

Black-throated diver

summer

Red-throated diver *Gavia stellata*
Length 55 cm (22 in). Slim bird which
sits low in water; upturned beak held
slightly upwards; young resemble
winter adults; only leaves water to visit
nest; resident in parts of Britain and
Scandinavia, winter visitor to other
European coastal waters. S 🖼, W 🖼

summer

Red-throated diver

Great crested grebe *Podiceps cristatus*
45 cm (18 in). Easily recognized by
prominent ear-tufts in summer and
dagger-like orange-yellow beak;
appears hump-backed in flight; often
submerges for long periods when
feeding; striped young often ride on
parents' back; resident throughout
most of Britain and Europe. 🖼, W 🖼

Great crested grebe

summer

winter

Black-necked grebe *Podiceps caspicus*
Length 30 cm (12 in). Recognized by
black neck and downward-pointing
ear-tufts; bill slightly upturned; breeds
in isolated places in Britain, central and
southern Europe; may be seen in
flocks. 🖼, W 🖼

Black-necked grebe

summer

imm.

Little grebe *Tachybaptus ruficollis*
Length 25 cm (10 in). Distinguished
from moorhen by smaller, tubbier
appearance; young striped; resident
throughout most of Britain and
Europe. 🖼

Little grebe

summer

winter

imm.

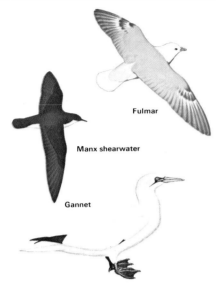

Fulmar *Fulmarus glacialis*
Length 45 cm (18 in). Glides on
outstretched wings; gull-like
appearance, but with distinctive
tubular nostrils on beak; straight wings
lack black tips; breeds in Britain,
Ireland and Scandinavia. ✉

Manx shearwater *Puffinus puffinus*
Length 35 cm (14 in). Long, narrow-
winged seabird which glides low over
water, but flicks over revealing pale
underside and then dark back; often
holds one wing low, 'shearing' the
water; nests in burrows on islands off
British and north-western European
coasts and in Mediterranean. ✉

Gannet *Sula bassana*
Length 90 cm (36 in). Cigar-shaped
body with long, thin wings; from a
distance, body looks very white, unlike
gulls which look grey; head yellow
tinged and wings black tipped in
breeding season; breeds on rocky cliffs
and islands off Britain, Iceland,
Norway and Brittany, winters at sea;
plunge-dives into water from great
height for fish. S✉

Cormorant *Phalacrocorax carbo*
Length 90 cm (36 in). Often perches on
rocks with half-extended wings; in
flight, distinguished from ducks and
geese by its long tail and bill; resident
on west coasts of Britain and Europe,
and Mediterranean, seen inland in
winter. ✉

Shag *Phalacrocorax aristotelis*
Length 75 cm (30 in). Head bears
distinctive crest in breeding season;
flight pattern similar to cormorant, but
bird is generally slimmer and smaller;
resident on west coasts of Britain and
Europe, and Mediterranean. ✉

Bittern *Botaurus stellaris*
Length 75 cm (30 in). Breeds in reed
marshes; very secretive; sits hunched
up, but extends neck when alarmed;
most active at dusk and night, when
booming, foghorn-like call may be
heard; resident throughout most of
Britain and Europe. ⊠

Grey heron *Ardea cinerea*
Length 90 cm (36 in). May be seen on
any stretch of fresh or sea water; sits
hunched whilst fishing, takes off with
lazy flaps of wings if disturbed; neck
held in 'S' shape in flight; nests in
colonies often in tall trees; resident
throughout most of Britain and Europe.
⊠, ⊠

Purple heron *Ardea purpurea*
Length 78 cm (31 in). Prefers denser
vegetation than grey heron; neck more
'S' shaped in flight than grey heron's;
breeds in southern parts of Europe. ⊠

White stork *Ciconia ciconia*
Length 1 m (39 in). Prefers marshes,
water meadows and grassy plains; may
nest near to human habitation and
fairly easy to approach; migrates in V-
formation; dagger-like beak; breeds in
Spain and parts of northern Europe.
S⊠

Spoonbill *Platalea leucorodia*
Length 86 cm (34 in). Long spatulate
bill characteristic; neck held
outstretched in flight; flocks fly in
lines; crest only obvious in summer
adults; breeds in Holland and Spain,
more numerous in the extreme south-
east of Europe. S⊠

Bittern

Grey heron

Purple heron

White stork

Spoonbill

181

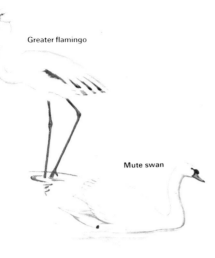

Greater flamingo

Mute swan

Whooper swan

imm

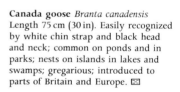

Canada goose

light-breasted

dark-breasted

Brent goose

Greater flamingo *Phoenicopterus ruber*
Length 1.2 m (47 in). Extremely long legs and neck, thick hooked bill distinctive; in flight the neck and legs droop and a trumpet-like call is given; resident in scattered colonies in southern Europe. ⊠

Mute swan *Cygnus olor*
Length 1.5 m (60 in). Orange bill with black basal knob distinguishes it from other swans; flies with neck outstretched; swims with neck held gracefully in an 'S' shape; resident in Britain and northern Europe. ⊠

Whooper swan *Cygus cygnus*
Length 1.5 m (60 in). Yellow bill with no basal knob; neck thin, straight and upright when swimming; Bewick's swan (*C. columbianus*) visibly smaller – 1.2 m (47 in) – with shorter neck and less yellow on bill; both birds winter visitors to Britain and north-west Europe. W⊠

Canada goose *Branta canadensis*
Length 75 cm (30 in). Easily recognized by white chin strap and black head and neck; common on ponds and in parks; nests on islands in lakes and swamps; gregarious; introduced to parts of Britain and Europe. ⊠

Brent goose *Branta bernicla*
Length 60 cm (24 in). Appears very dark and short-necked; rapid flight, usually low over seashores and bays; exists in two colour forms; light breasted and dark breasted; gregarious; winter visitor to Britain and western Europe. W⊟, W⊠

Barnacle goose *Branta leucopsis*
Length 63 cm (25 in). Only goose which
has white face and black neck; usually
seen on or near coastal stretches of
water; gregarious; birds seen in
summer are probably escapes; winters
in Britain, Ireland, Scandinavia and
Holland. W☒

Barnacle goose

Greylag goose

Greylag goose *Anser anser*
Length 80 cm (32 in). Bulky bird, with
ponderous walk and flight; pale grey
forewing and dark trailing edge of
wing conspicuous in flight; breeds in
parts of Scotland and northern Europe
(including Scandinavia), winters west
and south-west Europe. W☒, ☒, W☒

White-fronted goose

White-fronted goose *Anser albifrons*
Length 70 cm (28 in). White forehead
and heavily barred underparts
distinguish it from other grey geese;
two races: Eurasian (with pink bill) and
Greenland (with orange bill); noisy and
gregarious; winter visitor to Britain and
north-west Europe. W☒, W☒, W☒

Eurasian race

Greenland race

Bean goose *Anser fabalis*
Length 75 cm (30 in). Distinguished
from greylag by lack of pale forewing,
from immature white-fronted by bill
colour, and from pink-footed by yellow
legs; gregarious; usually seen flying at
dawn and dusk; winter visitor to
Britain, north-west and central Europe.
W☒, W☒, W☒

Bean goose

Pink-footed goose
Anser brachyrhynchus
Length 65 cm (26 in). Often mixes with
greylag geese in winter, from which it
is distinguished by being smaller and
darker, with smaller head and bill;
breeds in Iceland, winter visitor to
Britain and north-west Europe. W☒,
W☒, W☒

Pink-footed goose

183

Mallard *Anas platyrhynchos*
Length 58 cm (23 in). Commonest duck; eclipse males resemble females and young; distinguished in flight from shoveler by latter's heavier bill; resident throughout Britain and Europe. ▣, ▣

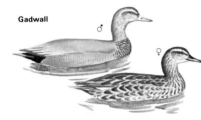

Gadwall *Anas strepera*
Length 50 cm (20 in). Eclipse males resemble females and young; in flight both sexes show black-and-white patch on trailing edge of wing, and chestnut patch on midwing; breeds in Britain and northern Europe, winters in west, central and south-west Europe. ▣, W▣

Pintail *Anas acuta*
Length 70 cm (28 in). Long, pointed tail a conspicuous feature, eclipse males resemble females and young; flies fast; winters in most of Britain and Europe. ▣, W▣

Wigeon *Anas penelope*
Length 45 cm (18 in). Fast flier; white oval patch conspicuous on male's wings in flight (grey in female); often seen in flocks; winters in most of Britain and Europe. ▣, W▣, S▬

Teal *Anas crecca*
Length 35 cm (14 in). Fast, jinking flier, usually in tight flocks; can rise very steeply; eclipse males resemble females and young; resident throughout Britain and most of Europe, summer visitor to Scandinavia. ▣, W▣

Garganey *Anas querquedula*
Length 38 cm (15 in). Conspicuous
white stripe over eye of drake; pale
forewing visible in flight; male has an
odd crackling call; breeds throughout
most of Britain and Europe, winters in
Spain. S ⊠

Garganey

Shoveler *Spatula clypeata*
Length 50 cm (20 in). Heavy, spatula-
like bill very distinctive; flies in
slightly head-down position; eclipse
males resemble females and young;
resident in most of Britain and Europe,
also breeds in north and east, and
winters in south-west Europe. ⊠, W ⊟

Shoveler

Shelduck *Tadorna tadorna*
Length 60 cm (24 in). Upright stance
similar to geese; pied plumage
conspicuous and males have distinctive
knob on bill; nests in burrows; breeds
on northern European and British
coasts, and in parts of eastern Europe.
⊟

Shelduck

Scaup *Aythya marila*
Length 45 cm (18 in). Male's colours
duller during eclipse; scaup usually
occur on coasts in winter, often in
deeper water than tufted duck or
pochard; winter visitor to Britain,
north-west Europe and Mediterranean,
breeding in far north. W ⊟, ⊠

Scaup

Tufted duck *Aythya fuligula*
Length 43 cm (17 in). Both sexes have
head crest – larger in male; appears
short-winged in flight; eclipse males
and young resembles females, but lack
crest; resident in Britain, north-west
and central Europe, also breeds in far
north and winters in far south. ⊠,
W ⊟

Tufted duck

Pochard *Aythya ferina*
Length 45 cm (18 in). In flight, neither
sex shows white wing-bars, but throat
and underparts contrast visibly;
resident in Britain, central and north-
west Europe, elsewhere breeds in far
north and winters in far south. ⊠,
W⊟

Goldeneye *Bucephala clangula*
Length 48 cm (19 in). Shape of head is
characteristic; large white wing-patches
visible in flight; forms tight groups;
wings make loud whistle in flight;
breeds in tree holes in Scandinavia,
Germany and Scotland, winters on
inland lakes, and coasts. ⊠, W⊟

Common scoter *Melanitta nigra*
Length 50 cm (20 in). May be seen
flying low over water, in line or in
tight flocks; breeds in far north of
Europe, including Britain, winters on
west European coasts. W⊟, S⊠

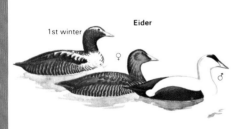

Eider *Somateria mollissima*
Length 60 cm (24 in). Flies low over sea
in loose flocks; white-above-and-black-
below pattern very distinctive on
water; heavy looking head and bill
distinctive also; resident in Britain,
north-west Europe and Scandinavia. ⊟

Red-breasted merganser
Mergus serrator
Length 55 cm (22 in). Low, long body
with distinctive tufted head and
hooked bill; eclipse males and young
resemble females; breed in Britain and
north-west Europe, winters in west and
central Europe. ⊠, W⊟

Goosander *Mergus merganser*
Length 63 cm (25 in). Outline shape
very similar to red-breasted merganser;
eclipse males and young resemble
females; nests in tree holes in Britain
and north-west Europe; winters in west
and central Europe. ⊠, W⊟

Goosander

Smew *Mergus albellus*
Length 41 cm (16 in). Very short bill;
drake unmistakeable in white plumage;
nests in trees by lakes and rivers, but
in winter also found in sheltered sea
bays; usually seen with other ducks;
breeds in far north, but winters over
most of Europe. W⊠

Smew

Griffon vulture *Gyps fulvus*
Length 1.1 m (44 in). Distinguished
from eagles found in similar regions by
former's short, square tail; head
protrudes less also; usually seen
soaring, sometimes in groups; resident
in Spain, Sardinia, Sicily and eastern
Mediterranean. ◮

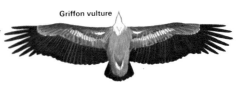

Griffon vulture

Golden eagle *Aquila chrysaetos*
Length 83 cm (33 in). Huge; usually
seen soaring on broad, fingered wings;
tail very noticeable, requires large
territory and hence not common;
resident in Britain, north and north-
east Europe, Spain and Mediterranean
countries. ◮, ◳

Golden eagle

Buzzard *Buteo buteo*
Length 53 cm (21 in). Plumage quite
variable; commonest large soaring bird,
usually seen circling slowly on air
currents; may be seen perching on
rocks and in trees; resident throughout
most of Britain and Europe. ▣, ⊞, ⊡,
◮, ◳

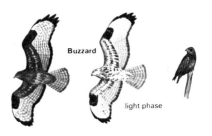

Buzzard

light phase

187

Rough-legged buzzard

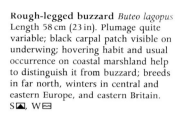

Honey buzzard

Rough-legged buzzard *Buteo lagopus*
Length 58 cm (23 in). Plumage quite
variable; black carpal patch visible on
underwing; hovering habit and usual
occurrence on coastal marshland help
to distinguish it from buzzard; breeds
in far north, winters in central and
eastern Europe, and eastern Britain.
S◰, W▱

Honey buzzard *Pernis apivorus*
Length 53 cm (21 in). Plumage quite
variable; base of wings more narrow
than buzzard's and barred; long,
straight-sided tail conspicuous feature;
breeds in Britain, central and southern
Europe. S◉, S◉

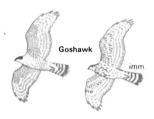

Goshawk

imm.

Goshawk *Accipiter gentilis*
Length 48–60 cm (19–24 in). White
undertail coverts and white stripe over
the eye characteristic, slower wing-
beats than sparrowhawk but fast flight;
females larger than males; resident
throughout most of Britain and Europe.
◉, ◉

Sparrowhawk

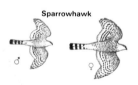

♂

♀

Sparrowhawk *Accipiter nisus*
Length 30–38 cm (12–15 in). Females
bigger than males; flies fast through
trees on short, broad wings;
conspicuous long, narrow tail; resident
throughout Britain and Europe. ◉, ◉

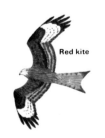

Red kite

Red kite *Milvus milvus*
Length 60–65 cm (24–26 in). Deeply
forked tail and long, angled wings
conspicuous in flight; white patches on
underwings help distinguish it from
black kite; breeds in central Europe,
resident in other isolated areas
including Wales. ◉, W▱

Black kite *Milvus migrans*
Length 53 cm (21 in). Lack of white
patches on undersides of long, angled
wings help distinguish it from red kite;
tail only slightly forked; often seen
near human environments; breeds in
central and southern Europe. ▣

Osprey *Pandion haliaetus*
Length 58 cm (23 in). Hovers over lakes
and rivers before plunging noisily into
water to snatch a fish; long, angled
wings; head small; plumage and eye
markings distinctive; breeds in north
and north-east Europe (including
Scotland), winters in extreme south-
west Europe. S▨

Marsh harrier *Circus aeruginosus*
Length 53 cm (21 in). Note grey on
wings of males; females and young
darker; prefers reed beds and other
marshy areas; flies low over the ground
in search of prey; widespread in
Europe in summer (including Britain),
contracting to southern Europe in
winter. ▨

Hen harrier *Circus cyaneus*
Length 48 cm (19 in). Breeds on
moorlands and in conifer plantations,
but winters on marshland; flies low
over the ground in search of prey;
breeds in north and north-east Europe
(including Britain), winters in south-
west and west Europe. ▰, W▨

Montagu's harrier *Circus pygargus*
Length 40 cm (15½ in). Narrower tail and
wings distinguish it from the marsh
and hen harriers; glides low over the
ground in search of prey; breeds in
most of Europe. S▰, S▨

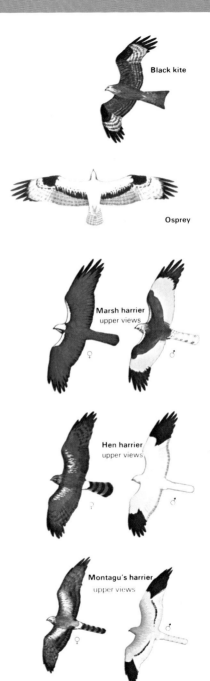

Black kite

Osprey

Marsh harrier
upper views
♀   ♂

Hen harrier
upper views
♀   ♂

Montagu's harrier
upper views
♀   ♂

189

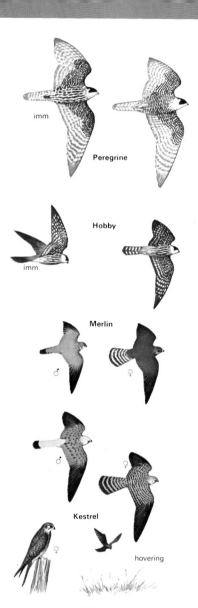

Peregrine *Falco peregrinus*
Length 40–50 cm (16–20 in). Broad, curved, pointed wings and shortish tail; powerful flier using shallow wing-beats, stoops from a height at great speed and strikes prey in mid-air; breeds throughout most of north and north-east Europe (including Britain), winters over most of Europe. S▲, ◨, W▭

Hobby *Falco subbuteo*
Length 28 cm (11 in). Long, sickle-shaped wings and longish tail; swift-like in flight; flies fast to catch insects and small birds; may nest in old crows' nests; widespread summer visitor to Britain and Europe. S◨, S◨, S◨

Merlin *Falco columbarius*
Length 30 cm (12 in). Direct, low flight, using fast wing-beats alternating with short glides; smaller than kestrel; breeds in north and north-west Europe, winters in central and southern Europe, resident in Britain. ▲, ◨, W▭

Kestrel *Falco tinnunculus*
Length 35 cm (14 in). Easily spotted when it hovers, head motionless, while it searches for prey; often seen by roadside verges; commonest falcon; widespread throughout Britain and Europe. ◨, ◨, ◨

Red/willow grouse *Lagopus lagopus*
40 cm (15½ in). Stout birds with short, rounded wings; different plumages of the two subspecies a result of long geographical isolation; low-flying; short bursts of wing-beats followed by glides; red grouse resident in Britain and willow grouse resident in Scandinavia. ◨

Ptarmigan *Lagopus mutus*
Length 35 cm (14 in). All white in winter, except for black tail; in summer wings and underparts white and rest of body mottled yellow-brown; resident in Britain and Scandinavia, and Pyrenees.

Capercaillie *Tetrao urogallus*
Length: male 85 cm (34 in); female 60 cm (24 in). Shy bird, easily recognized by huge size and turkey-like appearance; female distinguished from female black grouse by orange breast patch of former; resident in central Europe, northern Spain, Scotland and Scandinavia.

Black grouse *Lyrurus tetrix*
Length 50 cm (20 in). Gregarious bird of moorland/woodland margins; gathers at certain times of the year for noisy communal display at a site called a lek; lyre-shaped tail of male very distinctive; resident in Britain, north and north-east Europe.

Red-legged partridge *Alectoris rufa*
Length 35 cm (14 in). Upright stance noticeable; runs for cover rapidly if disturbed, only flying as last resort – flies low with short bursts of wing-beats followed by glides; resident in Britain, and west and south-west Europe.

Grey partridge *Perdix perdix*
Length 30 cm (12 in). Dumpy and smaller than pheasant, with much shorter tail; horseshoe mark on breast more prominent in male; runs fast; resident throughout Britain and northern Europe, except south-west.

♂ summer

Ptarmigan

♀ summer

Capercaillie

Black grouse

Red-legged partridge

imm.

Partridge

191

Pheasant

Pheasant *Phasianus colchicus*
Length: male 85 cm (34 in); female
58 cm (23 in). Common gamebird
extensively bred for sport; long tail
and short wide wings distinctive in
flight; gutteral call often heard from
undergrowth; resident through most of
Britain and Europe. ,

Quail

Quail *Coturnix coturnix*
Length 18 cm (7 in). Uncommon,
secretive bird rarely seen, although
'whet-my-lips' call is useful
identification feature; favours chalky
grassland soils; widespread summer
visitor to Britain and Europe. S⬚, S⬚

Crane

Crane *Grus grus*
Length 1.1 m (44 in). Larger size and
outstretched neck distinguish flying
crane from grey heron; grey colour
distinguishes it from ibises, storks and
spoonbills; may fly in V-formation or
soar; tail looks bushy when standing;
breeds in extreme north and north-east
Europe (excluding Britain) winters in
south-west Europe. ⬚

Water rail

Water rail *Rallus aquaticus*
Length 28 cm (11 in). Skulking bird of
thick vegetation, usually seen in hard
weather; long bill and legs distinctive;
makes squealing and grunting noises;
resident throughout Britain and
Europe. ⬚

Spotted crake

Spotted crake *Porzana porzana*
Length 23 cm (9 in). Very shy, prefers
dense vegetation; short bill and buff
undercoverts distinguish it from water
rail; call is repetitive, high-pitched
'wheet'; widespread summer visitor,
winters in south-west Europe. ⬚

Corncrake *Crex crex*
Length 28 cm (11 in). Call sounds like 'crex, crex'; more often seen than heard; breeds in fields and grassland; in flight, dangling legs distinguish it from young partridges and quail; widespread summer visitor, winters in south-west Europe. 🖾, 🖅

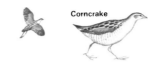

Moorhen *Gallinula chloropus*
Length 33 cm (13 in). Red bill and flicking white tail feathers distinctive; head jerks when swimming and tail held erect; resident throughout Britain and Europe. 🖾

Coot *Fulica atra*
Length 38 cm (15 in). White bill best feature to distinguish adults from adult moorhen; juvenile coot lack white plumage stripe of moorhen; appears more hump-backed when swimming; resident throughout Britain and Europe. 🖾

Oystercatcher *Haematopus ostralegus*
Length 43 cm (17 in). Distinctive pied bird with large orange bill; wing-bars visible in flight; winter and immature birds have white chin strap; call is 'kleep, kleep'; often forms flocks and may associate with other waders; resident in western Europe (including Britain) and Mediterranean. 🖃, S🖾

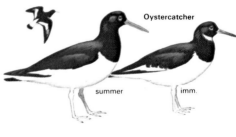

summer   imm.

Lapwing *Vanellus vanellus*
Length 30 cm (12 in). Adults distinguished by large head crest and contrasting plumage; rounded wings, showing black and white undersides, conspicuous in flight; often forms flocks; resident in much of Britain and Europe, visitor elsewhere. 🖾, 🖾, W🖃, 🖿

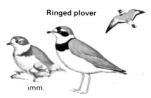

Ringed plover

imm.

Ringed plover *Charadrius hiaticula*
Length 20 cm (8 in). Well camouflaged
on shingle beaches on which it nests;
white wing-bar visible in flight; breeds
in Britain and northern Europe, (with
some residents in Britain) winters on
coasts of north-west, west and southern
Europe. ⊟

Little ringed plover

Little ringed plover *Charadrius dubius*
Length 15 cm (6 in). Pale pink legs;
darker bill than ringed plover; also
lacks wing-bar; different habitat also a
clue to identification; widespread
summer visitor to Britain and Europe.
S◪, S⊟

Kentish plover

Kentish plover
Charadrius alexandrinus
Length 15 cm (6 in). Upperparts paler
than ringed plover's; legs black; neck
band incomplete; resident of south and
south-west European coasts. ⊟

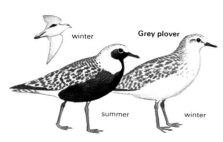

winter   Grey plover

summer   winter

Grey plover *Charadrius squatarola*
Length 28 cm (11 in). Greyer and
plumper than golden plover; note black
patches under wings in flight; face,
breast and belly black in summer;
winter visitor to Britain, north-west
and southern Europe. ⊟

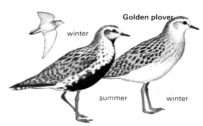

Golden plover

winter

summer   winter

Golden plover *Charadrius apricaria*
Length 28 cm (11 in). More widespread
than grey plover; lacks wing-bar,
underwing patch and white rump of
grey plover; outside breeding season
often found in large flocks, sometimes
with lapwings; breeds in Britain, north
and north-west Europe, winters in
west, south-west and southern Europe.
S▭, W⊟, W◪

Turnstone *Arenaria interpres*
Length 23 cm (9 in). Well camouflaged against rocks and seaweeds; notice short orange, yellow or red legs; black, brown and white wing pattern conspicuous in flight; breeds in extreme northern Europe, winters on western coasts. ▨

Snipe *Gallinago gallinago*
Length 28 cm (11 in). Characteristic zig-zag flight when flushed; orange-brown tail visible in flight; note long bill; resident in Britain, north and central Europe, elsewhere winters in west and south. ▨, ▭

Jack snipe *Lymnocryptes minimus*
Length 20 cm (8 in). Shorter bill, unmarked tail, and less twisting flight when flushed help to distinguish this bird from snipe; breeds in extreme north-east Europe, winters in west, central and southern Europe. ▨

Woodcock *Scolopax rusticola*
Length 35 cm (14 in). Dumpy body and long bill; flies adeptly through trees with clatter of wings if flushed; usually nocturnal, may be seen flying at dusk and dawn; resident in Britain and most of Europe, also breeds in Scandinavia and winters in southern Europe. ◉

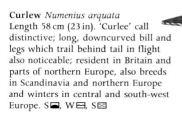

Curlew *Numenius arquata*
Length 58 cm (23 in). 'Curlee' call distinctive; long, downcurved bill and legs which trail behind tail in flight also noticeable; resident in Britain and parts of northern Europe, also breeds in Scandinavia and northern Europe and winters in central and south-west Europe. S▭, W▨, S▨

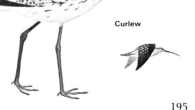

195

Whimbrel *Numenius phaeopus*
Length 40 cm (15½ in). Call is a series of
short whistles; striped crown
distinguishes it from curlew; breeds in
north-west and north-east Europe
(including Britain), winters in south-
west Europe. S ▭

Black-tailed godwit *Limosa limosa*
Length 40 cm (15½ in). Bill less curved
than bar-tailed godwit's; black-and-
white tail and white wing-bars
noticeable in flight; breeds in north
and central Europe, winters in Britain,
west and south-west Europe. S ▭, W ▭

Bar-tailed godwit *Limosa lapponica*
Length 38 cm (15 in). Barred tail
noticeable in flight, note also shape of
tail compared with black-tailed
godwit's; tumbles out of sky in untidy
spiral; breeds in extreme northern
Europe, winters in west and south
(including Britain). W ▭

Common sandpiper *Tringa hypoleucos*
Length 20 cm (8 in). Tail bobs when
walking; flies low over water; nearly
always seen near water's edge; breeds
throughout most of Europe, resident in
southernmost part of range. ▭

Green sandpiper *Tringa ochropus*
Length 23 cm (9 in). Smaller and with
shorter neck than greenshank; usually
seen singly or in small groups; breeds
in north and north-east Europe,
winters in Britain and western Europe.
▭, ▭

Wood sandpiper *Tringa glareola*
Length 20 cm (8 in). Longer legs and
bill distinguishes it from common
sandpiper; yellow legs protrude
beyond tail in flight; call is 'twee-twee-
twee'; breeds in northern Europe.
S ✉, S ▥

Redshank *Tringa totanus*
Length 28 cm (11 in). White trailing
edges of wings and white rump visible
in flight; orange-red legs and partly
orange bill also conspicuous; breeds in
north and east and winters in south
and west. ▥, S ✉

Spotted redshank *Tringa erythropus*
Length 30 cm (12 in). Very dark
summer plumage distinguishes it from
redshank; call is 'too-it'; breeds in
extreme north of Europe. W ✉, W ▥

Greenshank *Tringa nebularia*
Length 30 cm (12 in). White wedge on
tail is distinctive in flight; slightly
upturned bill; breeds in northern
Britain and Europe; winters around
Mediterranean. S ◨, W ✉, W ▥

Ruff *Philomachus pugnax*
Length: males 30 cm (12 in); females
23 cm (9 in). Colour of summer males'
ruff very variable; in winter males
resemble larger females; small head and
upright stance conspicuous; may form
small flocks; breeds in Britain and
northern Europe. ✉, S ◩, W ▥

Wood sandpiper

under view

upper view

Redshank

winter

summer

Spotted redshank

Greenshank

Ruff

♂ winter

♂ summer

Knot *Calidris canutus*
Length 25 cm (10 in). Distinctive red summer plumage; in winter, dullness and lack of features is a clue to identity; usually forms large, closely knit flocks; winter visitor to west and south-west European coasts (including Britain). W ▱

Purple sandpiper *Calidris maritima*
Length 20 cm (8 in). Dumpy looking bird; darkest small sandpiper; orange-yellow legs and bill base conspicuous at a distance; breeds in far north, winter visitor to west and north-west coasts of Europe (including Britain). ▱

Dunlin *Calidris alpina*
Length 18 cm (7 in). At a distance, flocks appear as shimmering black-and-white cloud; narrow white wing-bars and white sides of rump show in flight; resident in parts of Europe (including Britain), elsewhere breeds in north and north-west and winters in south and south-west Europe. S ▱, W ▱, W ▱

Curlew sandpiper *Calidris ferruginea*
Length 20 cm (8 in). White rump in flight distinguishes it from other sandpipers; distinctive red summer plumage; longer legs and bill distinguish it from winter dunlin; passage migrant across much of Europe, including Britain. W ▱, W ▱

Little stint *Calidris minuta*
Length 13 cm (5 in). Smallest European wader; notice black legs; often flocks with other small waders; passage migrant across much of Europe, including Britain. W ▱, W ▱

198

Sanderling *Calidris alba*
Length 20 cm (8 in). Runs jerkily along strandline following retreating waves; striking white wing-bar in flight; call is 'plick-plick'; winter visitor to west, south and south-west European coasts (including Britain). W⊟

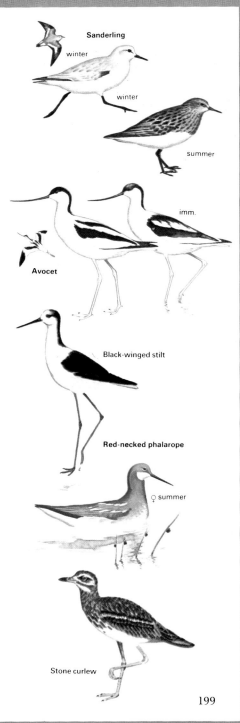

Sanderling

winter

winter

summer

Avocet *Recurvirostra avosetta*
Length 43 cm (17 in). Distinctive upturned bill and delicate black-and-white plumage; may be seen in groups wading or swimming; breeds in parts of southern and north-west Europe (including Britain), winters in west and south of Europe. ⊟

Avocet

imm.

Black-winged stilt
Himantopus himantopus
Length 38 cm (15 in). Readily distinguished by long, pink legs and thin, straight bill; dark plumage areas of juvenile are barred; breeds in south and south-west Europe. S⊟

Black-winged stilt

Red-necked phalarope
Phalaropus lobatus
Length 17 cm (6½ in). Summer plumage distinctive; usually seen singly or in small groups; fairly approachable; breeds in extreme north and north-west Europe, including Britain. ⊟, W⊠

Red-necked phalarope

♀ summer

Stone curlew *Burhinus oedicnemus*
Length 40 cm (15½ in). Streaked plumage; large eyes and distinctive head shape; may run to safety if disturbed; flies low over the ground; breeds in Britain, northern and central Europe, winters in south-west Europe. S⊡

Stone curlew

Great skua *Stercorarius skua*
Length 60 cm (24 in). Not widely distributed; may be mistaken for a short-tailed version of a young herring gull but note white wing-patches; may be seen in company of gulls; breeds on extreme north-west coasts of Europe, including Britain, winters in the Atlantic. S⊟, S▬

Arctic skua *Stercorarius parasiticus*
Length 45 cm (18 in). Commonest skua; 2 colour phases; may be seen chasing terns; shape of tail is useful clue to identification; breeds on extreme north and north-west coasts of Europe (including Britain). S⊟, S▬

Great black-backed gull
Larus marinus
Length 68 cm (27 in). Large size and darker wings and back distinguish it from lesser black-backed; legs pink; slow wing-beats; breeds in north and north-east Europe, including Britain, winters on north, south and west European coasts. ⊟, W▨

Lesser black-backed gull *Larus fuscus*
Length 53 cm (21 in). Commoner than great black-backed; back and wings slate-grey; legs yellow; breeds in north and north-west Europe, including Britain, winters in west, central and south-west Europe. ⊟, ▬

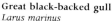

Herring gull *Larus argentatus*
Length 55 cm (22 in). Often encountered inland feeding on ploughed fields, rubbish tips, etc; larger size helps to distinguish it from common gull; resident on most British and European coasts and inland occasionally, also found inland in winter. ⊟, S▬, W▨

Common gull *Larus canus*
Length 40 cm (15½ in). Smaller and more slender than herring gull; yellow-green legs and no red spot on greenish bill; white on wing-tips distinguishes it from kittiwake; resident on many northern coasts and moors, including Britain, breeds also in Scandinavia, and widespread across south, south-west and west Europe in winter. ⊟, S◪, ⊟, W☒

Kittiwake *Rissa tridactyla*
Length 40 cm (15½ in). Dainty gull whose all-black wing-tips distinguish it from common gull; legs black; breeds on west, north and north-west British and European coasts, winters in Atlantic. ⊟

Mediterranean gull
Larus melanocephalus
Length 38 cm (15 in). Slightly heavier appearance, lack of black on adult's wings, and in summer blacker head, distinguish it from black-headed gull; breeds in extreme south-east of Europe, winters around Mediterranean. ⊟, S⊠

Black-headed gull *Larus ridibundus*
Length 35 cm (14 in). In summer bird has brown head and scarlet legs; black on wings helps to distinguish it from Mediterranean gull; resident in Britain and much of Europe, also breeds in east and winters in south and west. ⊟, S◪, W☒, W⊠

Black tern *Chlidonias niger*
Length 25 cm (10 in). Summer plumage unmistakeable; dark body with white undersides of wings and tail; usually feeds by taking insects from water surface; breeds in scattered colonies over much of Europe. S⊠, S⊟

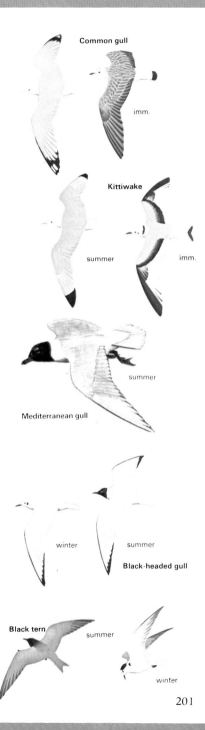

Common gull

imm.

Kittiwake

summer

imm.

summer

Mediterranean gull

winter

summer

Black-headed gull

Black tern

summer

winter

Sandwich tern

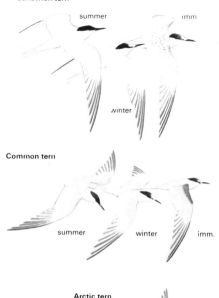

summer

imm

winter

Common tern

summer   winter   imm.

Arctic tern

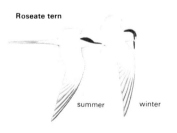

summer

Roseate tern

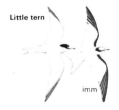

summer   winter

Little tern

imm

Sandwich tern *Sterna sandvicensis*
Length 40 cm (15½ in). Black bill has
yellow tip; legs black; breeds on coasts
of eastern and northern Britain and
Europe. S▨

Common tern *Sterna hirundo*
Length 35 cm (14 in). Lighter
underparts and black bill tip help
distinguish it from Arctic tern; red
legs; often seen in groups, plunging
into water for food; breeds in many
parts of Britain and Europe. S▨, S▨

Arctic tern *Sterna paradisaea*
Length 37 cm (14½ in). All-red bill and
lighter wing-tips distinguish it from
common tern; legs change from red to
black in winter; breeds in north and
north-west Europe, including Britain.
S▨

Roseate tern *Sterna dougallii*
Length 38 cm (15 in). Very pale, lighter
above than arctic or common terns, tail
longer and more deeply forked, flight
buoyant; breeds in Britain, winters in
extreme south-west Europe. S▨

Little tern *Sterna albifrons*
Length 22 cm (8½ in). Smallest European
tern; legs yellowish; flies with rapid
wing-beats; very vocal and active;
breeds on many European coasts,
including Britain. S▨

Razorbill *Alca torda*
Length 40 cm (15½ in). Thicker bill
distinguishes it from guillemot; young
and winter adults greyer; may be seen
flying in line low over sea in small
flocks; breeds in Britain and Europe,
winters in Atlantic and North Sea. ▭

Guillemot *Uria aalge*
Length 40 cm (15½ in). Slender bill
distinguishes it from razorbill; young
and winter adults greyer; may be seen
in small flocks flying in line low over
the sea; breeds in Britain and Europe,
winters in Atlantic and North Sea. ▭

Puffin *Fratercula arctica*
Length 30 cm (12 in). Large head and
bill conspicuous, particularly in flight;
nests colonially in burrows; breeds in
Britain and northern Europe, winters in
Atlantic and North Sea. ▭

Stock dove *Columba oenas*
Length 33 cm (13 in). Wings more
pointed than wood pigeon's, also
smaller; black-tipped tail and black
trailing edge to wings; may flock,
sometimes with wood pigeons; flies
faster than wood pigeon; resident in
Britain, western and southern Europe,
summer visitor to other parts of
Europe. ◼, ◿

Wood pigeon *Columba palumbus*
Length 39 cm (16 in). White collar and
plum-coloured breast distinctive; white
wing-bars visible in flight; wings make
clattering sound when bird takes off;
resident in Britain, western and
southern Europe, summer visitor to
other parts of Europe. ◼, ◿, ⊞

Razorbill
winter · summer
winter
Guillemot
summer
Puffin
summer · winter
Stock dove
Wood pigeon

203

Turtle dove

imm.

Collared dove

Cuckoo

Scops owl

Little owl

Turtle dove *Streptopelia turtur*
Length 28 cm (11 in). Thinner neck
than other doves and pigeons;
chequered wing pattern and dark tail;
soothing 'coo' call; breeds in most parts
of Britain and Europe, except
Scandinavia. S◼, S◪

Collared dove *Streptopelia decaocto*
Length 28 cm (11 in). Neck band is
readily identifiable feature; cooing call
is trisyllabic, with emphasis on second
syllable; resident throughout Britain
and much of Europe. ◪

Cuckoo *Cuculus canorus*
Length 33 cm (13 in). Male 'cuckoo' call
is best feature for indicating presence;
in flight (usually low over the ground)
may look hawk-like, but has rounder
tail, thin bill and pointed wings; note 2
plumage forms; breeds in all parts of
Britain and Europe. S◼, S◪, S◣, S◪

Scops owl *Otus scops*
Length 20 cm (8 in). Small with 'ear'
tufts; less squat appearance than little
owl; nocturnal, with bell-like call;
breeds in southern Europe. S◼, S◪

Little owl *Athene noctua*
Length 23 cm (9 in). Bounding,
woodpecker-like flight; partly diurnal,
and often seen perching on posts or
tree branches; pale eyebrows
conspicuous; yelping call; resident in
Britain and much of Europe. ◪, ◼, ◧

Tengmalm's owl *Aegolius funereus*
Length 25 cm (10 in). White face and
squarish head conspicuous; nocturnal,
except during Arctic summer; resident
in much of central and northern
Europe. ⊞

Snowy owl *Nyctea scandiaca*
Length 60 cm (24 in). Unmistakeable;
female larger than male with brown
spots; usually hunts during the day;
population varies: in some years found
in central and western Europe, far
south of Arctic breeding range. ◤, ◣,
W ⊟

Long-eared owl *Asio otus*
Length 35 cm (14 in). Recognizable by
long 'ear'-tufts and long face: flies with
slow wing-beats; calls with long, drawn
out hoot; nocturnal; resident in Britain
and much of Europe; summer visitor in
extreme north. ⊞, ◉, W ▨

Short-eared owl *Asio flammeus*
Length 38 cm (15 in). Diurnal habits,
together with dark wrist patches and
wing-tips, help to identify bird; flight
conspicuously bouncing or gliding, low
over the ground; resident in Britain,
central and western Europe, elsewhere
summer visitor in north and winter
visitor in south. ▨, ◉, ⊞

Tawny owl *Strix aluco*
Length 38 cm (15 in). Nocturnal, flying
on short, broad wings; calls an abrupt
'ke-vick' and 'too-whit-too-whoo' hoot;
most widespread owl; 2 colour phases:
brown and grey; resident in most parts
of Britain and Europe. ◉, ▨, ⊞

Tengmalm's owl

imm

Snowy owl

♀

♂

Long-eared owl

Short-eared owl

Tawny owl

rufous phase

grey phase

pale subspecies

Barn owl

dark subspecies

Barn owl *Tyto alba*
Length 35 cm (14 in). Sometimes seen during the day, but mainly nocturnal; ghostly, floating flight pattern; two subspecies: pale and dark, but both lighter than most other owls; resident in most parts of Britain (pale) and Europe (dark).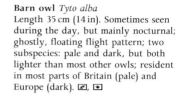

Nightjar

Nightjar *Caprimulgus europaeus*
Length 28 cm (11 in). Best encountered at dusk, when it may be seen searching for insects on the wing; buoyant flight; churring call may be heard; breeds throughout most parts of Britain and Europe. S▣, S▣

Swift

Swift *Apus apus*
Length 18 cm (7 in). Swept-back, crescent-shaped wings; short forked tail; very dark plumage except for throat; often forms flocks; very aerobatic; breeds throughout Britain and Europe. S▣, S▤

Alpine swift

Alpine swift *Apus melba*
Length 50 cm (20 in). Much larger than other swifts, with white underparts and brown breast band; flight very fast, often seen in flocks; breeds in southern Europe. S▲

Kingfisher

Kingfisher *Alcedo atthis*
Length 17 cm (7 in). Unmistakeable; small bird with electric-blue upper plumage that plunges from post or tree to catch fish under water; fast, whirring, low flight, can also hover; resident throughout most of Britain and Europe. ▣, W▤

Bee-eater *Merops apiaster*
Length 28 cm (11 in). Bright vari-
coloured plumage and pointed wings;
note shape of tail; may be seen in
flocks or solitary; may nest colonially
or solitarily; elegant flight, can also
hover; breeds in southern Europe. S⬛

Roller *Coracias garrulus*
Length 30 cm (12 in). Crow shaped, but
highly coloured; harsh crow-like call;
fast flyer; may perch on bush or tree in
the open, and then dart off to catch
prey; breeds in Spain, southern and
eastern Europe. S⬛, S⬛, S⬛

Hoopoe *Upupa epops*
Length 28 cm (11 in). Head crest, black-
and-white, barred wings and pink head
and breast make this bird
unmistakeable; crest is often raised and
lowered; breeds in most of Europe
except extreme north. S⬛, S⬛

Green woodpecker *Picus viridis*
Length 30 cm (12 in). Often encountered
on grassy rides and clearings; loud,
laughing call; yellow rump and green
underparts distinctive in flight;
resident throughout Britain and
Europe, except extreme north. ⬛, ⬛

Great spotted woodpecker
Dendrocopos major
Length 23 cm (9 in). Black head
distinguishes it from middle spotted
woodpecker and white wing-patches
distinguish it from lesser spotted; in
spring drums with series of rapid
blows lasting about a second; resident
in most parts of Britain and Europe. ⬛,
⬛, W⬛

Bee-eater

Roller

imm

Hoopoe

imm

imm.

Green woodpecker

♂

Great spotted
woodpecker

♂

207

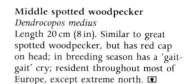

Middle spotted woodpecker
Dendrocopos medius
Length 20 cm (8 in). Similar to great
spotted woodpecker, but has red cap
on head; in breeding season has a 'gait-
gait' cry; resident throughout most of
Europe, except extreme north. ▣

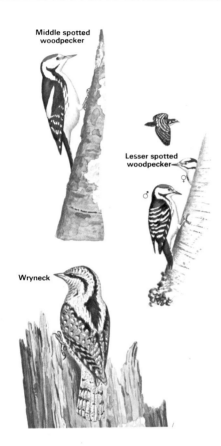

Lesser spotted woodpecker
Dendrocopos minor
Length 15 cm (6 in). Sparrow-sized;
lacks white shoulder-patches;
drumming higher pitched and more
rapid and for longer periods than great
spotted; usually stays up in trees;
resident in most parts of Britain
(excluding Scotland) and Europe. ▣

Wryneck *Jynx torquilla*
Length 18 cm (7 in). Flies faster than
other woodpeckers; skulking, tends to
hop on the ground; banded tail
distinctive in flight; breeds in many
parts of Europe (rare in Britain). S▣,
S▣

Short-toed lark *Calandrella cinerea*
Length 13 cm (5 in). Breast and
underparts lack streaked plumage;
centre of tail looks dark in flight;
makes high-pitched call on ground and
in flight; usually flies low, breeds in
southern parts of Europe. S▣

Crested lark *Galerida cristata*
Length 17 cm (6½ in). Broad wings and
short tail distinctive in flight; large
crest; sandy underwings and chestnut
tail edge also distinctive; runs fast;
often encountered in groups;
widespread European resident (rare in
Britain). ▣, ▣

Skylark *Alauda arvensis*
Length 18 cm (7 in). Often heard singing very high in the sky above: may be too high to see with naked eye; white outer tail feathers and trailing edge to wings; has small head crest; resident in most of Britain and Europe.
◩, ◪, S◻

Skylark

Woodlark *Lullula arborea*
Length 15 cm (6 in). Black-and-white wing-patches visible in flight; nests on ground but perches in trees; has shorter tail than skylark and tiny crest; resident in south-west Europe, breeds in most other parts (including Britain).
S◪, S◩

Sand martin *Riparia riparia*
Length 12 cm (4½ in). Colonial breeder in sand cliffs, river banks and quarries; fast, aerobatic flight; brown breast band diagnostic; buzz-like call; breeds throughout Europe. S◪, S◩, S◻

Swallow *Hirundo rustica*
Length 20 cm (8 in). Curved wings, red face, dark blue back and deeply forked tail characteristic; usually seen on the wing swooping aerobatically for insects; breeds throughout Britain and Europe. S◩, S◻

House martin *Delichon urbica*
Length 12 cm (4½ in). White rump, dark blue wings and white underside characteristic; stiffer flight than swallow; breeds throughout Britain and Europe. S◩, S◻

209

Tree pipit

Tree pipit *Anthus trivialis*
Length 15 cm (6 in). Spiralling song flight, which starts from tree and finishes back on the perch, is best identification feature; sharp 'tzee' call; breeds throughout Britain and Europe. S◧, S◧

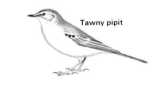

Meadow pipit

Meadow pipit *Anthus pratensis*
Length 15 cm (6 in). Browner legs than tree pipit; song flight steeply undulating; weak 'zeep' call; resident in Britain, north and north-west Europe, elsewhere breeds in extreme north and winters in south and south-west. ◧, ◧, ◧, ◧, W◧, W◧

Tawny pipit

Tawny pipit *Anthus campestris*
Length 15 cm (6 in). Adult has streaks only on head; juvenile has streaked breast also; longer tail and bill than other pipits; call is usually two notes; breeds throughout most of Europe. S◧

Rock pipit

Water/rock pipit *Anthus spinoletta*
Length 15 cm (6 in). Rock pipit is a subspecies of water pipit. Rock pipit darker and found on coasts, especially rocky; resident in Britain and north-west Europe; water pipit breeds in mountainous country, winters on inland wetlands; resident in southern Europe. ◧, S◧, S◧

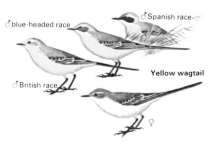

♂blue-headed race
♂Spanish race
♂British race
Yellow wagtail
♀

Yellow wagtail *Motacilla flava*
Length 17 cm (6½ in). Several subspecies exist, but yellow undersides and olive backs of males help identification, females and juveniles rather duller; breeds throughout Britain and Europe. S◧, S◧

Grey wagtail *Motacilla cinerea*
Length 17 cm (6½ in). Grey back, yellow undersides and long tail distinctive; juveniles duller; usually seen by water, twitching and flicking tail; resident throughout most of Britain and Europe.

Grey wagtail

White/pied wagtail *Motacilla alba*
Length 17 cm (6½ in). Pied wagtail is a British subspecies of white wagtail. Tail is wagged constantly; resident in most of Britain and Europe, elsewhere breeds in north-east Europe.

Pied wagtail

continental race

Red-backed shrike *Lanius collurio*
Length 17 cm (6½ in). Usually seen perching on bushes; note hooked beak; juvenile similar to female; breeds in many parts of Britain and Europe.

Red-backed shrike

Woodchat shrike *Lanius senator*
Length 17 cm (6½ in). More secretive than other shrikes, hiding among bushes and foliage; female duller version of male; breeds in southern Europe.

Woodchat shrike

imm.

Great grey shrike *Lanius excubitor*
Length 25 cm (10 in). Prefers more wooded areas than other shrikes, but may be seen in open country; may hover; resident in most of Europe, winter visitor to Britain.

northern race

southern race

Great grey shrike

211

Golden oriole *Oriolus oriolus*
Length 25 cm (10 in). Plumage of male
makes it unmistakeable; female can be
mistaken for green woodpecker, but
note different shape; breeds throughout
most of Europe. S▣

Starling *Sturnus vulgaris*
Length 22 cm (8½ in). Shorter-tailed than
blackbird, and iridescent plumage
shows when close up; flies with rapid
wing-beats; often seen near human
habitation; widespread British and
European resident. ▣, ▨

Waxwing *Bombycilla garrulus*
Length 17 cm (6½ in). Short yellow-
tipped tail and head crest noticeable;
may be seen in flocks, but occurrence
erratic; breeds in extreme north and
north-east Europe, winters in Britain
and central Europe. ▣, W▨

Jay *Garrulus glandarius*
Length 35 cm (14 in). Often raises crest,
giving an angular outline to the head;
weak, flapping flight on broad wings,
showing striking blue flashes and
white rump; resident throughout
Britain and Europe. ▣, ▨

Magpie *Pica pica*
Length 46 cm (18 in). In flight looks
black-and-white; very long tail and
rounded wings; young birds have
shorter tails; weak flier with
characteristic gliding flight; resident
throughout Britain and Europe. ▨, ▣

Alpine chough

Chough

imm.

Jackdaw

Rook

Carrion crow

Raven

Chough *Pyrrhocorax pyrrhocorax*
Length 38 cm (15 in). In flight very
rounded wings and square tail; alpine
chough (*P. graculus*) is same size, with
similar habits but soars more often;
both have patchy, mainly western and
southern European distribution; alpine
chough confined to mountainous areas
of southern Europe. ▲, ⊟

Jackdaw *Corvus monedula*
Length 33 cm (13 in). Small crow which
often forms flocks and is a strong,
sometimes aerobatic flier; call is a
repeated, high-pitched 'jack'; resident
in most Britain and Europe, absent
from far north. ▨, ◘

Rook *Corvus frugilegus*
Length 45 cm (18 in). Less stocky than
carrion crow with loosely feathered
thighs; colonial nester, usually seen in
flocks; faster wing-beats than carrion
crow; resident throughout Britain and
Europe. ▨, ◘

Carrion crow *Corvus corone*
Length 45 cm (18 in). Lacks the bright
feathers and white chin of rook;
resident in Britain and western Europe;
subspecies – hooded crow (*C.c. cornix*) –
has grey body and head, and is
confined to western Britain and eastern
Europe. ▨

Raven *Corvus corax*
Length 64 cm (25 in). Large crow with
heavy bill and long, wedge shaped tail;
often seen soaring, aerobatic flight; call
is a harsh croak; resident in mountain
regions throughout Britain and Europe.
▲, ▬, ⊟

213

Dipper *Cinculus cinculus*
Length 17 cm (6½ in). Looks like a large wren with white bib; perches on boulders, bobbing up and down; flight direct with rapid wing-beats; swims well, sometimes under water; resident throughout Britain and Europe. ✉

Wren *Troglodytes troglodytes*
Length 10 cm (4 in). Tiny, with short cocked tail; often keeps hidden in cover; song surprisingly loud; widespread resident throughout Britain and Europe. ⬛, ⬛, ⬛, ⬛, ✉

Dunnock *Prunella modularis*
Length 15 cm (6 in). Thin bill distinguishes it from true sparrows; hops, rather than runs; feeds on the ground; high-pitched, piping song delivered from exposed perch; resident in much of Britain and Europe, also breeding only further north. ⬛, ⬛, ⬛

Cetti's warbler *Cettia cetti*
Length 15 cm (6 in). Rufous upperparts and greyish white underside distinguish it from similar species; very loud 'cettee' song produced from cover; resident in western and southern Europe. ✉

Savi's warbler *Locustella luscinioides*
Length 15 cm (6 in). Tail long and rounded; song similar to grasshopper warbler but lower-pitched; often chooses reeds or bushes as song perches; breeds in Britain and much of Europe. S✉

Grasshopper warbler
Locustella naevia
Length 13 cm (5 in). Distinguished by song, sounding like a ratchet on a fishing reel; very shy, more often heard than seen; breeds throughout Britain and Europe, except for the south-west. S

Grasshopper warbler

Sedge warbler

Sedge warbler
Acrocephalus schoenobaenus
Length 13 cm (5 in). Note light eye stripe and square tail; song includes melodic phrases and harsh notes. Near vertical song flight; breeds throughout Britain and Europe, except for the south-west. S ⊠

Marsh warbler *Acrocephalus palustris*
Length 13 cm (5 in). Similar to reed warbler but paler legs; song varied and musical with much mimicry, but without reed warbler's harsh notes; breeds in Britain, central, northern and eastern Europe. S ⊠

Marsh warbler

Reed warbler *Acrocephalus scirpaceus*
Length 13 cm (5 in). Rather elongated forehead and rounded tail, spread out in flight; song contains grating notes, normally given from a reed stem; sometimes mimics other birds; breeds throughout Britain and Europe, except for the north. S ⊠

Reed warbler

Melodious warbler
Hippolais polyglotta
Length 13 cm (5 in). More angular forehead shape than *Phylloscopus* warblers; upright stance on song perch, delivers song with bill pointed upwards; breeds in south and south-west Europe. S ⊡, S ⊠

Melodious warbler

summer

215

Garden warbler *Sylvia borin*
Length 15 cm (6 in). Identified by complete absence of striking plumage characteristics; head very rounded; song similar to blackcap's but sustained longer; breeds throughout Britain and Europe. S⬛

Blackcap *Sylvia atricapilla*
Length 15 cm (6 in). Cap on head distinguishes it from other warblers; song, given from cover is a melodious warble; call is a harsh, repeated 'tack'; breeds throughout most of Britain and Europe, resident in southern Britain and south-west Europe. S⬛, W⬛

Whitethroat *Sylvia communis*
Length 15 cm (6 in). Distinguished by long tail with white outer feathers and white throat; song flight of male is an urgent, high-pitched chattering warble; breeds throughout Britain and Europe. S⬛, S⬛, S⬛

Lesser whitethroat *Sylvia curruca*
Length 15 cm (6 in). Dark cheeks can give hooded appearance; rather skulking habits; song is a quiet warble followed by several chattering notes; breeds in Britain and Europe, except for the south-west. S⬛, S⬛, S⬛

Sardinian warbler
Sylvia melanocephala
Length 15 cm (6 in). Very active small, capped warbler; fans tail in flight; loud chattering call and quick, melodic song usually given in aerial display flight; resident in south and south-west Europe. ⬛

216

Dartford warbler *Sylvia undata*
Length 13 cm (5 in). Appears rather
dark; long tail conspicuous, held
cocked upwards, often flicking; sings
throughout the year; resident in
extreme west and south-west Europe,
and southern Britain. ◙

Dartford warbler

♂

imm.

Willow warbler *Phylloscopus trochilus*
Length 10 cm (4 in). Small active
warbler, normally distinguished from
the similar chiffchaff by weak
descending song and paler legs; breeds
throughout Britain and Europe, except
for the south. S◙, S▨, S◙

Willow warbler

imm.

Chiffchaff *Phylloscopus collybita*
Length 10 cm (4 in). Chiefly
distinguished from willow warbler by
its repetitive 'chiff-chaff' song, also has
a 'hooweet' call; breeds throughout
Britain and Europe, resident in south
and south-east. ◙, ◙, ▨

Chiffchaff

Wood warbler *Phylloscopus sibilatrix*
Length 13 cm (5 in). Very active small
warbler, distinguished from others by
bright yellow throat; song is an
accelerating trill, often uttered in
flight; breeds in Britain and central,
northern and north-western Europe.
S◙

Wood warbler

Goldcrest *Regulus regulus*
Length 10 cm (4 in). Always on the
move, feeding high in trees; forms
small flocks with tits in the winter; call
is a high-pitched repeated note;
widespread resident in Britain and
Europe. ◙, ◙

Goldcrest

imm.

217

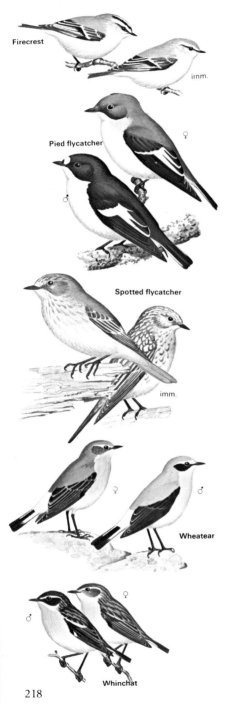

Firecrest *Regulus ignicapillus*
Length 10 cm (4 in). Distinguished from
goldcrest by eye-stripes; similar
behaviour to goldcrest; call is lower
and song is a repetitious 'zis'; resident
over parts of west, south-west, south
and central Europe, summer visitor
further north (including parts of
Britain). S◨, S◉

Pied flycatcher *Ficedula hypoleuca*
Length 13 cm (5 in). Catches insects in
tree tops from a perch; very active,
often flicking wings and tail; call is a
short 'wit' note; breeds in parts of
south-west and western Europe, Britain
and northern Europe. S◉

Spotted flycatcher *Muscicapa striata*
Length 15 cm (6 in). Very upright
stance on perch, from which it catches
flying insects, flicks tail; breeds in
most parts of Britain and Europe. S◉,
S◪

Wheatear *Oenanthe oenanthe*
Length 15 cm (6 in). Black-and-white
tail and rump pattern diagnostic,
especially in flight; often perches on
rocks or low bushes, flicking tail
frequently; breeds throughout Britain
and Europe. S◉, S◪, S▱

Whinchat *Saxicola rubetra*
Length 15 cm (6 in). Distinguished from
stonechat in all plumages by white base
to outer tail feathers; perches upright
on bushes, flicks tail; breeds in most
parts of Britain and Europe. S◉, S◪

Stonechat *Saxicola torquata*
Length 13 cm (5 in). Rather stockier
than whinchat; call sounds rather like
two pebbles being struck together;
song is a series of repeated high-
pitched notes; resident in Britain,
western and southern Europe, summer
visitor only to east. S⬚, ⬚

Stonechat

Redstart

Redstart *Phoenicurus phoenicurus*
Length 15 cm (6 in). Constantly flicking
reddish-brown tail; very active, often
catches insects in flight; breeds
throughout Britain and Europe. S⬚

Black redstart

Black redstart *Phoenicurus ochruros*
Length 15 cm (6 in). Darker than
redstart but similar in habits; often
uses old buildings for nesting sites;
resident in west and southern Europe;
breeds in Britain and central Europe.
⬚, ⬚

Robin

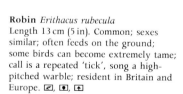

Robin *Erithacus rubecula*
Length 13 cm (5 in). Common; sexes
similar; often feeds on the ground;
some birds can become extremely tame;
call is a repeated 'tick', song a high-
pitched warble; resident in Britain and
Europe. ⬚, ⬚, ⬚

imm.

Nightingale *Luscinia megarhynchos*
Length 17 cm (6½ in). Very shy, more
often heard than seen; song is loud,
varied and musical, often uttered at
night though also during the day;
breeds in most parts of Britain and
Europe. S⬚, S⬚

Nightingale

Ring ouzel *Turdus torquatus*
Length 25 cm (10 in). Often seen in
flocks with other thrushes, especially
on migration; call note is a harsh
'chack, chack', breeds in north and
western Britain, north-eastern and
southern Europe, winters in the south-
west. ▲, ▬

Blackbird *Turdus merula*
Length 25 cm (10 in). Common; flight
undulating and jerky; tail is raised on
landing; raucous alarm call; melodious
song is given from a prominent perch;
resident throughout Britain and
Europe, except for the far north. ⬛,
▨, ⬆, ⬇

Redwing *Turdus iliacus*
Length 20 cm (8 in). Commonly seen in
flocks with fieldfares outside breeding
season; song is a variable flute-like
warble; breeds in north and north-east
Europe, winter visitor to Britain and
the rest of Europe. ⬛, W▨

Song thrush *Turdus philomelos*
Length 23 cm (9 in). Feeds in the open;
call is a weak 'seep'; resident in Britain
and western Europe, winters in south-
west, summer visitor elsewhere. ⬛, ▨,
⬆, ⬇

Mistle thrush *Turdus viscivorus*
Length 25 cm (10 in). Larger and paler
than other thrushes with bold
speckling on breast; undulating flight;
loud chattering call; resident in Britain
and much of Europe. ⬛, ▨

Fieldfare *Turdus pilaris*
Length 25 cm (10 in). In winter found in large flocks; wings closed briefly during undulating flight; loud 'chack, chack' call; winters in Britain, southern and western Europe, resident in central and northern Europe. ⬥, W⬥

Fieldfare

Marsh tit *Parus palustris*
Length 12 cm (4½ in). Best identified from the similar willow tit by call: a loud 'pitchu' and harsh 'tzee'; widespread British and European resident except for the south-west and far north. ⬥

Marsh tit

Willow tit *Parus montanus*
Length 12 cm (4½ in). Prefers wetter habitats than marsh tit; call is a grating and nasal 'tchay'; young birds hard to distinguish from young marsh tits; resident in Britain and Europe, except for the south-west. ⬥, ⬥

Willow tit

Crested tit *Parus cristatus*
Length 12 cm (4½ in). The only European tit with a head crest; song is a characteristic trill; widespread European resident, including parts of Britain. ⬥

Crested tit

Blue tit

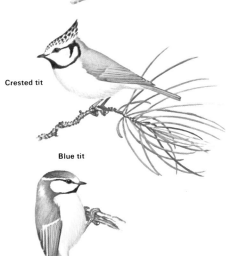

Blue tit *Parus caeruleus*
Length 12 cm (4½ in). Blue and yellow plumage characteristic; noisy and quite aggressive; scolding alarm call; widespread British and European resident. ⬥, ⬥, ⬥, W⬥

221

Coal tit *Parus ater*
Length 12 cm (4½ in). The only tit with white cheek-patches and white patch on nape of neck; call is a plaintive 'tseet'; widespread resident throughout Britain and Europe. ⊞, ◉

Great tit *Parus major*
Length 15 cm (6 in). Larger size distinguishes it from other tits; calls are many and varied but a loud 'tee-chur' song is characteristic; widespread resident throughout Britain and Europe, except for the far north. ◉, ⊞, ⊠

Long-tailed tit *Aegithalos caudatus*
Length 15 cm (6 in). Tail is longer than the tiny body; flight weak; often associates in family groups, widespread British and European resident. ◉, ⊠, ⊞, ◉

Bearded tit *Panurus biarmicus*
Length 15 cm (6 in). Male has distinctive grey head and black moustachial stripes; flight weak with fast wing-beats; characteristic pinging call; patchily distributed British and European resident. ⊠

Nuthatch *Sitta europaea*
Length 12 cm (4½ in). Climbs down as well as up trees; distinguished by bluish grey upperside and chestnut flanks; flight undulating; widespread resident throughout parts of Britain and Europe, except far north. ◉, ⊠

Treecreeper *Certhia familiaris*
Length 12 cm (4½ in). Very active,
creeping spirally up tree trunks
searching for insects; call is a single
high note; widespread resident in
Britain, north, north-east and central
Europe. ◙, ⊞

Treecreeper

House sparrow *Passer domesticus*
Length 15 cm (6 in). Associates with
man, often nesting in buildings; only
calls are repeated chirps; abundant and
widespread British and European
resident. ⊠

House sparrow

♂ summer

♀

Tree sparrow *Passer montanus*
Length 13 cm (5 in). Distinguished from
house sparrow by dark cheek-patch
and chestnut brown crown; sexes
similar; widespread British and
European resident. ◙, ⊠

Tree sparrow

Chaffinch *Fringilla coelebs*
Length 15 cm (6 in). Very common;
outside breeding season occurs in large
flocks, sometimes with other finches;
call is 'pink-pink'; British and
European resident, breeds in north-
east. ◙, ⊠, ⊞

♂

Chaffinch

♀

Brambling *Fringilla montifringilla*
Length 15 cm (6 in). Conspicuous white
rump and dark back in flight; often
seen in large flocks in winter; feeds on
the ground; breeds in extreme north of
Europe, winter visitor to Britain and
the rest of Europe. ◙, ⊠, ⊞

Brambling

♂ summer

♂ winter

♀

223

Bullfinch *Pyrrhula pyrrhula*
Length 15 cm (6 in). Both sexes have
dark cap and white rump; often seen in
pairs; plaintive whistling call;
widespread British and European
resident, except for the extreme south-
west. ◉, ◪, ⊞

Hawfinch *Coccothraustes coccothraustes*
Length 18 cm (7 in). Massive, triangular
shaped bill and striking white wing-
bar; rather shy, spends much time out
of sight in the tree tops; resident in
Britain and Europe, except for the
north. ◉

Serin *Serinus serinus*
Length 10 cm (4 in). Note striking
yellow rump in undulating flight; often
occurs in small groups; resident in
southern Europe, summer visitor to
central Europe. ◉, ◪

Greenfinch *Carduelis chloris*
Length 15 cm (6 in). Yellow on wing
and tail characteristic; flight deep and
undulating, call is a rather nasal
'tsweee'; British and European resident,
except for the north. ◪, ◉

Siskin *Carduelis spinus*
Length 12 cm (4½ in). Yellow rump and
tail-patches, much smaller and more
streaked than greenfinch; in winter
found in flocks, often with other
finches; resident in Britain, northern
and eastern Europe, winter visitor to
southern Europe. ⊞, W⊟, W◉, W◪

Goldfinch *Carduelis carduelis*
Length 13 cm (5 in). Adults have
striking plumage pattern; twittering
call, often given in flight; found in
small flocks in autumn and winter;
widespread British and European
resident. ▨, ▣, ▣

Linnet *Acanthis cannabina*
Length 13 cm (5 in). White wing and
tail-patches obvious in bounding flight;
mixes with other finches in flocks;
resident in most parts of Britain and
Europe, breeds in north and north-east.
▨, ▣, ▣

Twite *Acanthis flavirostris*
Length 13 cm (5 in). Flight is bounding,
typical of smaller finches; distinctive
nasal 'twee' call; resident in northern
Ireland and parts of Scandinavia,
winter visitor to southern Britain and
parts of northern Europe. S▲, W▤,
W▨

Redpoll *Acanthis flammea*
Length 12 cm (4½ in). Sociable bird
which often flocks with siskins in
winter, feeding in tree tops; flight
undulating; resident in Britain and
northern Europe, winter visitor to
central Europe. ▣, ▨

Crossbill *Loxia curvirostra*
Length 18 cm (7 in). Large bulky beak,
crossed at tip; the flight call, a metallic
'jip-jip', is unmistakeable; patchily
distributed resident across Britain and
Europe. ▣

225

Corn bunting

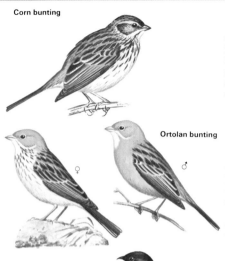

Corn bunting *Emberiza calandra*
Length 18 cm (7 in). Rather plump and heavy looking; jangling monotonous song delivered from a bush or post; resident in most of Britain and Europe, except for the north. ✈, ⊡

Ortolan bunting

♀ ♂

Ortolan bunting *Emberiza hortulana*
Length 15 cm (6 in). Adult male distinguished by greenish-grey head, female by yellow throat; widespread but rather secretive; breeds in Europe except for the west; occasional migrant to Britain. S✈, S⊡

Reed bunting

♂ ♀

Reed bunting *Emberiza schoeniclus*
Length 15 cm (6 in). Tail often flicked, showing white outer tail feathers; bodily patterned head of male is diagnostic; widespread British and European resident, breeds in north-east Europe. ▱, W✈, W⊡

Yellowhammer

♀ ♂

Yellowhammer *Emberiza citrinella*
Length 18 cm (7 in). Distinguished from similar cirl bunting by chestnut, not brown, rump; 'little bit of bread and no cheese' song of male unmistakeable; resident in most parts of Britain and Europe. ✈, ⊡

Cirl bunting

♀ ♂

Cirl bunting *Emberiza cirlus*
Length 15 cm (6 in). Facial pattern distinguishes male; rather secretive and retiring bird; resident in south, south-west and central Europe, and southern Britain. ✈, ⊡

Mammals

Hedgehog *Erinaceus europaeus*
Length 30 cm (12 in). Plump, spine-covered body, small head with pointed snout; usually active at dusk, but also nocturnal; makes hibernation nest of leaves and grass in undergrowth; occurs in most parts of Britain and Europe. ⬜, ⬜

Hedgehog

Pygmy shrew *Sorex minutus*
Length: body 6.4 cm (2½ in); tail 4.6 cm (1¾ in). Very small; long, pointed snout; tips of teeth red; active day or night; can swim and climb; nest a grass ball in cover; occurs throughout Britain and Europe, except south-west. ⬜, ⬜, ⬜

Pygmy shrew

Common shrew *Sorex araneus*
Length: body 8.7 cm (3½ in); tail 5.5 cm (2¼ in). Similar to pygmy shrew, but larger; fur grades from dark on back to pale underneath, with intermediate on sides; active day and night; climbs well; nest a grass ball in cover; occurs in most parts of Britain and Europe. ⬜, ⬜, ⬜, ⬜, ⬜, ⬜

Common shrew

Water shrew *Neomys fodiens*
Length: body 9.5 cm (3¾ in); tail 7.5 cm (3 in). Darker colour of fur helps distinguish it from other shrews; tips of teeth red; tail has double row of hairs; usually found in or near water; active day and night; occurs in most parts of Britain and Europe, except south-west and Ireland. ⬜

Water shrew

Mole *Talpa europaea*
Length 15 cm (6 in). Subterranean animal which betrays its presence by mole hills – mounds of earth – ejected at intervals in meadows and other fertile soils; plush body with tiny but powerful limbs, long snout and tiny eyes; active day and night; occurs in many parts of Britain and Europe. ⬜, ⬜, ⬜, ⬜

Mole

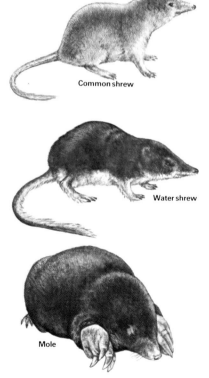

227

Long-eared bat *Plecotus auritus*
Wingspan 28 cm (11 in). Common bat, more easily identified than most due to extremely long ears; body small; emerges late, active all night, flies at 2–6 m (7–20 ft); roosts in trees, bushes, lofts; occurs in most of Britain and Europe. ▣, ▨, ▣

Pipistrelle *Pipistrellus pipistrellus*
Wingspan 25 cm (10 in). Smallest European bat, and quite common; emerges shortly after sunset; active during much of the year; twisting flight pattern; roosts in trees, caves, buildings; occurs in much of Britain and Europe. ▨, ▣

Rabbit *Oryctolagus cuniculus*
Length 40 cm (15½ in). Distinguished from hare by shorter legs, ears shorter than length of head and (usually) greyer fur; commonly encountered; active day and night, especially dawn and dusk; occurs in most of Britain and Europe. ▨, ▣, ▣, ▣, ▭, ▭

Blue (mountain) hare *Lepus timidus*
Length varies according to region: about 60 cm (24 in). Longer ears than rabbit; smaller than brown hare; found in upland regions, fur turns white in winter; less nocturnal than brown hare; often runs in wide arc; occurs in Scandinavia, Alps and uplands of Britain. ▲, ▭, ▣

Brown (common) hare *Lepus capensis*
Length varies according to region: about 65 cm (26 in). Longer legs than rabbit; black-tipped ears equal in length to head; mainly nocturnal, but sometimes diurnal; usually solitary; runs in zig-zag pattern; occurs in most of Britain and Europe. ▨, ▣, ▭, ▭

Red squirrel *Sciurus vulgaris*
Length 40 cm (15½ in). Distinguished by long, bushy tail, reddish fur and – in winter – ear-tufts; diurnal; extremely arboreal, moving skilfully through trees; may be seen on ground; occurs in most parts of Britain (local now) and Europe. ⊞, ⊡

Grey squirrel *Sciurus carolinensis*
Length 50 cm (20 in). Similar habits to red squirrel, but distinguished by larger size, greyer fur and lack of ear-tufts; diurnal; often seen on the ground; occurs in Britain and, locally, in northern Europe. ⊡, ⊞

Garden dormouse *Eliomys quercinus*
Length 30 cm (12 in). Black eye-stripe and long tail with bushy end distinctive; mainly nocturnal; often seen on the ground, especially near houses; nests in trees, holes, etc; occurs in most of Europe except extreme north. ⊡, ⊞, ✍

Edible dormouse *Glis glis*
Length 34 cm (13½ in). Smaller than grey squirrel, and with nocturnal habits; very agile and adept climber; nests in trees, holes, etc; occurs in most parts of Europe, but patchy in Britain and absent from south-west and extreme north. ⊡, ✍

Common dormouse
Muscardinus avellanarius
Length 15 cm (6 in). Large eyes, small ears and plump body distinctive; nocturnal; usually found on trees and bushes; agile climber; makes several nests – breeding, summer, and hibernation; occurs in most of Britain and Europe. ⊡, ⊞, ✍

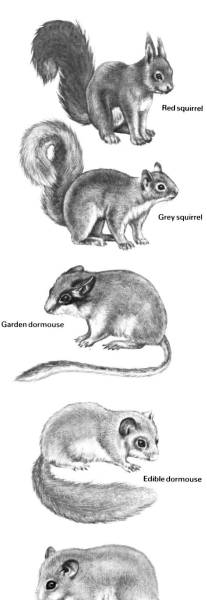

Red squirrel

Grey squirrel

Garden dormouse

Edible dormouse

Common dormouse

229

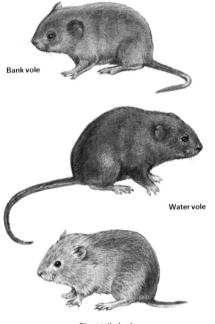

Bank vole *Clethrionomys glareolus*
Length variable, but about 20 cm (8 in).
Clearly visible ears and longish tail;
active day and night; runs fast and
climbs well; nest is made within
burrow system; occurs in most of
Britain and Europe. ⬛, ⬛, ⬛

Bank vole

Water vole *Arvicola terrestris*
Length 36 cm (14 in). Rounder face,
shorter ears and tail distinguish it from
brown rat; often makes a 'plop' as it
lands in the water from its bankside
nest; active day and night; occurs in
much of Britain, south-west and
western Europe. ⬛, ⬛

Water vole

Short-tailed vole *Microtus agrestis*
Length 18 cm (7 in). Grey-brown fur
helps to distinguish it from the redder
bank vole; more diurnal than common
vole; can swim, but seldom climbs;
may be seen in groups; prefers moist
areas, occurs in much of Britain and
Europe, except parts of south-west,
south and Ireland. ⬛, ⬛, ⬛, ⬛

Short-tailed vole

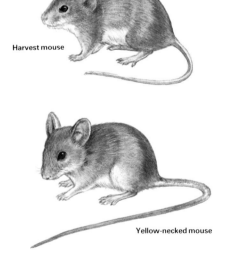

Harvest mouse

Harvest mouse *Micromys minutus*
Length 12 cm (4½ in); half this length
comprises tail. Reddish colour,
prehensile tail and small size help
identification; active mainly by day;
climbs well, especially on corn stalks
and reeds, in which ball-shaped nest is
built; occurs in much of Britain and
Europe. ⬛

Yellow-necked mouse
Apodemus flavicollis
Length 20 cm (8 in). Yellow collar on
throat distinctive; mainly nocturnal;
climbs and jumps well; may enter
houses; nests under or among roots or
in holes; occurs in many parts of
Britain and Europe. ⬛, ⬛

Yellow-necked mouse

Wood mouse *Apodemus sylvaticus*
Length 20 cm (8 in). Throat collar much less complete than yellow-necked mouse's; mainly nocturnal; climbs and jumps well; may be seen in groups; nests in burrows, but may occupy bird's nest; occurs in most of Britain and Europe. ⬛, ⬛, ⬛

Wood mouse

Fox *Vulpes vulpes*
Length 1.1 m (3½ ft). Coloration quite varied, but often reddish, with (usually) white-tipped tail; mainly nocturnal, but sometimes hunts by day; builds a den in a bankside; occurs throughout Britain and Europe. ⬛, ⬛, ⬛, ⬛, ⬛

Fox

Badger

Badger *Meles meles*
Length 95 cm (37 in). Large, shy, mainly nocturnal mammal with fur which appears black and white; moves with trotting motion; sett is built in quiet woodland bank, usually among tree roots; occurs in most of Britain and Europe. ⬛, ⬛

Stoat *Mustela erminea*
Length 40 cm (15½ in). Sinuous-bodied; black tip to tail; active day and night; ranging far and wide in search of food; can climb and swim; investigates all likely hiding places for prey; occurs in most of Britain and Europe. ⬛, ⬛, ⬛, ⬛, ⬛, ⬛, ⬛

summer

winter

Stoat

Weasel *Mustela nivalis*
Length 30 cm (12 in). Eel-like body; habits similar to stoat; smaller size and tail lacking black tip distinguishes it from stoat; occurs in most of Britain and Europe; absent from Ireland. ⬛, ⬛, ⬛, ⬛, ⬛, ⬛, ⬛

Weasel

231

Polecat *Mustela putorius*
Length varies, but about 60 cm (24 in).
Uniformly darker and bigger than
stoat; distinctive face mask; mainly
nocturnal; swims well; nests in holes;
occurs in most of Britain and Europe.
▣, ⊡, ⊠

Otter *Lutra lutra*
Length 1.3 m (4 ft). Wide, flat face with
small ears; distinguished from other
aquatic mustelids by large size and
webbed feet; rarely seen; usually hunts
along rivers, sea lochs, etc, at night;
swims well; occurs in most of Britain
and Europe. ▨, ▤

Pine marten *Martes martes*
Length 75 cm (30 in). Yellow or cream
throat-patch distinguishes it from
polecat; also slightly more fox-like head
than rodent-like head of polecat;
mainly nocturnal; climbs well; nests in
hollows or old bird and squirrel nests;
occurs in most of Britain and Europe.
⊡

Beech marten *Martes foina*
Length 75 cm (30 in). Throat-patch
white; heavier looking than pine
marten; nocturnal; bounding gait;
climbs well; nests in holes and hollows;
occurs in much of Europe, except
extreme north. ▣, ⊡, ⊠

Wild boar *Sus scrofa*
Length 1.6 m (5 ft). Unmistakeable;
large, hairy and pig-like; young
striped; nocturnal; usually found in
groups, rooting about in the soil for
food; often heard snorting and
snuffling; occurs in much of Europe
except extreme north. ▣, ⊠

Red deer *Cervus elaphus*
Length 2.5 m (8 ft). Males' antlers rounded in cross-section; mainly nocturnal; usually seen in herds; originally forest animals, many populations now live on upland areas; occurs throughout Britain and Europe. ▣, ⊞, ▱

Roe deer *Capreolus capreolus*
Length 1.6 m (5 ft). Males have very small antlers and tail; white rump shows in winter; mainly nocturnal; usually seen in herds or groups, but solitary individuals also encountered; occurs throughout Britain and Europe. ▣, ⊞, ◩, ◪

Fallow deer *Dama dama*
Length 1.6 m (5 ft). Males only have flattened antlers; in winter spotted coat pattern less distinct; mainly nocturnal; usually seen in herds; barking call; occurs throughout Britain and Europe. ⊞, ▣

Mouflon *Ovis aries*
Length 1.3 m (4 ft). One of several species of wild bovine found throughout Europe; others – such as feral goat, ibex, chamois, musk ox and saiga – may also be encountered. ◮, ▱, ◪

Common seal *Phoca vitulina*
Length 1.9 m (6 ft). Shorter muzzle and rounder head distinguishes it from the grey seal; colour variable, usually grey-white or yellow; often seen bobbing up and down offshore, but hauls on to quiet beaches; occurs around coasts of Britain and Europe, down to Mediterranean. ▱

Red deer ♂ summer
♀ winter

♀ winter
♂ summer
Roe deer

Fallow deer ♂ summer
♀ winter

Mouflon

Common seal

233

Bibliography

General books

Discovering the Countryside with David Bellamy (series) (Newnes)
Nature Watcher's Directory by David Marsden (Hamlyn)
Severn House Naturalist's Library (series) (Severn House)
The Amateur Naturalist by Gerald Durrell (Hamish Hamilton)
The Book of Nature Photography by Heather Angel (Ebury Press)
Where to Watch Birds by John Gooders (Pan)

Identification guides

A Field Guide to the Insects of Britain and Northern Europe by Michael Chinery (Collins)
A Field Guide to the Reptiles and Amphibians of Britain and Europe by E.N. Arnold and J.A. Burton (Collins)
Collins Guide to the Freshwater Fishes of Britain and Europe by Bent J. Muus and Preben Dahlstrøm (Collins)
Pond and Stream Life edited by John Clegg (Blandford)
The Country Life Guide to Animals – their tracks and signs by R.W. Brown, M.J. Lawrence and J. Pope (Newnes)
The Country Life Guide to Birds of Britain and Europe by Bertel Bruun (Newnes)
The Country Life Guide to the Seashore and Shallow Seas of Britain and Europe by Andrew Campbell (Newnes)
The Mammals of Britain and Europe by G. Corbet and D. Ovenden (Collins)
The Natural History of Britain and Northern Europe (series) (Hodder and Stoughton)

Index

Page numbers in *italic* refer to illustrations